My Life as a Jesuit in Dachau

MEMORIES

— OF A —

DEVIL

D1264457

FATHER CHESTER FABISIAK, S.J.

Published in the USA

Printed in the United States of America
ISBN   978-1-7321170-0-6 (paperback)
        978-1-7321170-1-3 (hardcover)

Interior design by Darlene Swanson • www.van-garde.com

"Live only for today, and be peaceful on this day."

Memories of a Devil, by my beloved uncle, Father Chester Fabisiak, S.J., is a memoir of life in Dachau, the Nazi concentration camp.

This memoir is being published posthumously.

Father Chester wrote this memoir in Spanish during his first postwar missionary assignment in South America. Twenty years later, the manuscript accompanied him to the United States, where he ministered for the next 30 years. The memoir passed from hand to hand, from one translator to another, only to return to Father Chester in its original form every time.

It was returned one last time on the day of Father Chester's funeral. There, I became the manuscript's next recipient.

Years passed, and I faced a seemingly endless array of difficulties in seeing the memoir through to publication. However, I considered publishing this book to be not only an honor but a duty, to both my uncle and society.

Memories of a Devil communicates a profound message about the fragility of human nature. It reflects on the nature of human will persistently challenged by God and evil. It also presents a vivid, horrifying picture of human beings capable of the most profound cruelty toward others. The memoir reflects on how souls and minds embedded in a dominant, destructive group ideology can readily and blindly influence other people.

Father Chester Fabisiak, S.J., was ordained in June 1939. He was young and ready to serve God and humanity. However, three months later, Hitler invaded Poland. Father Chester was arrested along with his religious brothers. Ultimately, he was sent to the infamous concentration camp, Dachau.

The repugnance of the camp and the evil within it pierced Father Chester's body, but failed to conquer his soul. His great faith in God allowed Father Chester to escape death numerous times. His courage and imaginative methods of avoiding the enemy's onslaught gave him hope – and a little joy – and kept him and others alive.

After the Allies liberated Dachau, Father Chester continued with his missionary devotion. He spent his life glorifying God every day and passing God's innumerable blessings onto the world. God's divine power had brought him back from the worst horror imaginable.

Father Chester's life was one of undying victory through the joy of serving God and celebrating his love for others, life, and his Heavenly Father. His fight for justice lives on in my heart, and in the many other hearts he touched.

May this memoir teach us about the past, inspire us to live each day, and guide us into a more just future.

Submitted in Loving Memory by a Forever Grateful Niece,
Dr. Danuta B. Fabisiak

AN ACKNOWLEDGMENT:

"I DON'T KNOW OF ANY other way to express my gratitude to the Lord for allowing Father Chester into our lives, other than by sharing my thoughts with you and hoping that you will share this letter with the rest of the world.

...A couple of months later, I picked up my children from school
I asked what was wrong, but they started crying.
They told me Father Chester had just died.

We sat in the parking lot at school and cried for a long time. My eyes are flooded with tears as I am typing this now, only wishing we had made it a point to tell Father Chester how much we appreciated the influence he had had on our children. I wanted to tell him that he was the one who made such an incredible impact on children's lives.

He carried children's stress on his own shoulders, helping them through their rough times and through adjusting to their responsibilities. He made them laugh and he loved them dearly.

I have never in my life known a person to have this effect on people other than Christ."

Very truly yours,
Parishioner

"Father Chester served the Church of the Blessed Sacrament since 1981. His warm presence was felt at area nursing homes, retirement residences, and daily Masses. Both adults and children looked forward to visiting with him as he walked through the neighborhood. The children of Blessed Sacrament School feel honored to have been taught by him during their religion classes. His animated storytelling and pleasant nature will be fondly remembered by each student.

Despite the hardships of having been detained in a concentration camp and experiencing difficulty with his eyesight, he was eternally positive and forgiving. His saintlike qualities will be forever remembered by everyone who was fortunate enough to have crossed his path.

Thank you, Father Chester, for allowing us to share in your extraordinary life!"

Blessed Sacrament School

Springfield, Illinois

FATHER FABISIAK'S ACKNOWLEDGMENTS

I WOULD LIKE TO EXPRESS my deepest feelings of gratitude for Miss Emma of Cochabamba, Bolivia, who had the sorry job of correcting my knowledge of the Spanish language. Without her generous help, my journal would never have appeared for publishing.

I am sincerely grateful to my friends in Springfield, Illinois and Dearborn, Michigan, who provided photos of Dachau.

I am eternally grateful to everyone who helped me during the war and in the years that followed. Some of their names are unknown to me, and there are so many others, I cannot mention them all here.

Some photos are included after the text of this book.

PROLOGUE

It never occurred to me that my writings might one day be a book. After the war, I worked in almost all the countries of South America and found myself surrounded by people whose curiosity about the Holocaust—or "The Phenomenon," as they had heard it called through international communication—could not be satisfied. Their knowledge of the war came from newspaper articles and radio broadcasts and had never been fully confirmed. I was a living witness. I am a Jesuit priest, and I was a prisoner of Dachau for five years. Through my own experience, I did—and I still do—authenticate the horrors and the truth of the war.

Most people in those Latin American countries, so far from the borders of Europe, tried to reject images of unsubstantiated atrocities and much of the war itself. They believed it all to be propaganda against a small country, a country whose greatness somehow now shone in their collective mind like the sun on a celestial firmament. I was sent there to fulfill my religious duties, but I had also survived the war, and my existence gave credence to its devastation, to its breadth and scope, and to the undeniable atrocities that had been inflicted upon me and countless others.

People around me, compelled by an understanding of the facts of the war and a growing antagonism toward its injustices, not only lent an ear to the story of my experience but also encouraged me and, later, pushed me to write it all down. Many offered to finance its publication. Finally, after many months of thought, I started gathering material about the events I experienced in different jails and, ultimately, in the infamous concentration camp of Dachau.

Naturally, this book tries to present material in a readable narrative, accessible to anyone. It is not an attempt to present data scientifically or to prove the occurrence of events using specific days and hours of the day - nothing of the sort. It is, instead, a set of historical facts based on actual events I experienced. It is not based on the fruit of imagination. It is not a creation of a passionate hatred for an enemy. I lived these events, and I am recounting them with all truthfulness.

In this book, the reader will often see references to "a German/the Germans." (The author wishes to clarify that he expressly refers to Germans compelled to operate under Nazi rule and law.) I want to elucidate that I have no desire to generalize, denigrate, or defame an entire population. I wish to distinguish between individuals who are great and noble Germans, and those whose inhuman conduct has darkened the name of all Germans.

Human society knows well that life cannot exist without mutual confidence in one's fellow man, that even the smallest cell of it strives to live in relationships between people. Before the war, great politicians of the day took the supposed promises of "der Führer" to be sincere. On whatever premise that decision was based, whole nations gave way, and Adolf Hitler was able to unleash a war that for him and for the world would have incalculable consequences.

The societies involved in the massacre that was the Holocaust were tranquilized by the advocacy of supposed moral principles.

Others, who in some part must have understood Hitler's instincts, did not have the level of maturity necessary to comprehend the reality. Many people adopted a passive acceptance of the least dangerous path, one that would not deflate the illusion that all would be well.

The war began on September 1, 1939, and news of it traveled across Europe like the projectiles of a machine gun. Hitler's insatiable appetite for power was not yet understood, and in Germany his promises of restoring national honor and pride were still new. Older generations of Germans were consoled by the knowledge that their country, the Germany of their past, was not barbaric but a cultured society of gentlemen and ladies, and so, for Germans, there was nothing to fear. They did not recognize that their noble culture, which had been built on a deeply religious foundation, was now allowing a single individual to be elevated beyond his human station.

Germany trusted Hitler in a haze of political myopia, with the single-minded simplicity of doves when, in truth, the European situation demanded people with the keen instinct of serpents.

Austria and Czechoslovakia were quickly overcome, overwhelmed by the strength of the German troops. Still, with the honor of drunkards, the Polish government continued assuring its people and the entire world that the danger did not exist. There was no possibility of war because der Führer himself had given his solemn word, his counterfeit promise, that there would be no new conquests.

The whole world fed off this mad farce even though the moment we had least anticipated had already arrived. On September 1, 1939, every Polish newspaper suddenly and unanimously launched its terrified voice in the declaration, "War! War!" It was unavoidable. Hitler's lie, however carefully presented, left no room for truth or compromise. The media announced to the world that war had struck Poland, initiated by the Third Reich, and Polish cities crumbled under the weight of German bombs.

TABLE OF CONTENTS

THE BEGINNING

ON SEPTEMBER 16, 1939, GERMAN troops entered our city, Poznan, Poland, and our welcome could not have been colder. I was in my house, a residence for Jesuit brothers. Seven of my religious brothers had already been drafted to defend our country. I wanted to enlist to fight for the rights of the nation, but every time I went to the conscription office, my request was denied. My vision was poor, and I had to receive treatment for my eyes daily so that my condition did not deteriorate. The physician who had been treating me was a young woman of remarkable character, an admired professional, and a qualified ophthalmologist. However, she also had great physical beauty. Because of that combination, her office was soon filled with German men, many of them members of the Gestapo. The doctor's office became a valuable source of war news, and I looked forward to my daily visits, sometimes going there hours before my appointment.

One day, she told me she had learned that I was on the list of people whose freedom troubled the Gestapo. She said she knew the secrets of the Gestapo, that they were ruthless and cruel, and that I should flee to Lublin without delay. She wanted me to take all her machines and instruments. She was frightened for her own safety, and she told me that if she were to die, I must sell her equipment for the money, which I would surely need. I did not take her seriously; I assured her that we were safe and that we would not need to leave our home.

It seemed peculiar that the terrible Gestapo would tell their secret plans to this young doctor, a Polish girl, even though she was charmingly beautiful. I had a very clear impression of the ethical nature of most German people. I felt sure that I could not expect anything bad of them. In truth, this young doctor was risking her life with each indiscretion, each secret revealed while demonstrating her compassion and morality. Who knows how many lucky men and women encountered her, or how many lives she saved?

At our religious residence, we celebrated Mass during the customary hours with great faithfulness, and we prayed for peace as the situation in our city of Poznan became increasingly unstable. Poznan is located near the German border, and sometimes we instinctively ran to protect ourselves from the sounds of German bombers flying overhead. News of the war was frightening, but the sounds of day-to-day life were quiet enough, and our Father Superior, who spoke perfect German, assured us we had nothing to fear. German troops greeted us courteously on the street, and we continued thinking that the young Polish doctor, who had tried so hard to warn us, had been wrong. We returned to prayer, attempting to regain a sense of inner peace and tranquility.

One morning, in the corner of the city's plaza, I saw a truck heavily loaded with bread. Soldiers of the Wehrmacht, the German army, were handing out food to the poor. A uniformed German soldier, his gun strapped to his shoulder, was eating some of the bread meant for the poor, devouring pieces with a voraciousness greater than that of any of the beggars. This act seemed only a small irony at the time, but it came to represent an escalating aggression and foreshadowed many of the unhappy events that were to follow.

FLOWERS AT THE FOOT
OF THE MONUMENT

PEOPLE WHO VISITED POZNAN BEFORE September 1939 saw the statue of a Polish martyr rising out of the plaza next to the university, a monument to the Sacred Heart of Jesus. Every day, more and more of the faithful deposited flowers at his feet and prayed for his help and protection. When this first began, German soldiers made a peaceful effort to disperse those who congregated there. But soon, anyone bringing flowers to the foot of the statue or standing there to pray was locked in jail for three days. It had become a crime to worship openly. I was arrested along with others. While in prison, we heard that the statue, whose heart was made of pure gold, had disappeared.

I talked with a man who said he had asked a German soldier about this blasphemous theft. The soldier had replied, "And you, what have you done with Bismarck?"

"But sir," the man had said, "what does this have to do with Bismarck? The figure of the Sacred Heart is the image of our God."

The soldier had replied, "I do not know Polish ideology, but first I am a German, later a Catholic."

In the evening, we heard shooting. Later, we learned it was the soldiers amusing themselves by taking shots at the statue, which they then blew up, its pieces thrown to the wastebasket of the city. A sign was placed near the rubble: it read, "Here lies the great pig of Poland."

New Visits From The Gestapo

Let us return to the events that took place in our house. The Gestapo had come to our door before, but they had been courteous and left us unharmed. On September 21, 1939, they came again, walking through the rooms with a new forcefulness. Their words were still very courteous, but these "Hitler supermen" forgot their high status and began plundering our belongings, filling their pockets with small objects that had almost no material value. From Father Wladyslaw Wiacek, they took a package of handkerchiefs his father had given him. From me, they took an alarm clock they found on my desk, which was a sentimental gift from my family. We priests talked among ourselves about the radical differences between the old and new German generations, how these atheistic, materialistic, and immoral young men epitomized their current slogan and their evolving misguided belief, which was: "The more cruel a German, the more of a man."

A curfew was imposed, and no one was allowed to walk along the streets at night. However, on September 22, my sister-in-law, Marysia, came to our house in the late evening, well past curfew. She was extremely upset and nervous, and kept saying that we should go with her, that we should dress like civilians and leave immediately. She insisted that if we did not, we would be taken to jail the next day and eventually to Dachau. We had heard the rumors of a concentration camp called Dachau, but we did not believe it existed. It could not possibly exist. I left to speak with my Father Superior, who rejected everything Marysia had said. He told me rumors like this had been circulating for some time now, that these were scare tactics used to silence the opposition. He said it would be impossible for the Germans to create such a place as the death camp.

I returned to tell my brother and his wife that I could not leave with the rest of the family because, as a Jesuit priest, I must obey my Father Superior. My brother sounded almost desperate when he said goodbye. He said he had failed to keep our family together and that he knew he could no longer ensure our well-being.

Our Father Superior's faith and confidence in the incomparable German education and philanthropy did nothing to calm all the brothers in the house. Instead, some of us were in opposition to one another. We were ten against three. Ten were convinced we should leave Poznan immediately, while the Father Superior and his supporters defended their position of there being nothing to fear. He had the "enormous weight of experience" on his side, which also represented religious authority, and this demanded our ultimate obedience. This was the most critical moment in our lives as young priests, one that would determine the entire course of events to follow. Father Superior, wanting to be prudent under uncertain circumstances, gave each of us a small amount of money for any eventuality.

September 23 dawned timidly over the city, carrying an indefinable vapor of autumn. As usual, I went to the young doctor who treated my eyes. This time, she said she had seen a list of people condemned to go to concentration camps, and that my name and the names of my Jesuit brothers were among them. Now it was possible to believe that what she was saying could be true. But it was too late.

JAILED

When I returned to my house, I pressed the doorbell, which sounded with the same metallic whine as always. The door opened as it had done thousands of times before. However, instead of the amiable Brother Doorman, who would receive me with a smile on his lips like a small boy, a pistol appeared and I heard a voice say, "Stop."

An agent of the Gestapo brutally dragged me by the chest through the front door while saying, "We have been expecting you. Enter."

Another soldier kept his pistol drawn and would not allow anyone to move. The Gestapo stole everything they could find, including food, which they fixed as a banquet for themselves, along with the wine, which had been allotted for the celebration of Mass.

I began to understand Psalm 104:15 from the sacred scripture of the Bible, "Wine that gladdens the heart of a man," because it was making the German soldiers more pleasant. They began consoling us, joking and assuring us that we had been denounced, accused of belonging to various German organizations. They said they did not believe these accusations and would take us to prison for only a few hours. A fast examination would be made, our names would be cleared, and we would be released immediately.

I must add, with sadness and with pain, that they gave their firm and complete word, but that lies and hypocrisy overcame their humanity .

After their banquet, their good humor was surprising. They allowed us to walk onto the patio, where an imposing map of Europe hung on the wall. We were looking at the map when one of the soldiers approached us. With his hand, he made a huge gesture, as if to erase all of Poland.

He asked us, "*Polen, wo bist du?*" "Poland, where are you?"

My companion, Father Wiacek, answered him with an impressive seriousness. "We have lost her, it is true, but the day will arrive when Poland will occupy all of this." Then he put his fingers on the map of Germany.

The logical reaction would have been for this member of the Gestapo to be furious. Instead, he burst out laughing, as though he had heard an exquisite joke, perhaps because he did not measure the importance of what was being said.

Before leaving our house, we were permitted to return to our rooms to gather our belongings, but all our things had already been stolen and taken away. What reason could there be for the high officials of the Gestapo, so cultured and educated, to steal in this blatant way? It was lawful for the Gestapo to rob religious, poor men, like birds of prey. If we took one Deutsche Mark from these soldiers, we certainly would have been shot for committing an atrocious crime.

At two o'clock that afternoon, a military car arrived and we were taken to the Mlynska Street jail. We crossed a solitary street and, with the sun in our eyes, walked slowly in front of an old car, forcing the driver to reduce his speed. This innocent action was an occasion for the Gestapo agent to show his true affections.

He said, "*Ah, solche polnische schweine,*" which means, "Polish pigs."

If it is true that the mouth speaks what is in the heart, then the pig, by his own mouth, declared his way of thinking.

The Gestapo took us through a gate. One of them said, "*Zugang,*" which means "pass," and told us to wait in a holding area. Even then, my older Jesuit brothers continued talking about the excellent education of the Germans, apparently hoping that soon an army chief or some official would come and tell us we had been falsely accused and that we could go home.

Hours passed and, finally, a guard came and took us to our cell. He told us to enter. A large table with two long benches and two camp beds constituted the only furniture, and there was a small window with iron bars. The guard closed the door and locked us in with a huge key.

Father Superior had not been with us at the time of our arrest. He appeared on his own after turning himself in to the Gestapo. He was brought to our cell and we were reunited as the religious community we had once been before September 1939. He told us that our residence, which had always been a place of communion and prayer, was now being used as offices for the Gestapo.

Our faith was fed by the illusion that one moment, the door would open and our innocence would be revealed. However, that moment did not arrive, and we began to feel desperate and lose hope. We kept looking into one another's faces, and the only thing we could see was that we were prisoners.

Three days passed without the door opening. No one brought us a piece of bread or a glass of water. This abandonment and neglect was radically disappointing, especially for the older brothers and their theory of the Germans' superior and humanitarian nature. At dawn of the fourth day, the door opened and we received our first meal: a clay-like piece of black bread and black coffee. Some of the brothers were semi-conscious, so weakened by their fast that they had to be roused to eat. I refused the bread, knowing it would make me sick, though I drank some of the coffee. I resisted the rotten bread for one more day, when I finally mustered the courage to knock on the cell door. Soon the guard appeared. I showed him my state of health and told him I needed white bread or I would become violently ill. He listened calmly, then left without saying a word. My companions reacted harshly to what for them had been insolent behavior on my part; the next day the guards brought a piece of white bread and I could finally have something to eat.

A dry, blowing noise in a neighboring cell worried us. We had heard this noise each morning since our arrival but could not figure out what it was. Another prisoner, having seen a brief glimpse of the area from which the sound was coming, said it was the blow of a chopping blade, beheading any Pole condemned of a crime.

We were living like animals without the ability to change our clothing, wash, or shave. The guards finally brought in someone they called "the barber" to shave us. He acted crazy, and when he started his task, he poked each of us with a knife against the face, acting foolish at the same time. We had to laugh at him even though our faces bled throughout the ordeal and my entire face was in pain. We thought that if we were to die by his hand, it might as well be between ridiculous outbursts of laughter.

We were hungry, our cell was becoming filthy, and family members and friends were trying to help by bringing us food and clothing. The Gestapo began asking them for more and more rare and expensive things, saying these things would make our lives as prisoners easier. Our families made many sacrifices to help us. Of course, the Gestapo kept everything, living like wicked kings. We felt certain that the regular soldiers of the German Wehrmacht shared none of these luxuries, and that only the Gestapo benefited.

One of the brothers was in poor health, suffering from tuberculosis. Father Rosemann received no medical treatment and was in agony, coughing and spitting constantly. The cell felt like a tomb where he was being buried alive. For those Germans who watched his suffering, a human life held no value. Only the megalomania of Hitler's doctrine, only the life of Adolf Hitler, was important. We all gathered around Father Rosemann, tending to him as gently as we could. Remarkably, he managed to survive that prison cell.

Black and dirty, we continued until almost the end of November. On one of those days, the Gestapo took each of us and stood us before a long table. Our names were written in the jail registry. I was the youngest and smallest of the group, and I always tried to place myself last, so that I could observe the order of events. In this way, I was able to hide my watch and a small amount of money before they questioned me.

When my turn arrived, they asked me, "How much money do you have?"

I said, "I do not have anything."

They said, "No watches either?"

"None."

"How is it you do not have these things when all the others have them?"

I told them I was the youngest and had not had time to acquire much in life. They took the cross I had received from the Boy Scouts.

"What is this?" an officer asked.

"A Cross," I said.

"I know it is a Cross, but what organization is it from?"

Not knowing how to say "Boy Scouts" in German, I responded that it was a standard organization for youth, similar to the Hitler-Jugend, or "Hitler Youth." The officer raged with fury because I'd had the nerve to compare our Polish youth with Hitler's German youth. I felt his first brutal slap across my face. One of the others tried to explain who the Boy Scouts were. However, the officer clung to the idea that it was a military organization and that being a member of it was a punishable offense by decree of the German authorities. I remembered reading in the newspaper that anything representing a military organization was to be turned into the authorities, and any pertinent information or secrets were to be revealed.

I said to him, "Why would I show you the cross if it was military?" I told him the only purpose of the Boy Scouts was to develop a young person's character and provide a foundation for a national religious conscience.

When the officer heard this, he threw the cross to the ground. I calmly picked it up and put it back in my pocket. That cross accompanied me to Dachau, where I lost it; I don't know how or where. I hope its loss was providential, as the sowing of redemption in a horrible Calgary of humiliation, degradation, and suffering.

While we were in that cell, we remembered past times and examined our plans for the future (though any plans at this period were a fantasy). This was when I learned about the events that had occurred at our house while I was absent on the day of our arrest.

MY SISTER-IN-LAW HAD REASON

ALL THE FATHERS HAD ALREADY celebrated Mass except for one, who stood at the grand altar of our church before a numerous and faithful congregation. The Mass was almost finished when German shouts were heard, and German soldiers surrounded the church and our house, which was attached to the church. The Father was allowed to complete the Mass. Afterward, no one was allowed to leave the church. The congregants were held inside, and the soldiers took all the Jesuits into the house under armed guard. The priests were accused of shooting out the front door of the church, aiming at the German soldiers.

One of the priests asked, "Who fired against you?"

No answer to this question was forthcoming other than that the act had been "seen." The soldiers said they had seen the priest who had fired shots at them escape out the window of the church, his white shirt flying. This was despite the fact that all the priests were present (except for me, and I was visiting my brother). Finally, the women and children were allowed to leave the church. The remaining men were searched thoroughly, as though they were criminals, and then released.

A large crowd of people had gathered in the street. A man approached one of the soldiers and asked the cause of our arrest.

The soldier responded, "We cannot be calm while the Jesuits are free."

There was no reason for our arrest other than lies that had been told about us. My sister-in-law and the young doctor had warned me to leave Poznan, and I had not listened. Now it was too late. Those lies told against us, because of our faith, made me think about the lies that the emissaries of Pontius Pilate had told against the most innocent of men, Jesus Christ. Not one of us doubted the destiny that awaited us.

WATCHING THE MOUTH
OF THE MACHINE GUN

ONE NIGHT, SEVERAL TRUCKS STOPPED outside the doors of the jail. We were told to climb into them and that if any of us tried to run away, we would all be executed. It was the sweet norm of "all for one." Soldiers with machine guns rode inside each truck, and an armored tank with a gigantic machine gun mounted on its roof followed. A motorcycle led the way. We left the city of Poznan in complete darkness, with no idea in which direction we were going or what course our destiny would take.

After a long haul, far from our city, we stopped and were made to get out. We walked for about 80 meters through a large field. Then we were told to stand and form a single line. The lights of the trucks were directed at us and the mouth of the machine gun, with its deadly eye, was focused on us. We all understood our situation; in a few moments we were to die, there in the middle of that dark field. We were Catholic priests who had faithfully served God, and we tried to prepare for death calmly, silently requesting absolution from one another. As the soldiers prepped the machine gun, an officer approached and asked if we wanted to have our eyes covered. Each of us responded that we wanted to confront death with our eyes open.

I did not feel any fear, which is hard to comprehend because

I am an emotional person. I have thought about this many times and have never found an explanation. Perhaps my years of religious life had given me a strange sense of security. Perhaps my deep faith in God was giving me strength. I was curiously preoccupied with what the impact of the bullet would feel like. Just then, a military car arrived; the Gestapo official and a man in the car had a conversation we could not hear. Then the car drove away toward Poznan.

FACING NEW DEATH

THE GESTAPO OFFICER SPOKE WITH the other soldiers and we were ordered to return to the trucks. We were still wearing our summer clothes, and at this point we felt colder than fear. After another long ride, we stopped in a small plaza. It became apparent that the Germans had no idea where they were or what to do with us. They began going from door to door, shouting, threatening people, looking for a place on this sweet Polish earth to put us. They were brutal, throwing people into the street while examining the houses. They came to the home of a Jewish family. There were thirteen priests, and this house was far too small, so they went on to another Jewish family, who owned a cereal business and had a larger house. The Jewish families were taken away, and we were divided between the two houses, with seven older priests, including Father Rosemann, brought to the first house. We felt only gnawing hunger, cold, and fatigue.

We were closed in and sealed off. Then, finally, the insufferable Gestapo left us for a short time during the night. We looked for food in every corner, but all we could find were fish scales and crumbs of bread. It was Saturday, the Jewish Sabbath. We did not know what had happened to the Jewish families. The Gestapo was robbing their businesses, loading packages and the bulk of their belongings into trucks and taking them away. Days passed, and the soldiers came to check on us often, entering with a fury and threatening our lives if anyone tried to run. We felt we were condemned to live and die in those rooms.

We were living without eating. During one of the Gestapo's visits, we were desperate enough to speak up and say that several days had gone by without our having anything to eat.

One of them answered, "You must thank Hitler. You live only due to his magnanimity. In fact, you all should have died a long time ago, like miserable dogs."

We were being condemned to die, not by gunshot but by slow starvation, and no one outside the two houses would ever know. We had not yet heard of the prototypes of Perfect Kolbe, which would come later; prototypes of death by hunger, or of his theory that debilitated, starving people could be easily cowed and controlled.

One of my companions, Father Franciszek Siemianowicz, was an audacious and decisive man who had many plans for escape. We agreed that it was preferable to die from a gunshot wound than in this slow, agonizing way, with intense physical pain and dizziness, and we knew we must act without delay. We talked about a thousand projects, a thousand illusions. However, we were in such a weakened physical condition that we could not even create real projects. While hunger devastated our physical resistance, those sweet illusions adequately nourished our spirits. I cannot say that God listened to our prayers because we did not pray to be rescued; however, it seemed that He understood our situation and arrived in time.

One day, we were permitted to step onto a patio behind the house. Through a wooden fence at the back, I heard a feminine voice call softly, "Are you one of the priests the Germans brought here?"

"Yes," I said.

"I am Polish," she said. "Do you have enough to eat?"

"Nothing," I said. "We have had nothing since we arrived."

"Here, have a little bread," she said, and threw pieces of bread over the wall, as well as garlic sausages.

The food fell onto the ground, as though it had come from Heaven. I thanked her and ran with insane joy into the house, holding my precious cargo like a boy with a great new toy. We divided the food among ourselves and would have devoured it like hungry wolves but for the words of our dying brother: "Slowly, slowly, if you want to live." He was teaching us how to eat again, slowly, to ease our discomfort. In this way, Father Rosemann, forgetting his own agony, helped save the lives of his hungry brothers.

The next day I was able to stand near the fence and talk with the woman who had given us the food. I learned that we were in the town of Golina and that the other priests were in a house separated from us by about 150 meters. I was overly eager to talk to them and to make sure they were still alive. After the next visit from the Gestapo, I climbed over the fence and ran to where the others were staying. They had found wheat bread in their house, and although they were still starving, the nutrients in that bread had kept them slightly better and healthier-looking than we were. I did not understand their condition, as I thought that flavorful white bread must be healthier. (Later, I learned that the richness of vitamins was superior in wheat.) Instead of being glad to see me, the priests were terrified that the Gestapo would arrive while I was there, find me missing from the other house, and kill us all. One of the elders accused me of being a crazy person who was completely irresponsible and "more dangerous than the devil himself." Perhaps he had a point, considering the circumstances of the moment, but he did not know that one day this dangerous devil would be his salvation.

I rushed off. On the way back, I passed in front of a bakery brimming with bread. I remembered the money I had hidden from the Gestapo; I always carried it with me, and I quickly bought as much bread as I could carry. I ran to the house of the kind Polish lady, left the bread, and once again ran back to the bakery to buy as much as I could carry. I made two runs from her house to where we were staying, throwing everything over the wall, then climbed back over the fence. I was never caught. We ate until we were satiated and still had enough for the following day. Who could imagine the joy I felt in feeding my brothers and seeing the immediate danger of our death from hunger disappear!

During this time, our companions in the other house continued eating wheat. Against everyone's will, I made a new trip to buy bread and cold cuts for them. It calmed their hunger and fear somewhat; it was food that strengthened their weakened energies. I had to flee quickly from them, as the terror of the Gestapo had not disappeared. This was our one providential chance, the finding of food, that saved us from death but did not create any fundamental solution to our problem. We always faced a dilemma: to die of hunger or to be shot. We did not have the smallest doubt that the Gestapo wanted to see us die of hunger and that few deaths could be more horrible. Such circumstances compel men not only to try bold acts but to attempt heroic ones, for we felt we had a right to a natural life. Some of us planned to flee, accepting all consequences for our actions. However, most of the brothers were opposed to our plan. Against our will, we agreed to postpone our escape until an undetermined time.

The Gestapo visited us day and night; the night visits were far more brutal and frightening, as the Gestapo often appeared completely drunk, making excessive and nasty threats. One very early morning, I noticed their intense eagerness to finish removing the business materials of an unfortunate Jewish family. This time, I suppose, due to negligence, they left the door of the warehouse open, and we could finally enter to see what was there. However, the Gestapo become furious and made us face their cannon. They put their revolvers to our temples and our chests, threatening us for our audacity. One of the brothers, Janek, already exhausted and sick of their violent threats, opened his cassock and offered his chest, shouting at a soldier in a clear voice, "Kill me at once. I am not afraid of you."

The soldier's reaction was the opposite of any we had thought possible. He turned shame-facedly and walked away.

CHANGE OF THE GUARD

MANY DAYS PASSED, AND THE Gestapo decided to put us in the hands of the local police. They would leave us in the two houses, guarded by the police, and would come back from time to time to check on us. We were not to be released. As soon as they had left, we went to the head of the town and told him of our impossible situation and of what had been done to us. He said he knew nothing of this, that the police in Golina were Austrian, and that we could work with them. From the beginning, they granted us more freedom in every way. However, they could not provide us with food, so I was put in charge of organizing a provisional plan. We would be allowed to go out and look for food, but we would all have to present ourselves in our quarters three times a day.

Immediately, I went to find the woman who had first thrown bread and sausages over the wall. She was very kind and offered to find food for each of us, but it was impossible for her to feed all thirteen. A doctor in the town would help, and the parish priest, old and kind, committed himself to finding food for the brothers in the first house. Of course, we were terrified of being caught, knowing the penalty would be death.

Taking advantage of our conditional freedom, we organized a group of good people who wanted to help the brothers in the second house. All these people, whose economic conditions were already difficult, performed acts of extraordinary charity so that we might have anything we needed. They performed heroic feats, risking their lives every day on our behalf, knowing the Gestapo would shoot them if they were caught. I, too, felt a true sense of reward, being able to help maintain my own "family." The parish priest also tried to find all that was necessary so that we might have what we needed to celebrate Mass. Thus, we resumed our religious life, which had been completely interrupted. The only thing we lacked was the Roman Breviary prayer, included in our lost sacramental books.

The police granted us more and more freedom. On some days, we were no longer asked to present ourselves three times a day; one of us could be there to speak on behalf of the others. We took advantage of this and tried to alleviate Father Rosemann's continued suffering. The chief of police came to visit Father Rosemann, whose condition was so terrible that the police chief did not know what to say. However, he was afraid of the Gestapo, so he denied our request to move Father Rosemann to a hospital.

The parish priest told us his sister was an official at a hospital in the city of Lodz and that if we could somehow arrange permission for a transfer, Father Rosemann could be placed there. The opportunity presented itself almost at once. The chief of police happened to be at the house. At the same time, the town pharmacist, who was a fervent Catholic and a brave Polish woman, was visiting. She had brought liquor for any of us who wished a drink, calling it "a remedy for many evils," and she began offering it to the policeman. At first he refused to drink with us, alleging that he was prohibited from drinking with prisoners. However, soon he decided to have a small one and then another and another. Eventually, he was completely drunk. With the pharmacist's help, we obtained written permission from the chief of police to transfer Father Rosemann to the hospital in Lodz, as well as permission for an essential travel companion.

For this position, there were two candidates. One was Father Henry, whose height and large bearing contradicted his single-minded fear of facing death. To escape our situation, which brought some of us to the brink of madness every day, Father Henry wanted to be the patient's companion, the one who would help him along the way. I was the other candidate, and I did not have much difficulty yielding my place to such an immense Jesuit. We obtained permission for the safe conduct of both men. Some of our friends in the town provided money for the trip and for the purchase of two suits of clothes. In this way, two of the brothers got out. Father Henry was to conduct himself carefully, discuss nothing of our situation with anyone, and return to us as soon as the patient was admitted to the hospital.

The patient arrived at the hospital, where the priest's sister received him with affection, and he continued to live for some time. Father Henry was to return to our house prison, but he conducted himself quietly and in such a way that the police worried very little about his absence. Because of their trip, we managed to communicate with our friends who remained at home in the city of Poznan. They now knew where we were located and sent food and clothing – as much as they could give to us and to the townspeople of Golina. Because of them, we were even able to exercise charity, giving clothes to people in the same condition as – or worse off – than we were. Our friends in Poznan demonstrated so much concern and Christian charity that at times we could not accept what they offered; they were experiencing many difficulties themselves and were not rich people.

FRIEND OF A JEWISH FAMILY

A VERY NICE JEWISH FAMILY still lived in one of the houses next door. The oldest son was fulfilling his military service, and the oldest daughter was a teacher at a school for Jews. The other children were smaller. The teacher was a pretty young woman and notoriously flirtatious. She liked taking walks in front of our windows, dressed differently every day, and she had good taste in clothing. The father had a small business, and they all lived together quite comfortably. We established a profound friendship with everyone except the teacher, whose conduct disturbed me. On the other hand, why not give glory to God for making her so extremely pretty and attractive? Naturally, being against anything false, I did not say that she did not please me. The fact that she was Jewish was not a problem, and I felt attracted to her. I liked her, and I did not doubt that she, also, was interested in my small figure.

In truth, we could end up as a happy pair, but I did not know how to respond to her feminine hints, and I did not know how to make the most of the situation. "The one who goes too slow evidently arrives late; the one who goes too fast takes the chance of never arriving." I walked too slowly, and she went too fast, and for that reason I do not have a lovely wife and that family does not have a husband for their dear daughter. We both lost, but thank God for this favor.

I spent many hours with the younger children in this family, speaking to them about the Sacred Scripture, mainly the Old Testament, and teaching them some Catholic orations. They all showed extraordinary interest in my informal classes, in which they were learning and enjoying themselves.

In one of these classes, a clear-eyed young boy asked me something I could never have anticipated. "Sir, where are you from? You must be Jewish because you know all the things our rabbi has taught us." This "conversion" boy came from a house and attended a synagogue where the rabbi explained the history of the Old Testament to children and their families.

I answered him, "And why am I not Jewish? Our parents were Jewish, and we are their descendants." This was an ambiguous answer, but I was trying not to disillusion the boy. He took it in a literal sense. When the class was finished, the boy ran to give this news to his father, who also took it in the literal sense.

One day, the father of the boy came and asked to speak confidentially to me. In a very serious tone, he said, "Father, tell me, what are you doing with my children?" This question and the tone in which it was proffered troubled me greatly, as I feared that the children had said something bad or scandalous about me. He complicated things even more by saying, "I do not know what you are doing with my children. You are undoing my whole family."

I said to him, "What is this about, sir? In what way am I undoing your family? Please explain yourself."

He said, "I don't know, but the fact is, they have never behaved this way before. They hardly finish their food, and nothing can keep them in the house. All they want to do is immediately come and be with you. What do you say to them so that they do not want to leave you for a single moment? It is as though you have become more important than I am."

I answered him, "Sir, I speak to them about the Old Testament only, and I have also taught them some Polish orations."

He looked apprehensive, then burst out laughing. He had been well-informed all along about what I was teaching his children and had come to express his gratitude for and joy about the advances his children were making in their knowledge of the Sacred Scriptures. The situation had also given him the luxury of playing quite a disagreeable joke on me.

He had another important subject to talk about, and this gave me a chance to get back at him. His children had told him of their suspicions that I was Jewish, and he had come to clarify whether this was true.

I asked him, "Are you going to doubt my Jewish origin? Look at my facial characteristics. Do I not look Jewish?"

He examined my face and, after a while, responded, "Your face is not absolutely Jewish, but your hair does not leave the slightest doubt. Sir, if we are talking cause and effect, the apple part of the tree, you have a Jewish head and are, therefore, a Jewish person."

Thus, with his own argument, I convinced him that I was Jewish. Then he asked, "Why are you not a rabbi?"

I answered, "Because I do not know Hebrew. Also, I am now a Catholic priest. I would like to be a rabbi but prefer to continue being a priest because I do not see any possibility of becoming a respectable rabbi. I lack a library. I do not have anyone to teach me Hebrew. Mainly, I do not have the money to pay for my studies."

But the good Jew, with admirable fervor, persisted in obtaining my conversion, telling me that I would be very appreciated, that I could fill a vacancy left by the previous rabbi, who had died at the hands of the Germans. At my disposal, he put the rabbi's precious library and gave me his word that he would install me in a beautiful house, where I could start and finish all my required studies. Also, there was no problem with my learning Hebrew. His daughter was an excellent teacher and an exceptionally beautiful girl. She could teach me quickly and could become my wife if I accepted her freely.

Those were difficult days and circumstances, and they had been almost unendurable. However, though this had started as a joke, a whole life's plan was being set before me. This could be a serious, pleasant life, filled with an encouraging promise of happiness – the life of a rabbi whose community would appreciate him and who would have a beautiful wife. It was a highly attractive prospect.

The fact that I could find a woman appealing did not shock me. That she was young, with the promise of a splendid future, and that she felt something for me, a miserable little man, was not a surprise. I remembered the saying which went something like this: "The fortunes of the ugly, the pretty, and the desired are similar. The man is much like the bear; the ugly one can catch the prettiest fish." What more can one desire? But she was not to be for me, and neither was I for her. I had already found my life's path, one I would travel until my natural death unless I was to die at the hands of the Gestapo.

After that, every time I saw the Jew, he smiled affectionately, recalling what had passed between us, a joke I would remember all my life. He had adamantly wanted to convert me to his religion and had failed to do so. If every Catholic demonstrated such a desire to make conversions, there would be no diversity on earth. The man's children no longer came to talk to me, nor did they want further teachings from the Bible. The only explanation I could think of was that they feared that one day I would shower their heads with baptismal water.

Saving a Young Jewish Boy

THE GESTAPO HAD BEGUN ORGANIZING Polish Jews into groups to be sent to the work camps. From the beginning, their treatment was completely unjust. It was inhuman; the Jews not only suffered from verbal insults but from physical blows – a brutalism that German acts craved as a means of serving their privileged position and notorious physical "superiority." The Jews protested. Many of them would not go to work, and then were attacked. Their numbers gradually diminished.

The Gestapo united with the local police in a network known as the Volks Deutsche; some of them were Polish by birth, and many of them were Germans staying in Poland. They began questioning the oldest son of the Jewish family next door. That young man, terrified by what they might do to him, tried to escape by running. The Gestapo ran after him. As he came out from the back, I told him to hide in our house. The door to our basement was so well-disguised, it was almost invisible; anyone who did not know the construction of our building would have no idea it was there. He quickly went through the basement door, and we placed a small table and two chairs against it. Two of the brothers sat there playing a game of chess.

Our front door was violently flung open and the Gestapo looked everywhere for the young man. They accused us of hiding him. Although they had no proof, they told us that our house was the only place he could have run. They said they would kill us if we were hiding him. They threatened and yelled and searched every corner, but he did not appear. Eventually, the Gestapo had to give up their search and leave, and he was able to get away. One young man's life was spared.

A Grand Mystery:
Kindness Without Measure
or Cruelty Without Limits

GOLINA WAS A VERY SMALL city. During this time of the German occupation, the Gestapo had stolen from the townspeople most of their food and every article of value. These people no longer had the essentials for daily life; many of them began buying and selling on the black market. An item had to be purchased very cheaply, then taken to the city of Poznan, where it could be traded for money or some necessity. Of course, the German authorities made this activity a crime. If a person was caught carrying merchandise, the articles were confiscated. That person was then fined or taken to jail, and sometimes taken to German work camps. Like always, the poor didn't have much to lose; consequently, they took these risks every day.

A soldier came from outside the town of Berlin to take charge of the local post office. The Gestapo commanded him to take provisions twice a week to German soldiers in Poznan. He was a very ugly man physically and – deformed by the spirit of Hitlerism and making all the pretensions of being a "superman" – he acted in a brutal way towards others. However, he had an underlying level of kindness that often prevailed, one rare enough that I must mention it.

This soldier knew everyone in the town and was aware of any movement on the black market. Instead of arresting people, he helped them sell their merchandise.

To a woman standing by the side of the road, he would say, "Matka, jutro mieso," which means, "Mother, tomorrow there will be meat." He would take her packages of goods and sell them himself, getting a much better price than the woman could have obtained. He did this for many people throughout the months and was always scrupulous in returning their money. He confessed to me that he had great sympathy for them and that he was very satisfied when he could help the "matkas." On the other hand, if he discovered the trading of contraband that did not require his help, he would become furious and threaten death to anyone caught. He would then go to the house of the incorrigible sinner and show them the "legal" way of conducting this illegal business. After these negotiations, he would experience a paroxysm of happiness, as if he had won a grand battle.

Another paradox was his treatment of the Jews. He said he hated them and he boasted of his anti-Semitism so that many Jews trembled just to hear his name. He was a confessed Protestant and he fixated on breaking up mixed marriages. He often spent an entire day looking for these situations. He burst into one household where the husband was Jewish and the woman Catholic. He screamed at the top of his voice at the husband, who was hiding behind a cabinet, until the poor man came out and fell to his knees in fear. The soldier told the couple that they must separate and that it was vile for a Catholic and a Jew to live together. However, he did not arrest or hurt them. The grand racist, considering this as one more triumph in his life, walked away.

He visited our house and spent hours trying to convert me

to Hitlerism. I told him my conversion was impossible because I was convinced Hitler was wrong, and I would break his arguments with my own.

Then he would say, "Wait until tomorrow. I will come back with better reasons." Another day, he came into the house screaming loud arguments, talking about the philosophy of Nietzsche.

When I saw and heard him, I said, "Why do you scream so much? Do you think I'm frightened by this small display?"

Instantly, he quit screaming and asked that he be excused. The only portion of Nietzsche that he seemed to absorb were the words "man and superman," with emphasis on some men becoming supermen.

I asked him, "What is a man? What is he made of? Aren't all men made of water and air?"

He responded, "Well, then, what is a calf? Are they all the same?"

I asked, "Are you and a calf the same?"

He became furious, saying I had insulted him when he had always treated me with respect. We went on and on like this, having these ridiculous conversations. He often left in a rage, saying he would return the next day to renew his intentions to convert me. Then, one day he did not return. He had given up on the conversion.

Once, like a little boy, he presented himself to tell me about his problems. During one of his excursions to a neighboring town, he had found a mule. The thought occurred to him to take the mule home, but he did not know how to carry out his plan. He emphasized the joy his wife and children would have with an animal so docile and hairy, but, he asked, "How would I take this mule all the way to Germany for them?"

I told him that as a member of the Gestapo, he could easily

transport himself and the mule on a cargo train. The only problem was that no trains ran between Berlin and his house, which was 18 kilometers away. He could solve this problem by riding the mule for the remainder of the way. He loved this solution and, after while, came to say goodbye with real happiness. He had forgotten the fury he felt after our discussions in the past.

Some hours later, he returned extremely irritated and said, "Damn you. Go to the devil with your advice." He was convinced that I was mocking him, that if his wife saw him riding on the back of a mule, she would say, "Who is more of a mule, the one on four feet or the one on two feet? One mule is mounted on another." The poor man was completely within his rights.

I said to him, "Let's look for a better way." The following idea occurred to me. "Whenever you decide to take the mule home, write your wife a letter telling her you will be three or four days later than the real date. Then, as you get close to your house, get off the mule and walk the rest of the way, avoiding any inconvenience that might occur." This idea seemed sound, and he went on his way, arranging to buy the mule and obtaining the necessary papers for travel.

In those days, he proceeded with extravagant emotions, almost unreal, like a doll or something different from whom he might be in reality. I had the feeling that after the war, he would resume his normal life and return to quieter reflections and his true God, having grown apart from himself not through maliciousness but through ignorance.

Triumph Of The Tribune

This same German soldier who had lost interest in debate became entirely focused on military events at the western front. He concentrated his attention on the march of his countrymen toward Paris. The fall of Paris would constitute the end of Paris and the complete triumph of Germany over all of Europe. In the post office where he was stationed, the soldier placed a great map. He could observe and mark the German troops' advances with pins and flags of different colors. Every day, the positions changed with the news he received from his commanders. The town of Golina, where we were still being held, was to prepare for a celebration that would occur as soon as Germany occupied Paris. The soldier talked and dreamed of inviting the Führer to attend this event.

The original plan of his "genius" brain was to erect a gigantic tribune or raise the platform, where officials could be elevated during the festivities. To develop his idea, he recruited as many Jews as he could find, who at this time were still living in the town. Having been terrorized before, brutally and inhumanly treated by the Gestapo, the Jews immediately presented themselves for work. The soldier made a rudimentary drawing and began considering himself an honorable commander. He could be heard whistling happily as he distributed tools and work. His instructions were that once he blew his whistle, the workers were to congregate and erect the tribune perfectly, in the shortest time possible. Again and again, they repeated this operation. The goal became building the tribune within five minutes of the whistle's blow. The little flags on the map were approaching Paris, and the soldier became very agitated because the construction of the tribune was still taking thirty-five minutes. It became apparent that he would have to be satisfied with this as the fastest time. He began feeling akin to Napoleon, exercising electrifying control over his subjects.

Elsewhere in Europe, the war was raging. Paris fell, and thirty-five minutes after the soldier heard the news, the tribune was installed. It was a double triumph for the soldier – the fall of Paris signifying German control, and the tribune being constructed within thirty-five minutes. The victory deeply pleased him, and he offered the Jews many barrels of beer, as much as they wanted, purchased with money from his own pocket. The Jews themselves were momentarily pleased because they knew that this was the only thing standing between them and a never-ending chain of suffering. After this event, the soldier left them alone in relative calm and treated them in a surprisingly humane way. The other priests and I felt that he was a divided man – a faithful follower of Hitler's brutal command, yet at times showing decided kindness toward others. A fight for his soul raged inside him.

THE FAMILY OF BRZEZINSKICH

OUR LIVES TOOK ON A sense of regularity, almost as though the situation were normal, with few new visits from the Gestapo. The police were not our friends, but they treated us tolerably, and our friends in Poznan helped us obtain our breviaries and our sacred glasses for the celebration of Mass. Our families were able to visit us; I received mine twice. They became our group of friends, along with other people from the town of Golina who wanted to help us.

The Brzezinskich family, whom we barely knew, never tired of helping us, and demonstrated their sincere sympathy for our situation. If any members of that honest and kind family heard that we needed something, they went about finding it for us. The head of the household was a pharmacist whom the entire town admired for his honesty and excellent citizenry. He gave us the gift of necessary medicines. He also ensured that we received food every day. Another member of this family was the proprietor of the mill and of electricity. I will never be able to thank this family enough. They were able to warn us just before the Gestapo arrived to take us to the concentration camp.

The Brzezinskich family was composed of two single sisters and an admirably attractive grandmother. Their brother lived in Warsaw. Every year, the daughters of that brother came to spend their vacations with their aunts in Golina. By mutual agreement, after the vacation was over each year, the relatives took turns accompanying the girls back to Warsaw. This year was the older sister's turn. The year of the war, Maria, the younger sister, had a prophetic and significant dream. Two weeks before the war exploded, she told us about this dream at breakfast the day after she'd had it. Naturally, no one believed her, but they enjoyed hearing her tell the story. It was like listening to one of the tales from *A Thousand and One Nights*. Unfortunately, this story became reality two weeks later.

She told her dream like this. "I dreamt it was not my older sister who accompanied the girls to Warsaw; instead, it was me. My sister was sick and asked me to go in her place, and I gladly agreed. It happened to be the night of the first of September, and when I arrived at the capital, I saw German airplanes bombing the city. We all ran to the girls' father's house. Planes were flying over us, but none of them dropped a bomb on us. I saw some houses destroyed from the bombs and many people running in the streets. Looking up into the sky, I saw two eagles, one white and the other black, fighting furiously in the air. In a moment, I saw the white eagle fall to the ground and the other one clawing its chest, devouring it into pieces. Then I clearly heard a voice: *'This is how Poland will die, but not forever.'* And then, seconds later, I saw a light on the horizon, accompanied by a voice that said, *'Poland will live.'*"

This was where the younger sister's dream ended. When I heard her relating this dream, I thought it seemed laughable, and I gave it no importance. She told many people about this vivid dream, again, two weeks before the start of the war.

Essentially, almost all the events of her dream were identical to what happened two weeks later. People can think what they will, but everything she dreamed came true, except for the resurrection of Poland. The older aunt became sick, and the younger one traveled with the girls to Warsaw. Once they reached the capital, they witnessed an air attack by the Germans like the one in Maria's dream – the perfect realization of that terrible night. Two planes fought overhead, and one of them fell to the ground in pieces. Who is capable of a response to this phenomenon? I abstain from making any comment. The only thing I will relate is that I heard Maria's dream from her lips, recounted in identical detail, two weeks before the military events were to occur.

THE FLIGHT

THROUGHOUT THIS ENTIRE TIME, WE were prisoners in the town. The proprietor of the mill had a well-hidden radio and kept us informed about news at the front, although much of what we heard was German propaganda. We were aware of some of the daily events of the war and the situation that now reigned over our land. The radio was the bridge of news. It became evident that we must escape before the Gestapo returned to Golina.

The oldest son of the proprietor was a member of a secret organization against Hitler. We arranged with this young man to plan for my escape and the escape of my fellow prisoners. However, an escape project was to be made for all of us, and our Father Superior was adamantly opposed. He knew we faced certain death if we were caught, and he did not want to hear talk of this escape. We did continue to talk, though, and all but one of us were determined to leave. In the end, it was agreed that each of us had the right to try to save his own life.

Without our ever hearing the name of any member of the secret organization that would help us, the plan took shape. The proprietor of electricity would turn off all the street lights and we would flee at night, wrapped in darkness. His son obtained everything we would need to ensure our safety – disguises, money for the trip, false documents, and a place for us to stay. Finally, the day arrived when we were to flee. Each of us disguised himself, received the money and documents, and took his first steps toward freedom. It was apparent that God had us in His hands. That same day, after we were gone, the Gestapo arrived to take us to a concentration camp.

I moved from place to place. Finally, one day I arrived at my family's house. My father had been so worried, and he spoke to me about my sister-in-law, Marysia, who still lived in Poznan. He was frightened because no one had heard any news of her. Because my new traveling documents were in perfect order, I went to Poznan to find her. Our friends affirmed that our church in Poznan had been converted into German headquarters and that the church doors were sealed. However, the Gestapo had sealed only the rear church doors, so it was possible to enter through the front doors and ascend to two rooms in the church tower – a perfect place to hide. The Gestapo did not know about the small door connecting the church to the tower rooms. Through that door, I could go out into the church itself while they slept. Those tower rooms were freezing, as the heat had been turned off all over Poland, but my friends brought me food and I lived in relative comfort. I could go quietly into the church to celebrate Mass, and I could visit my sister-in-law, who lived not far away. However, it was rumored that a German colonel was staying in her house.

IN THE ARMS OF
A GERMAN COLONEL

MY FIRST VISIT TO MARYSIA'S home confirmed that what I had heard was true. A German colonel lived in her house but was not there when I arrived. My brother was away in the military, and only Marysia and the colonel were staying there. Weeks earlier, the Gestapo had come to her door. They had thrown her out of the house, taking all her furniture and possessions. A German colonel moved into the house, though when he heard of Marysia's situation, he insisted that she be returned to her home. The Gestapo tolerated this, yielding to the colonel's demands, but only if Marysia lived there as his servant.

Once the Gestapo left, the colonel said to my sister-in-law, "Lady, you are not my servant but the lady of the house." He seemed to have a conscience, which was hard to find during that time. He was a man with a quick temper, yet he appeared to be honest, someone who possessed a sense of justice. He treated Marysia with respect.

After one of my visits, I descended the ladder from the back window, as was my custom, and ran right into the colonel. He knew who I was from a photo in the house and asked if I was a priest.

He shook my hand and said, "Come, we need to talk."

I did not know how to respond, as I was unsure whether this

was a malicious trick or a sincere attempt at discussion. After a lengthy conversation, I began to trust that he was an honest man with good intentions. He said that what he most desired was to locate my brother and return him to Marysia in good health. The colonel asked me to visit him every day and said the Gestapo would be no problem. If they caught me, I was to call him and he would defend me against them. A friendship was growing between us, and he invited me to attend a movie with him. However, this was too dangerous and I refused.

In all our conversations, he would ask, "What do you think of the war? Who is going to win?" He saw that I could not respond adequately, and he went on to say, "I understand you very well. You cannot give me your honest opinion. This is logical because you are Polish and I am German. I am going to tell you what I think. I am not Catholic. I am Protestant, a Protestant who positively believes in God and practices religion with a moral conscience. And I would say that if God indeed exists, Germany must lose this war. Germany must pay for all the cruelty done to the Polish, cruelty that you could not imagine, which I have seen with my own eyes. Germany will lose this war."

In the streets, there was a rumor that a Jew had returned to the city and was hiding in the church. It was very dangerous, as the Gestapo was looking for him and would no doubt find me as well. I immediately changed residences, staying in a place far from the church. I remained hidden there for three days. However, the colonel found me and gave me his ballpoint pen. He asked if I would bring him religious medals for his wife and two sons, even though they were not Catholic. He said he would help my brother, who by now was in a German prison. He said he would take the proper procedures with the authorities so that I could return to my home.

I planned to flee on the fourth day, though I went to talk to him first. He embraced me as though I were a true friend. He said that he cared for me like a brother and that he would accompany me to a safe place. Being accompanied anywhere by a German colonel was an appealing idea, though it would raise suspicions wherever we went. Also, it would compromise him as a soldier, so I did not accept. He insisted that he give me money, which also seemed to be a complication. The possibility of it falling into Gestapo hands posed a threat, and I would be unable to explain how I managed to carry anything of value. I was not completely desperate and thought my usual state of poverty would suffice.

THE BETRAYED

THERE WERE RUMORS OF MY capture, so I was forced to remain hidden. I managed to return to my father's house, where I stayed for a very short time. I was running from the Gestapo but also from the gossip of kindly townspeople. Through their idle talk, they spread word about my location and unknowingly compromised my safety.

I fled by train to Kalisz even though Poles were prohibited from traveling, and I experienced problems – interventions and violent insults – all along the way. However, I was able to arrive at the house of the Franciscan Fathers in Kalisz, which was already filled with Germans. They had allowed the priests to remain in their lodgings, and we discussed among ourselves the terrible circumstances that had affected us all. The Fathers took care of me in their best spiritual way; however, I met a young girl from a poor Polish family who would soon be the cause of my imprisonment. Despite the comfort there, I did not stay long and moved quickly to an orphanage. I did not realize that the young girl was in the service of the Gestapo and that her mission was to spy on the priests' actions.

Sometimes I walked around the city as though I were free. Another Jesuit often accompanied me, a brother whom I had known throughout my religious studies. One day, he informed me that within twenty-four hours, he would have a chance to flee. He entrusted me with this information and asked if I would pick up his watch from a shop where it was being fixed, then bring it to him before he was to leave.

I wanted to accompany him and knew how to obtain crucial documents in which my first and last name would be German. These documents were completely valid and signed by the German authorities. Thus, I now had with me the papers that gave me liberty of movement in all countries that the Germans occupied – all the territory of the Reich. The young girl followed my every footstep. Ultimately, acting against her conscience and to avoid death at the Gestapo's hands, she agreed to prove her loyalty, with me as the victim. When I returned from the watchmaker's shop, the police were waiting for me. They looked at my papers, positioned themselves on either side of me, and took me to jail.

In those circumstances, I could do nothing. It was useless to run, guarded as I was. I looked for a chance, even a street with many passersby, but the streets on which our steps echoed were deserted. There is a saying that a shipwrecked man will grab at anything that floats. The same thought occurred to me, and I tried to get rid of the false documents, thinking that without them, nothing serious could be proven against me. My guards were a couple of authentic *Volks Deutsche*, "snotty boys," recruited for the unfortunate function of arresting Polish and German citizens. I started crumbling the documents in my pocket. I don't know if this was a sign of boldness, prudence, or inexperience on my part, but I was hoping this might enable my release.

At the headquarters, I was brought to the chief, who was uninterested in my presence. I stood leaning against the wall for many hours. Finally, I timidly asked if I might sit, as I was drained and experiencing an alarming weakness in my feet. The chief made a gesture for me to sit, then continued with his own business as though I did not exist. It was well into the night when he began asking me a series of questions, completely as a formality, and said that my pockets should be searched. The soldier searching me was surprised to find little pieces of paper and nothing else; he became impatient with me. I thought that only one of two things would happen: they would reconstruct my documents, in which case my future was dark and dangerous, or they would be unable to remake anything of my papers, and I would be safe.

They took me to a small cell with no windows and only a cement floor upon which to lie. Abandoned in this dark prison, I tried to rest while the soldiers worked to repair my papers. If they did, they would see a photo of a person very much like myself, with a German name, but with no German blood in his veins.

At eight o'clock the next morning, one of the police officers opened the door. In a fierce voice, he directed me to accompany him to the chief's office. I understood that we were not about to engage in entertaining conversation. The chief said he knew my way of speaking was not authentically German, and he had concluded that I was involved in high espionage. He said I would soon be put in the hands of the Gestapo.

IN THE HANDS OF THE GESTAPO

I KNEW VERY WELL THAT falling into the hands of the Gestapo, who were famous for their cruelty, was the equivalent of the prelude to hell. One could not expect kindness from an organization whose members glorified being authentically German, not by their manliness, but by their cruelty. I also knew that the Gestapo cared little about the actual truth and that being accused of a crime could be enough to seal my fate.

The place of interrogation was an ugly room with a very large table strewn with papers. Leather whips – used for torturing the imprisoned – leaned against the wall. Sitting in a revolving chair behind the table was a young man with a cigarette between his lips. He was perhaps too young for this level of responsibility and importance, and his sympathetic countenance disguised the blood of a wild animal. There, in that room, I looked for something that would be in my favor and give me a string of hope.

The interrogation began. The chief started by reciting my *curriculum vitae* and the history of my work, saying that I was involved in espionage and that I was an active member of an anti-German organization. He said it would be stupid of me to not admit my acts and divulge the details of the network of spies to which I belonged. I had nothing to tell him.

He maintained complete self-control while insisting that he

wanted the truth and that he knew my false name to be Modok. He wanted all information and all other false documents in my possession. He seemed satisfied with my child-like responses that told him nothing; his demeanor was calm and patient. He then came after me and beat me with all his strength, raining heavy blows upon my back and my whole body. He expected that, through pain and fear, he could force my shameful confession and deep contrition, thereby gaining every particle of information I had withheld.

However, he was wrong, first because I knew nothing to tell, and second because I became like a mule. Whipped instead of treated gently, I became angrier. Imitating the splendid example of that stubborn little animal, I tightened my lips and would not say a word. For this discovery of my own character, I must thank them. It helped save my life and the lives of any I could have named. I began to understand my mother's saying, that if you treat someone badly, it is worse than being that same devil and that you can obtain everything you want by treating another in a proper manner. The Gestapo did not recognize this basic tenet, which was why they lost the war.

I was returned to my cell, and my body hurt so much that any movement created additional suffering. I was convinced that my injuries were more severe than I could imagine. Several days passed. Then the Gestapo came to take me back to my previous room.

After we entered, a man dressed in civilian clothes stood behind me. He said, "Father, tell them the truth. The young girl told them everything."

This was how I knew she had informed on me. She and her family had been threatened with death unless she spied for the Germans. I was one of a group whom she had denounced. I did not condemn her because I knew that her life required these activities.

When I entered the room, I heard dark laughter. The Gestapo seemed very excited. One of them was telling a story about three Polish men who had tried to flee and had been captured. They men had been condemned to death.

The Gestapo were laughing when one of them began to question me. "Father, would you like to tell the truth today?"

Though I was so weak I could hardly stand, I answered, "I give you my word that if you try to hit me again, I will not utter a single sound. I prefer to die and leave my skeleton here." I said it with such energy that they all began to laugh harder, very satisfied with themselves.

"Tell us what you have done and where you have been since the first of September 1939."

To this question, I briefly answered that I had been at my father's house taking care of him. Immediately, they asked for his address, then took pictures of me from all angles. The chair where a prisoner sat to have a photo taken had an enormous needle on one side. As the picture was taken, the operator would press a button and the needle would stick into the body of the prisoner, causing him to scream in pain. Another prisoner had informed me of this, and so I avoided one more painful injury by sitting carefully on the chair.

One of the Gestapo was sent to find my father, a man who would never tell anything but the complete truth. He had permanently instilled in us, his sons, his great love of the truth.

"Do you know this man?" the Gestapo asked him.

"If I do, he is my son," was his answer.

"Where has your son been from the beginning of the war until this day?"

My father was about to say, "I don't know," when he closed

his lips and hesitated. Then, without knowing why he was saying it, he responded, "He has been here with me the entire time."

This was the first innocent lie of his life, and it saved me. It is hard to explain such an event regarding my father, but I had been trying to send him ardent messages through my mind, begging him to say the right thing, knowing that my life depended on it. After the war, I spoke to my sister, Wladzia, the only witness to this conversation. She said that it suddenly seemed to occur to my father to give that answer.

Now they directed all their attention on my passport. "Why do you have a passport?"

"For the purpose of visiting my religious brothers."

"Where are their houses?"

I explained that there were many, in Poland, Germany, and Czechoslovakia.

"Which houses have you visited? Where did you get a German name?"

If I responded to that, many people would be in trouble. I said, "From a German friend of mine."

"Why not use your Polish name?"

I told them that I knew there would be suspicions if I used a Polish name and that I would have been denied a passport. They asked about the money I carried and the watches, one of which was mine.

"You have stolen the other watch," they said. "And how do you have this much money?" I was carrying one hundred and twenty-five Deutsch marks. I explained about my companion who had asked me to pick up his watch from the watchmaker's shop and told them that my father and my brother had each given me money.

"Don't you know it is prohibited for Poles to carry this money?"

I said I certainly did not know this.

With no proof or real concern for the truth, they stamped "THIEF"on my papers. I was taken to another cell.

In Jail For The Second Time

THE JAIL WAS AN OLD building with an exterior aspect that was worse than the reality, sizable and gray. My cell was for those sentenced to death. It was minuscule and dark, with a tiny, narrow window at the top of the interior wall – a window from which one could never see outside. The smallest piece of sky was barely visible at midday. Weak rays of light fell upon the straw mattresses that served as our beds.

Both my companions had received their sentences – condemned to death. One of them awaited his day to enter the other world, declaring that he was not in much pain because he felt that he had not sinned greatly. His crime was to own an old revolver, which had been found in his home during an ordinary search of Polish houses. He passed his nights chained up, with handcuffs on his hands. Surely, he died. He disappeared from the cell one day, and I never heard news of him.

My other cellmate was young, and he had been condemned to prison for life. A revolver had been found in his house as well, one that his father-in-law had used in the First World War. He was the father of two little girls and the owner of a small farm. The Gestapo had brutally tortured him in his own home. The man could not imagine living his entire life in prison and had practically stopped eating. The food was not so bad, and it would have been sufficient to preserve his physical strength. However, most of it went back to his guard. The man spent his days in one of the four corners of the cell, speaking not a single word. We could not make him talk to us. He cried so much, his eyes were very sunken, dark, and sore. His heart was entirely torn. The only subject that interested him was his family, his two daughters, though we tried not to mention them or any family matters because he would drown in desperation and exhibit symptoms that made him seem crazy. The situation was unbearable; his emotional suffering made every moment almost intolerable.

One day, he was called out because his lawyer was trying to revise his sentence. He was to appear for the second time before the judge. When he returned, his punishment had been changed to ninety-nine days. I was certain he had been cleared of all unlawful responsibility; he had the face of a satisfied man and was able to speak.

I said to him, "I congratulate you, and it makes me happy for your good fortune. Perhaps you will soon see your family."

I tried to shake his hand, and he let out a crazy laugh. "*They condemned me to death.*"

I asked, "How is this possible?"

He said, "It is true. They condemned me to life in prison, but according to the German code, that life is only ninety-nine days."

This became a time of the craziest emotional disparity. It was true. This young man had been condemned to die in ninety-nine days, which was the saddest, most terrible news that no one could have predicted. However, the young man's response was happiness. The light returned to his eyes, and he was happy to speak, which he did constantly. It was not vulgar or monotonous talk, but funny stories and jokes, making us laugh, enough so that we all thought *we* were going crazy. The atmosphere in our cell was so lively, if it hadn't been for the presence of our jailers, we would have forgotten we were in prison. The young man's voracious appetite returned, and he was never satisfied with the amount of food he received. He had no shame in asking us for a portion of our food, which at first, we offered with pleasure. Finally, we had to say, "NO," or we would have nothing left to eat.

The oddest thing was that his happiness was not a passing mood, something that varied from day to day. Even the handcuffs placed on him at night did not affect his sense of humor. We had figured out how to loosen and remove the handcuffs, which could be done easily, but he preferred to keep them on. He counted the days remaining in his life, according to the law, from the day of his sentencing. I tried to offer him a confession, but he always responded that he had nothing to confess; his conscience was clean and he had no regrets.

One morning we awoke and he was happy as always. He immediately began telling us about his dream of the night before. He had been mounted on a brown horse, fast as an arrow, and the two of them were galloping far, far, with no end in sight. Suddenly, the horse was gone, the young man's head had disappeared, and he was alone in an unknown place.

I said to him, "I hope they don't cut off your head today as happened in your dream." We all laughed like crazy men, placing no importance whatsoever on all this.

We were waiting for breakfast when our cell door opened and the soldiers called out our delightful companion; with enthusiastic gestures, he said goodbye to us. Days passed and we learned nothing of his location; we felt submerged in an ocean of questions about him. The jailers finally told us that on the day he was taken out of our cell, he had been put to death by beheading. His dream coincided with his execution, which he had awaited with such peculiar happiness. These events were strange and unexplained.

THE GESTURE OF A NOBLE AUSTRIAN

IN THIS JAIL WAS A certain guard, an Austrian citizen, a Catholic, with a strong body, a red, amiable face, and a big stomach. He gave the impression of a laborer, and he had very negative feelings toward any type of brutality. Once he found out I was a priest, he tried to get close to my cell to exchange a few words with me, leaving me with a drop of hope for a better future.

He came to my cell one day and said that he felt very bad that I had been arrested and that perhaps he could find me a job that would help me work my way out of prison. His offer moved me, but I also knew that all the other soldiers and officials in the jail treated the Poles with extreme brutality, so I kindly responded that I could not accept. He was clearly trying to help me, but he understood my fears and never mentioned the subject again. I knew I was to be called before the judge the next day and I would await his judgment.

That night, I had a dream that I didn't give special importance. However, I talked about it with my cellmate, just to fill some of the long, confining hours. We had both been advised that we awaited death, so the dream had no real impact, but I awoke from it feeling dazed and I wondered about its significance.

I dreamt that I was in the presence of the judge, who was a

tall man, bald and with a cold aspect. He had extremely long arms that ended in fists like those of a ferocious animal. He raised his voice a lot, launching insults at me, looking like a man who would devour me to relieve his fury. He judged and condemned me.

THE JUDGE

AT LAST, MY TURN ARRIVED to go before the judge. Two officers put handcuffs on me. Like a thief and a dangerous bandit, I was taken to an empty room. Inside it were tables, a circular desk, and a few steps up where the accused was to stand. The officials entered, and the man in the middle caught my attention, his presence touching the marrow of my being. He was tall and thin like the handle of a broom, with a long neck and a large head, disproportionate in size, more squared than angular. His cheekbones jutted out, and his high, broad forehead had many wrinkles. He was bald but with a beard, and his long nose pointed far down, making his face look brutal. He resembled an alien creature, although within his interior was a human heart. My fervent hope was that his immortal soul still contained some image of God. He lifted his long arm in a firm way, the gesture of the Führer. "Heil Hitler." His voice did not resemble his body; it was more like thunder trying to intimidate me, the one he called the insolent Jesuit.

Before saying a word to me, he had clearly found me guilty. My legs were so weak that everything sank beneath me. A cold sweat covered my body, taking away my resistance. My heart beat as hard as the whip of the Gestapo, and I felt incapable of opening my mouth.

The judge began reading the accusations, his voice filling the room. I was so dazed with fear, I did not understand a word.

He stopped from time to time to look at me. In those moments, I could only yield, crushed not by guilt but by fear. "When did you become a spy and who were your collaborators?"

A legal officer was present, supposedly to defend me, but I couldn't think or speak. Finally, I said in Polish, "I don't understand."

The officers exchanged insults. The judge said, "It is written here that you speak perfect English."

I knew I had to answer or be condemned to die. I was able to say, "This is the first lie that is told against me."

The judge did not stop talking but attacked me over and over on the same issue, yelling at me and presenting the case against me as though it were well-known. Something changed inside me. Fear no longer dominated me. Almost like in the dream, I was suddenly able to give precise responses to each of the judge's questions. It had been a dream, but I prefer to think of it as a beam of love from the sky, helping me through my most critical moment.

The judge said, "I will not present any further facts because your guilt is proven here, with your signature."

I answered, "The signature is not valid. I signed only because of the violence and beating."

He said, "The document is valid to me." With each statement, the judge became more like a truly wild animal, condemning and insulting me, calling me insolent, a badly educated priest, a depraved man, and a liar who would not admit his mistakes. I told him my only mistake was to have taken a German name instead of my Polish name and that the remainder of the accusations were false. He did not take any more time with me but continued screaming and throwing insults.

He stood, irritated, and with a gesture of fury, said, "I am going to punish you, you insolent Jesuit. You will remember me all your life." The legal officer was not allowed to speak or take part in the process. The sentencing was brief: the workforce for an indeterminate time, and then the concentration camp. After the judgment, I was returned to my cell.

ZACHTHAUS-SIERADZ CELL 13

TWO WEEKS PASSED AND THEN I was transferred to the jail in Zachthaus-Sieradz. It was the beginning of 1940. This was where I remained until November 13 of that same year.

The name of the prison indicated its character. Three large adjoining buildings formed the shape of the prison. They were new buildings, modern, very comfortable, clean, and sanitary. The cells were on the sides of the buildings in a triangular shape, creating a spacious central room where prisoners would gather, guarded by the authorities. I was given cell number 13, a large room with a long window that overlooked the outside. The sun's abundant rays filled it, creating an effect completely opposite of the dark memories of my previous cell. Eight beds with sheets and blankets had been placed against the wall, which had armoires that stored eating utensils. There was one large "tub" for all of us.

All the inhabitants of cell 13, eleven others and myself, were young, of Polish descent, all in the flower of life and full of optimism even though everything was certainly not well. We felt that our cell was one of the privileged, with good living conditions, although the environment did not favor education unless it was in thievery. One of the young men was so young, he was almost a little boy.

Thus, we were twelve, like the apostles. Four of us left the cell every day at certain hours to function as barbers of the jail. After breakfast, they would travel from room to room, with guards watching vigilantly. They served as a partial link between the imprisoned and the free world, and we all benefited from this. The news was transmitted by way of the barbers, and after some months, they generally enjoyed quite a bit of liberty, with no one especially interested in them once they were inside each cell. They cut the hair of the cooks and often received extra food, some of which they brought to us. No one bothered to check their box, which held their hair-cutting instruments but could also keep a good sausage.

MARIO

IN OUR CELL, THE REAL leader was Mario. Everyone respected him, and no one contradicted his orders. He was a short, muscular young man with a well-formed body. He had a small mouth and eyes that moved like a bat's, missing nothing. He had an extraordinary ability with words and could use them to intimidate most of the other prisoners. He was very agile but conceited, and he acted as though he were the only real man among us. He was a natural bully whose intense, penetrating eyes terrorized those around him; anyone who tried to confront him would be beaten and left lying on the ground.

Mario acted like a brute, but he had delicate, feminine ways when he thought no one was observing him. He had long, shiny nails like a woman's and was always clean and tidy. His stories, though, were the dirtiest I had heard in my life, and his mouth was like the foulest human thesaurus. His previous nocturnal excursions to homes that were not his, his frequent encounters with the police, his tales of his love adventures and his thievery – these passed the time for many of the prisoners, though they did not necessarily believe much that Mario said. He knew only a few German words, but he understood his superiors very well and was able to instill confidence in them. Once he became aware that I was a priest, he demonstrated more respect and pretended to act like a gentleman with me while being rude and disrespectful to the rest.

Mario was adept psychologically. He could ascertain the other prisoners' needs, and he always carried an extra portion of food or a cigarette in his bag. The food wasn't so bad in prison, but at times it was not enough. Mario would bribe a prisoner with food, then become violent. Though he was an insupportable brute who loved humiliating others, he was also an essential companion, bringing food and generously distributing it to us when he had more than enough for himself.

Once Mario knew my priestly character, he began trying to subjugate me to his will by offering his daily ration of food, which he didn't need; he ate in other cells and had stored food here and there for his own consumption. He became violent and bossy, using crude language and telling foul jokes and stories about my private life.

I knew I would have to face him, and I finally said, "Silence, you rabble. Because you are corrupt, do you think everyone else around you is corrupt?"

All the prisoners started to laugh. While he sneered and laughed with them, overcoming and defeating the poor priest, I knocked him down with a blow to the nose. Of course, he beat me badly, and the first person who came to help me was Stasiek, the smallest prisoner, actually still a little boy. His physical strength could never have saved me, but he set an example for the others. He awoke the boldness in one other prisoner, and now we were three against Mario. He was like a wild animal and could have easily defeated us, but because we resisted him, stood up to him, and humiliated him, he backed away. From then on, he acted more cordially toward us all.

STASIEK

STASIEK, THE YOUNG MAN WHO was the first to help me, was very sweet, innocent, and happy. He enjoyed the affection of all the prisoners in the cell. Being from a poor family, he had no choice but to help his widowed mother, so he began stealing. For this he was put in prison, waiting months without hearing a sentence or knowing what his fate would be. He was a pious boy and confessed to me, asking me to not go even one night without praying for him, his mother, and his country.

The barbers brought this boy a large portion of fresh bread, and while chewing, he used some of the breadcrumbs to build a statue of the Furher. We all observed his delicate and artistic work and helped him hide it from the authorities; it was exquisite and very realistic. However, with so many visits from officers and with German soldiers coming and going, this could not remain a secret for long. They soon discovered this likeness of their "god." At first, they did not know what to think, but considering the artistic and realistic nature of the statue, they became interested in its maker, little Stasiek. They admired his qualities and talent and provided colors so that the Führer might have his precise uniform.

On another occasion, the officers discovered that Stasiek had made model airplanes that were quite realistic, and his case was brought before the authorities. Members of a special military commission came to see him and asked him if he would like to study sculpture under their guidance. Stasiek was interested in studying, and he could also see the possibility of his freedom. In this way, he disappeared from our lives, but not from our hearts. We never knew what became of him.

THE TACITURN GENIUS

ONE DAY, A NEW PRISONER joined our cell. Now we were thirteen prisoners in cell 13. He was a tall, thin young man with a sad demeanor. At first sight he appeared intelligent. Taciturn did not take part in any of our conversations. Almost daily, he sat against a wall, meditating upon who knows what matter. He seemed to be ruminating over anguishes unknown to us. Knowing that I was a priest, little by little he began opening himself to me. He was distrustful, and he did not want to touch upon any matter related to himself or his history.

He was making a thick rope out of thin strips of paper, and we did not know what the thing would become. In the first days when he did not speak a single word, we saw him go in circles in the cell, seeking and testing various objects. What was he thinking and for what reason did he need those objects? It was a true mystery to us, and we started to believe he was completely crazy. However, the young, crazy Taciturn carried out more work in one week than any of us, inventing a machine out of nothing. We had been working with our hands and had nothing to show for it, while he worked using his brain and invented a new machine.

In our conversations, I came to know a little about his life. He was from a very poor family and had always dreamt of becoming an engineer. Though economically this was impossible, his desire grew stronger daily. "I want to be an engineer," he'd declare emphatically.

This was all he thought of. He proceeded through secondary school, buying his books by working at a small job and by having food one day and none the next. He knew nothing of the charms of young girls and became a hermit, struggling to realize his aspirations. He succeeded in finishing his studies in Krakow, learning French while he was there, and then an even bigger insanity – he decided to go to France. While in Calais, he found work and continued to improve his French. Soon, he was teaching classes to French children. His economic situation was still dreadful, and he used the same strategy – eating one day, fasting the next until he finally achieved his golden dream and received his engineering degree, crowning himself with success. He worked in France but wanted to return to his native land. When he did, the war surprised him.

Taciturn began working in military workshops and on submarines. Everything was going well for him; he was doing what he felt was a crucial task and he was privy to military secrets.

One day, a chief inspector from Berlin, aware of Taciturn's Polish accent, called him away from his work section, stating, "If you are speaking less than original German, I will put you out."

He was then put out on the street, where he did not greet the German police. Because of this, they gave him a slap. When he defended himself, they threw him to the ground. That was how he ended up in cell 13 at Zachthaus-Sieradz.

Because of his act against a German police officer, Taciturn awaited death by German justice, but not by Divine decree. The secretary of the jail announced that some paperwork had arrived and that the chief inspector had ordered Taciturn's immediate freedom. He never really believed he would remain alive.

He said to me, "Today they will forgive me, but tomorrow they will kill me."

After a few days, the director of the jail appeared at our cell, acting extremely friendly. He took the engineer away. Taciturn never returned, and our contact with him was severed, so we never heard any more news of his life.

A Saved Bounty

The Germans were accustomed to giving us unpleasant surprises, and on the days when we least expected them, they would enter our cell and turn everything upside down, including us, from head to toe. One of these visits put us all in danger. On this day, the barbers had returned to our cell with an extraordinary bounty – two kilos of cold meat, which they had received from the kitchen after cutting the cooks' hair. As usual, no one stopped them or checked what they were carrying. It seemed as though our eyes would pop out of their sockets. Our mouths were watering at so rare and appetizing a feast. However, every joy in this world can have a short existence. Before midday, the barbers came to tell us that we were about to have an inspection and that we were to hide the cold meat well. Our problem was where to hide something when all the items in the cell were in plain sight; even a needle would be obvious. We had two solutions: to put everything in the tub (which we used to relieve ourselves) or to eat everything, which we could not do quickly enough, as the inspectors were already in the next cell.

An idea occurred to me, and knowledge of German psychology helped me devise a plan. I sat on the tub and fired enough gas out into the room to make a terrible odor. I don't know how I did it, but when the inspectors stepped into our cell, I kept passing gas; they held their noses and tried not to breathe the lethal air. The cold meat was hidden in a blanket behind a group of prisoners and would be discovered if I did not perform well. Squeezing my stomach with both hands and showing the inspectors such pain on my face, I acted as if I were giving birth to five children. My posture and the unpleasant smell were an embarrassment to the soldiers, who couldn't leave quickly enough. The hidden treasure, as well as the reputation of the barbers, who were trembling like autumn leaves, had been saved.

Mario was the first to hear our victory story, and he ardently embraced me, the hated priest, admiring the whole adventure and saying, "I suspected that you were a bad man, but now I see you are a devil." In this way, I gained an odd respect from Mario and the other prisoners.

SAVED BY A SONG

MARIO WAS A GOOD SINGER. Many times, lying on the mattresses, we listened to his soft voice through an entire repertoire of songs from past days. He sang with extraordinary feeling, and one song dampened many of our eyes every time. It was about a man wrongly imprisoned. Each time Mario sang this song, it seemed new and fascinating.

When Mario went before the judge, this song changed the outcome of his ruling. It seemed to us that Mario's sentence had been unjust (he was to spend the remainder of his life in prison) but without any witnesses, he could not adequately defend himself. His lawyer prepared a slim defense. Mario prepared his song as his own defense. When Mario performed the song in court, in front of those representing the legal system and the general public who filled the room, his rendition was marvelous. His voice and his poignant composition, which were actually telling his own story, moved everyone there so much that a significant part of his sentence was reduced and he regained some part of his freedom.

I am much grieved that I am unable to remember the song, although I heard it sung many times by Mario, who delighted in singing it and who sang it so well. It was like something out of another century, though it was recent, written during his days confined to his cell. He sang it with genuine feeling through an abundance of tears shining in his tiny, knowing eyes.

GAME OF CARDS

ACCORDING TO GERMAN REGULATIONS, THE imprisoned could not play cards in their cells. In our cell, though, two men were united by their skill at thievery and by their attention to card playing. Of course, they paid no attention to the no-card-playing rule, enjoying their games every day.

The guards had a small hole through which they could look without being noticed. The two young men sat in front of the hole to demonstrate their lack of concern about being caught. One of the guards silently put a key in the door and burst in to catch the two card players; he found nothing, turning over the entire cell, searching the men, and finding no cards.

The next day, the scene was the same as before, with an additional guard joining the procedure, both of them making a thorough and laborious search for the cards. They knew who the two individuals were, having seen them many times through the hole in the door, but could not find the evidence. Once again, they left the cell empty-handed.

On the third day, the two friends did not stop playing and were doubly happy to frustrate the guards again. On the fourth day, the two guards were accompanied by the jail director, who searched both men in the nude, as well as the rest of us, without finding the cards. The director was embarrassed to be put in this position with no cards to show for it, so he asked the men what they had done with the cards. He threatened them with punishment. The two men said they could only tell the truth – that they had no idea where the cards had gone. The director became vehement and threatened to hurt the men. However, they said they didn't understand why he kept threatening them when he held the cards in his own pocket the entire time.

He reached into his pocket and, as if by black magic, he held the cards. He was paralyzed by what seemed to be impossible and left the cell, though not before the two men craftily removed the cards from the director's pocket. These two were specialists in robbery; every day, when they played cards in front of the spy hole, the guards came in and found the cards in their own pockets. As they left, the thieves took back the cards and set up to play again. This small drama was an amusing distraction during our long days.

ATTENTION TO THE IMPRISONED

WHILE IN JAIL, THE SICK could see the prison doctor twice a week. We were always asked what level of pain we had, a low number or a high number. If the number was very high, the guards would see that prisoner first, with the intention of convincing us to not ask for the doctor again. With a high number, a prisoner was taken to the ground floor to an area where a guard waited with a stick in hand. The guard would tell us to remove all our clothes, then would entertain himself in a sadistic way by beating us with the stick, in particular around the genitals. He would ask if we felt sick; when anyone said yes, he would hit that person harder until the prisoner said he felt fine and no longer had to see the doctor.

During this time, I suffered from awful pain in my molars, and my whole face became swollen. The sadistic guard took me to the holding area and asked if I had pain. When I said I did, he began hitting me, and I was not taken to the doctor. The next day and the next were the same; the guard asked if I had pain and hit me brutally when I answered yes. The same thing was happening with other prisoners; to avoid being beaten, one of them removed his own teeth with a pair of scissors. Finally, I got a guard who was less sadistic and who took me to see the dentist.

The dentist was a lieutenant who attended patients in his

Wehrmacht uniform. He had an amiable aspect, a triangular face, and a smooth, rounded beard. He was thin and taller than medium height, and had an energetic voice. He expressed a sincere interest in the health of his patients and, compared to other Germans in prison, was more courteous and far less brutal. When I told him I was a priest, he could not hide his feelings. Forgetting the differences between us, he said that he had been a student of the Jesuits of Berlin and that he owed his education to them. Then he told interesting stories of his student life. I spoke openly and with confidence to him, not feeling suspicion or danger of any kind. He could not remove my teeth, but he prepared to put gold crowns on them. He warned me to not tell anyone about this, ever, because he was never to place gold crowns in the mouth of any Polish prisoner.

Just then he was moved to another location, a site entirely unknown to me. I never saw him again or heard about where he went, and I never had the crowns put on my teeth. However, I learned a valuable lesson from him. He behaved like an authentic German but also like a good person. His higher education notwithstanding, the cultural dream of Germans becoming "supermen" was, at least in this man, founded on true Christian ideals. Though I was an inferior Pole and a foul prisoner (and he was a hated German), he had demonstrated a genuinely Christian attitude toward me. Before he left, knowing that I could write in German, he contacted the chief of the jail, asking him to employ me in his office.

THE SECRETARY

ONE DAY SOON AFTER THAT, I was called to the chief's office. He was an illiterate man who was round rather than thin and of medium height. The chief extended his hand to me. This was incredible for a German to do within the walls of the jail.

He seemed very friendly and asked, "Father, would you like to work in my office?"

"I have never worked in an office, but if you teach me what to do, I will do it gladly," I responded.

He told me he had never worked in an office either, and that there wasn't a great deal to do, but that it was better to pass the days here than in the prison cell. The chief took me to the prison tailor because anyone working in his office had to look "decent." I received a different prison suit of clothes and a pair of shoes. I seemed like a new man.

The chief's job was to write a report each week for his superiors; his job depended upon this. For a man with little education, he knew how to keep up the appearance of a well-educated person. However, he needed someone who could write his report in perfect German. Above all, the Jews from Lodz would have done the finest job, but from the beginning, they were hated and would never be allowed to do this work. I was the only one who could write in a Gothic script. The work chief believed that the

Gothic style was an expression of a strong, energetic soul that was authentic to the Germans – one that would best represent him. Thus, I became the secretary. I would take the chief's dictations, a job all the other inmates envied.

The next day, I presented myself at the office. The chief spoke very little but showed me simple things to do that kept me busy from 8 to 11:00 a.m. At 10:00 a.m. was something called Brotzeit, which meant one could smoke or eat at that time. Every day, the chief offered me a cheese sandwich, positioning himself at the window in case anyone should look in. He said, "While I smoke, you eat this sandwich, but I must watch so that no one sees me giving you this bread. Perhaps the law would allow this, yet it is better to be careful."

Aside from the easy work and the right to Brotzeit, I was earning a daily paycheck of 14 pfennig (a pfennig was about a penny), the amount noted in a book. With my new charge as secretary, my prestige in the cell grew. Mario no longer imposed his authority over us and had forgotten his pretensions and immoral stories. Though we had lost two of our companions, the little artist Stasiek and the thoughtful engineer, we lived somewhat well and in harmony in our cell. By the time I left Steradz, I was notified that I had a payroll coming off a small number of marks.

The chief was a man-devil toward others, but he never touched me or treated me badly. The only unpleasant moments happened during official visits from the inspectors, who occasionally reviewed all the work areas. During these visits, the chief called me to appear in front of the inspectors. He mocked me and said a litany of blasphemies in front of me, which I had never heard him do before.

He spoke against the *Schwarze Mutter*, "The Black Madonna"

the Virgin Mother, venerated by the Polish people in the sanctuary at Czestochowa. His favorite statement was "Despite all the trust put in her and the many Polish prayers made at her feet, she laughed at them and did nothing against the military force of the Germans." Satisfied with his blasphemies and content with the smiles he received from his visitors, he sent me back to my place.

At the beginning of May, the chief received transfer orders. He and a group of prisoners would be going to a new location to work, Kotzine. The chief, who had the authority to move me and any of my comrades at any time, asked me delicately if I would like to be transferred with him. I answered that it was not my decision, that it depended on the Gestapo. He said that the Gestapo would not be a problem, and by mid-May we were on our way.

I Traveled To Ostrow Wiekopolski

(The Happy Young Men)

THE GESTAPO DID REMEMBER ME, and I became part of a transport of prisoners sentenced to the work force. About 150 of us would first be taken to Ostrow, a large city in the western part of Poland. This was one more step to the place that awaited, the prison sentence that would have no end.

In the small jail at Ostrow, it was my turn to occupy the already famous cell where Cardinal Dalbor had been imprisoned during the time of *Kulturkampf*, the "culture war," and the Prussian Chancellor of Iron, Otto van Bismarck. A sufficient number of beds was available for all the Polish prisoners, some of whom had put their noses into politics. They were an admirable group, aware of what was in their future, sadder than one can imagine because of documents against them – documents in the Gestapo's hands. And yet, they were some of the happiest young men I had ever seen in my life, happy and brave. They had decided to die in defense of their country and to feel some happiness in their last moments. It was much like the atmosphere of a convent, men in private prayer and in common daily meditation, with ongoing religious discussions and political gatherings, filled with a serene peace that amazed anyone who saw them or participated.

As it happened, all the cellmates were Catholic, not only because they were sons of Catholic fathers and had been baptized but also because of their experience and education. Like all other men, they loved their families and suffered very much at the separation from their homes. They loved each other as well, as companions who had been in combat, which encouraged them to stick together. They enjoyed an extraordinary and profound bond, having withstood torture by the Gestapo, who had tried in vain to make them name people who could be arrested and imprisoned. They were proud of their part in the fight against German oppression, and through their own sufferings they helped save the lives of their companions and others.

Their attitude dominated all their acts. When they kneeled to pray, which they did a couple times a day, they weren't motivated as much by respect or fear but by a necessity inside them, one that came from the heart. It was the necessity to be in contact with God and to make of their lives an offering for their beloved country.

I think my presence helped them. Not only were they able to share their experiences, but I could hear their confessions and prepare them for their final days. In truth, they still did not feel the extent of their death sentence, but it was the only possibility their future held. Our time became almost totally devoted to confession and discussions of religion and patriotism. In the mornings and afternoons, we had two hours of meditation and private prayer. During these times, the men confessed their faults and defects, and we discussed the best ways of uniting with God.

In this cell, my companions knew one of their jailers well. He was a Polish man who had worked as a guard since before the war. He was strong, round, and, by his looks, healthy – the father of a large family. He had declared a desire to help us, his jailed countrymen, and for this reason found himself in some danger, accused of being openly contrary to the State. This man, knowing well the stories of all the young prisoners, came to inspect our cell almost every day. He had little trouble obtaining bread for us. My being a priest quite affected him, and he began focusing his love and attention on me. In addition to the ordinary packet of bread, there was another, smaller one, "of something better and finer," for the Father. No doubt his gifts played a significant role in maintaining our common happiness; we never knew hunger because of the gifts of our jailer, Mr. Kazimierczak. He had chances to change his work location but instead he took every opportunity to help us.

Almost every day, he took me out of my cell to clean the jail's inner patio. This was not real work, but my friend gave me a broom with which I went round and round, always looking busy. Three times a week, we went into the city and, with some of the other young prisoners, packed up a great deal of German cereal. Our work consisted of transporting bags of cereal from one place to another, transferring food along the roads where soldiers awaited their cargo. Because of Mr. Kazimierczak's indulgent character, these excursions gave us many chances to change our clothing and escape. The German chief could see this laxity, and Mr. Kazimierczak was told that he would be transferred soon, along the rails to an unknown post.

Another young prisoner and I planned our escape. We were able to communicate with his family, whom the German occupation had not yet affected and who were ready to resolve any problems related to our escape, including providing a safe place for us to hide, one which had already been determined. The time and place were set, a car was prepared, and everything we needed was ready. However, we did not go. Mr. Kazimierczak had been exceptionally kind and vigilant in watching over us, and he was the father of a large family. If we escaped from his guard, it would be the end of him. We decided to wait for another opportunity, to flee at a time when he would not be implicated. Our collective conscience was relieved of the burden of taking him away from his family, and possibly ending his life. However, another time to escape never came.

The Mechanics

ONE DAY, WHILE WE WERE in our cell, the director of the jail presented himself in search of an auto mechanic. Unfortunately, none of us had any mechanical knowledge. However, three of us stepped forward as though we were automobile specialists.

It was a daring ruse. The director took us to the patio where his car was parked, damaged during his trips throughout the villages in search of provisions. He did not know what the car needed, but he had confidence in our expertise and left us to our work.

We looked at each other, asking ourselves, "Do you know something?"

As foreseen, out of everyone's lips came the same answer: "*NADA.*"

Nevertheless, we rolled up our sleeves and went to work. We touched everything within reach of our hands. The motor remained silent.

An officer passed by, asking us about the work we were doing and who owned the car. "It belongs to the director of the jail. It is very bad, but it won't be too long before we have it running," we told the officer.

He told us that instead of fixing it, we should do something to be certain it would never run again. He said it with such seriousness, we felt euphoric. It was a good sign when the Germans were already divided among themselves.

Without knowing anything about mechanics and by touching everything in front of us, and by blind coincidence, we got the car in running condition. We noticed a package inside – a liter of butter, which was a greatly denied delicacy. We took it directly to our cell. Thanks to the Polish bread guard, we found ourselves in our cell with no time to lose. We devoured the buttered bread, then threw the container out the window. Happy and satisfied with our combined feat, we were talking about our divine luck when the director entered. We could not satisfy his desire to see the butter again. He flew into a rage, then sent the entire cell in search of his treasure. Finally, he was convinced that we were honest, and we emerged triumphant in this very small way.

AUTUMN IN RONAU

I RECEIVED MY NEW WALKING orders and new equipment for transport: a bit of bread, summer clothes, proper attire for a prisoner, and instead of shoes, Swedish socks. Early in the morning, the transport was formed, destined for the workforce. In between the Polish were seven Jewish men; I was the only priest. We traveled small roads under guard to a town called Ronau, land that was still in Poland. This was a big farm with an abundance of work horses and a wooden shed with a thatched roof. The cement floor of this shed became our room of life.

We had barely stepped into this new place when we heard the words, "If one person tries to escape, you will all be executed."

It was the eleventh day of November, and the camp was frozen due to the cold. In the afternoon, we received the instruments for work, and we immediately went onto the land. Each man was assigned an area where he was to dig deep holes eighty-five by thirty centimeters in size. The dirt was already frozen, and before we could dig we had to tear the ice cap off the dirt. The amount of work we were to accomplish increased every day, and a Volksdeutch passing near me said some words I did not understand: "Learn to work with your arms more than your eyes if you don't want to die soon." I did not have time to think about this, and tried to do the work, my feet injured and bloody through the Swedish socks.

Trying to comply with the orders, I tore at the ice cap with a pick. Water began spraying out, covering the entire area. It seemed rational to move little by little, seeking a place to keep digging a hole, but I made no real progress. One of the other prisoners denounced me to the overseer by saying, "The priest does not want to work. He feels he is better than the rest of us." Without ascertaining whether this was true, the guard hit me across the head with this whip. I fell to the ground, covered in blood and growing numb; I lay in the freezing water with no one to help me. I don't know how long I was there, but when I regained consciousness, I was freezing and dazed with pain. One of the others close to me yelled to get to work or I would feel another blow, but I could not move. I leaned on my shovel and waited to see what God would allow. Soon the guard who had hit me came over and said, "Pastor, I hit you, and you may not have deserved it." I was allowed to rest for some time until the pain in my head subsided.

That first day was relatively brief; before 5:00 in the afternoon we were inside our shed. The whole episode was frightening, as was the fact that the Germans wanted their prisoners to appear happy, to walk and sing in a lighthearted way. They demonstrated a German song and how to sing it with the proper feeling; we all sang in different languages, using words we had tried to translate, with nothing matching. Naturally, it sounded ridiculous and offended the honor of their town. Thus, the system was changed, and we were no longer forced to sing. Instead, we were to march at the command of, "One, two, three," elevating our feet high to imitate a victorious army. Unfortunately, it was not a happy occasion but a tragic one. Often, the Swedish socks came loose and flew into the air like snowballs, barefoot men with bleeding feet chasing after them. Instead of happy marching children, now and then someone would scream as they received a blow from these strong and terrible men. The chief of the jobs evaluated the situation and, changing tactics, made everyone line up in two silent, straight lines. We were sent to see the chief of the workforce camp.

THE CHIEF OF THE WORKFORCE CAMP

HERE WAS A VERY CURIOUS man, of medium height with broad shoulders, but thin in the waist like a little girl. He had a serene aspect and was of a somewhat advanced age, and he spoke carefully, in a low voice, without ever using his hands. His indifference and coldness of manner, along with his slow and even voice, made us all nervous; we were aware that something like cold meat – not a heart – was covering his chest, and that human misery would not disturb his equilibrium.

When the chief planned a form of punishment, the devil himself could not have deciphered his thoughts. He gave the impression of a man devoured by ambition and the power to control, but truly failed at being a man of any strength or one who could make decisions of major importance. He was like an inaccessible statue with an inscrutable mask, someone who occasionally had furies and tantrums and who seemed to have no soul. Then we discovered that one of his sons had been killed during the Blitzkrieg against Poland; we thought this might have been the reason for his icy demeanor, his hatred, and his cold, calculated cruelty toward the Polish.

The food was kept out in rural places, and in those camps, our job was to create channels in which water would run. The chief determined that our digging of holes or channels should progress twenty-five to thirty-five meters over the course of half a day. The cold made this work impossible and, consequently, resulted in our failure every day. At the beginning, an abundant amount of potato soup, beets, and bread was available for four people, but gradually our food was reduced so that we might work harder. We were beaten and whipped, also to make us work harder. Of course, it all had the opposite effect; the fearsome man made the punishment worse with each failed effort. We might have been able to rest on Sundays, except that even on that day we went to work on empty stomachs, sometimes for ten hours. Because of the lack of food, the cold, the beatings, and the terrible work conditions, some of the prisoners were on the verge of death.

When they said they were unable to work, the chief used the German system to cure them: "Those who cannot work have no right to live."

We had a choice: die a little later in the work camp or die instantly under the brutal blows and kicks of the chief of the workforce.

To provide a complete image of the chief of the workforce, a small detail is worth remembering. The first Sunday after our arrival in Ronau, he entered our barracks, said some words, and encouraged us to write to our families. Naturally, there was no obligation, but each of the imprisoned had the right to send two letters per month to his family. The letters were to be written in German, and many of the prisoners asked for my help. I could do this for them; I acted as their instrument, writing and transcribing what they dictated.

Because of their fears, the messages were almost always the same, with little variation: "I'm here. I'm well. I don't need anything. Do not worry about me. I am in good health and I expect to reunite with you all at home."

My letter was different from the rest. Writing to my sister-in-law, Helena, in Kozmin, I clearly explained my situation, in no way hiding the dark aspects of our lives in the workforce camp. I wrote that I did not have the least hope of seeing her again or leaving the place alive.

The chief read all the letters, then put them in his office. The following week, he entered the barracks with a bundle in his hand – our letters, which had been intercepted. He picked up one of them, opened it slowly, called the prisoner who wrote it forward, and read it aloud. As a letter was read, each prisoner was reprimanded for not telling the truth. The chief, our defender of truth, ranted that our families had the right to know about us, and he gave us a list of reasons for not telling unforgivable lies. However, he did not hit anyone. I was like a mouse under a broom, expecting the worst because my letter had told the truth, providing the gruesome details of our life in prison.

To my surprise, the chief read my letter aloud slowly. Presenting it as a model, he stated, "That is how a letter should be written. Write what you feel; don't send your families a thousand lies."

The next time the prisoners wrote letters, they did not spare the brutal details, which in the past we had been forbidden to talk about. The chief's words encouraged the prisoners to relate their experiences with brutality in the camp; they didn't suspect the price they would soon pay. I wrote a bland letter, not saying much of anything because I thought the chief would not send it to my family anyway.

Again, the commander appeared with the bundle of letters in his hands. It had been a well-prepared trap. He told us, "For having written so many bad things against me and my companions, all of you will receive what you deserve." Two soldiers let loose blow after blow on each of the men, cruelly punishing them for their honesty. My letter was declared a model and was sent directly to my sister-in-law. To let me know they had received my communication, my brother-in-law, Stanislaw Jozefiak, sent a man disguised as himself to visit me. I did not know this man; on a Sunday, he presented himself at the prison as Stanislaw Jozefiak. I saw this person looking at me with happiness, and I responded with huge smiles, though I had no idea who he was.

The man opened his arms to me and exclaimed, "*Czesiek, Jak sie masz?*" "Chester, how are you faring?"

I answered, "*Swagier, jak ci sie powodzi?*" "Brother-in-law, how are you?" I really was *Czesiek,* but he would never be my *swagier.* We continued our masquerade, hugging and kissing. To this day, I have no idea who that man was. At least he saw me, and he must have carried news of my health and well-being back to my family. I don't know why he was willing to risk his life in this strange way, performing such a magnificent charade. Also, knowing the Germans as I did, I could not understand how it was possible to deceive them so easily, resulting in their allowing an unknown man into the prison. Of course, the prisoners were afraid to write letters, not knowing how or what to write and always fearing the same dire consequences.

Tilly, The Chief Of The Works

IF THE WHOLE WORLD WAS afraid of the principal chief of the work camp, there is no way to express the fear instilled by the presence of Tilly, the chief of the works. He was no more than thirty-five years old. Because of his skinniness and inflexibility, he seemed taller than he actually was. The lower part of his body was disproportionate to his superior upper trunk. He had very long, extremely thin legs and shoes like long canoes. When he walked or stood, his knees were a well-arched form, enough so that a large bird could easily walk between them. He looked like a human skeleton covered in a black uniform, which made the shadows of his character very fearsome. His head was narrow, his eyes lost in his dense nasal pocket. His nose was very long and ended in a curved hook, and he had a little mouth whose upper lip protruded over the lower. When he smiled, he did not open his mouth; instead, keeping his teeth tight, he laughed, "*Ji, Ji, Ji,*" his jaw sharp and pointed, his face resembling an angry bird or rooster.

His rifle was never armed, but an iron stick or anything heavy imposed punishment on the guilty. It was all very simple: not being able to finish your work due to physical exhaustion, not lining up in rows at exactly the time determined, arriving early at the place where prisoners were to stand, dragging one's hurt feet covered in their own blood during the song we had to sing when returning to the barracks, doing anything at the wrong distance from the chief – all were unforgivable crimes that demanded a beating. He watched us closely, quietly moving nearer like a panther, waiting for some loosening in our task that he could confront. He would look away as though he didn't care, then would fall on us like a wild animal, heaving blows with no compassion, hitting us anywhere and everywhere the strikes landed. He usually knocked his victim down, beating him, using his boots against the poor man's throat, chest, and stomach. During all this, he did not raise his voice, but crazy and furious, he was unable to stop his own hatred. He would look at the tortured victim, full of unexplainable and superior satisfaction, and, finally inspired in some unknown way, begin to preach furious sermons that he directed at everyone.

Once this clearly psychopathic chief had spent himself in this manner and was fully satisfied, he showed visible relief. He changed, trying to become a more understanding man, one who seemed to have human feelings. They say the devil is not as dark as he is painted, and Tilly may not have been as bad as I have painted him. Before all of us he declared himself a violent, animalistic man, committing the errors of a man; then he seemed to recognize his faults – the sign of a man who may be larger or better than he appeared.

Helper Of Anthony

BEHIND US CAME A GROUP of people who specialized in working with tubes of cement, mending the water channels and other projects on which we were working. Among them was a Polish man, Anthony. When he became aware of my presence, an imprisoned priest working at his side, he wanted to help me. Anthony told the chief of the labor camp that he would be responsible for security, assuring him that none of us would try to escape; in return, I was to have a little more food than before. The chief agreed on the condition that I never ate in front of the other prisoners and that I was never to receive cigarettes to take back to the barracks. Cigarettes had no value to me because I was not a smoker, but the gift of bread, or injection of vitamins, was how some "good days" began. Anthony brought me news of the world and of the camp Velico, and he was able to communicate with people who could lend us service if needed.

Working every day in Anthony's company, I was given a pack of cigarettes. It was dangerous to have them, but I took them to distribute to other prisoners who were smokers. Unfortunately, as I held them in my hand, someone passed by and denounced me to the chief of the work camp. He called me out in front of the other prisoners, saying, "Give me the cigarettes," in a low, threatening voice.

"I don't have any," I lied.

"Someone saw you receive a pack of cigarettes from Mr. Anthony."

"It's a lie," I said.

He had me searched, which was not hard because I had nothing in my pockets. They took off all my clothes, interested in all my organs, visible and invisible. They looked between my legs, in my behind, under my arms, and in my mouth and found nothing. I had hidden them very well. I was sent to get dressed, and they were convinced that a malicious lie had been told against me. My innocence shone like the rays of the sun, and from then on I was completely trusted by the chief of the work camp, who became my protector.

I dressed myself and got back in line with the cigarettes hidden on me in just the same way. What happened to the cigarettes? It was easy and really foolish. Because of the cold, I had a pain in my throat and had wrapped it in a cloth made from a handkerchief. Inside the handkerchief were the cigarettes. When I got naked, the only thing I wore was the cloth around my neck. Mr. Anthony, who had also been under suspicion and was relieved at the outcome of the search, was very interested in knowing the trick of the cigarettes. When I showed how I had done it, he was most surprised, not by my cleverness but by the lack of ability on the part of the soldiers and the chief of the work camp to search me completely.

It seemed that the work we had been assigned in Ronau was coming to an end; one day the chief received orders to transfer our small group of prisoners to a new place of work, Kotzine.

KOTZINE

THE PLACE DESTINED FOR THIS next phase of our lives was a little house, a granary with a small storage area for wood. Vigilantes had occupied the house, and the storage held potatoes for the workers to eat. The wooden walls of the barn house had big holes, large enough for a man's fist to pass through. The entire camp was open, with no fence. The first group's work was to create a sleeping area for all the imprisoned, with the help of some free people from the rural area who were carpenters. They were to put down wooden floors that would serve as our beds. Of course, no one thought about making lavatories, as the whole camp was open and we could use the ground outside for that purpose. We were to build a wire fence with sharp points at the top, designating the area that would contain us. At Ronau it had been freezing, not only in the barracks but also while we dug the channels, standing in freezing water up to our knees. In Kotzine, the work was the same, except now summer was approaching and the weather wasn't as cold. Again, we were to dig a channel. This time, it was to be over eight feet deep and almost twenty feet wide at the top, with walls fortified by high, sharpened sticks.

The hardest work consisted of shoveling the dirt from the bottom of the canal and carrying each shovelful to the top of the hole. This took all of a man's strength. No matter how strong the man was, the straight slant of the walls and the weight of the shovel made the job almost impossible. This work was not only irrational, but also counterproductive, with all the men working at a task that seemed impossible to execute. The prisoners could see this clearly, yet somehow the German soldiers could not grasp the situation or were unwilling to make a change.

This place quickly became a site of torture and double suffering – first, because of the impossibility of completing any of the work, and second, because of the exhaustion that followed. In the beginning, I went with the rest of the workforce and was immediately aware that I would not be able to tolerate the work or exhaustion for very long. Then, my protector, the chief, came to help me, sending me into a beautiful field like a plateau, with a panorama of wildflowers. There, I cut wood into long sticks for use in lining the channel. The chief told the vigilantes and other officers, "No one can tell the pastor what to do. He depends on me." That was all he said, and afterward, I was protected.

I knew that my position was an enviable one – performing somewhat clean work, exerting no huge effort, and having the beautiful vista of a great forest extending for two kilometers along a dirt path. At the end of the path sat houses belonging to rural farmers, as well as an immense valley covered with cultivated fields and open plains filled with flowers.

THE COMEDY OF A FUGITIVE

SEEING THE FOREST JUST BEYOND us awoke in all the prisoners yearnings to plan their escape and their salvation. However, only one of us on the workforce tried to run. It was incredibly dangerous, but taking advantage of the relative closeness of the forest, a young prisoner from Lodz tried to flee. His attempt was very serious, but it provided us with a comedy of errors as we watched.

The fugitive started running toward the forest and was well outside the range of the German soldiers before they saw him. All at once, they started yelling and running around, threatening to shoot to kill and aiming their rifles, which, at this time, were not loaded and were unable to fire one shot. They started yelling at the rural people who lived near the edge of the forest, stating that they needed horses, but those people either did not hear or were not interested in helping.

Following the example of the first prisoner and realizing that none of the guards had bullets, a second prisoner began running toward his freedom. We could not help ourselves and had a real laugh over the event. The second prisoner ran fast, trying to catch up to the first prisoner, while the guards remained confused, inactive, and utterly humiliated.

A farmer emerged from one of the rural houses, not with a rifle or any intention of catching the escaped prisoners, but followed by a nasty-looking dog. The first prisoner had reached the forest, and the second prisoner was close behind, when the dog attacked the second prisoner. He fought body-to-body with the dog. Who knows how it would have ended had the dog's owner not been able to separate them. The guards caught the prisoner, who cursed the dog and lost his chance for escape; he was taken back to the other inmates. He quietly wished the first prisoner luck and never forgot his encounter with "that damned dog." We realized that the German soldiers did not trust one another and were very poorly organized. They had appeared to be terrible as armed men, but they could not communicate with one another in a crisis and were barely able to recapture an escaped prisoner without the help of a dog.

However, in the afternoon we were told that the Gestapo had surrounded the rural houses and the forest and that soon the prisoner would be in the hands of justice; if they were unable to find him, he would die of hunger while in hiding. In the days to come, the chief happily gave us every detail of this poor man's capture, his wounds and, finally, his execution and miserable death.

THE CARPENTER

THE CAMP DID NOT HAVE enough tables on which the imprisoned could eat. Some thirty people, after long hours of work, received a moment of rest in an open space (the "dining room") to serve themselves soup and occupy whatever chairs were available. The others stood or sat on the floor.

Finally, the chief thought about making some tables and benches. Looking at us with his malicious, penetrating eye, he said, "I do not trust any of these people to do this job." Then he said, "Pastor, come here. Do you know any carpentry?"

I replied, "I know it." We were afraid of the consequences if we answered him with a negative.

"Do you really know it?"

I replied that I did.

He asked again for a third time, like Jesus did with the Apostle Peter. After providing the same answer every time, I received the task of making the tables and benches. The chief told me I would be working alone and that there was no rush to finish the job.

I did not have the slightest idea about carpentry or how to make a table or a bench. However, there was the wood, and there were the tools, and I was to set to work. The new carpenter now had the apparatus to do the job, though for the least mechanical of people, it was like trying to measure the distance to the stars.

Before starting the work, I studied our one table, which seemed simple enough – some boards with three cross pieces to hold them together. I studied the instruments. Knowledge must have come out of necessity. I made five tables and benches in three-and-a-half days. On the fourth day, I notified the chief that the tables were ready, and he stood there with his mouth open.

He did not know how to hide his admiration. In front of everyone, he said, "This pastor is not only for praying. He knows how to work well." I did not care about his compliments, but in this unusual way, I had begun to learn carpentry, which I hoped might help me in the future.

THE SOLDIER WAITER

THERE WAS A NEW SOLDIER at Kotzine. He was a model of health – other than his face, which was as red as a tomato and round like a full moon. He had a very noticeable stomach and a neck almost as wide as his head. He had a kind mouth as well, and he was in excellent humor no matter what the circumstance. He acted in no way like a German soldier, except for the fact that he kept his distance from us, more as a convenience than for any other reason, perhaps out of fear that his superiors would see his kindness toward us. While his comrades watched him, he had to pretend to be a vigilant, cruel soldier; however, when he acted rough and severe with us, it came out so poorly we had to laugh. We found it most interesting to see him try to be an authentic German man in this situation, making terrible threats we knew would not become reality. We all felt his compassion coming from a sincere heart; in the Germans' opinion, those qualities could stem from profound human defects. He never hit any of the prisoners; on the contrary, he appeared to have a sincere interest in us. I had an excellent relationship with him.

This kind soldier melted with pleasure when anyone flattered him. Because he seemed to take care of us, we first started calling him "Gentleman Waiter," and then other names to indicate his kindness. I called him "Colonel." He would state humbly that it was not true, that he had never done anything to deserve those words, degrading himself as a man and a soldier. However, we could see his joy and pride at being thought of in this way by the men around him.

At this time, I once again began experiencing excruciating pain in my molars, and my entire face was swollen. Though the chief of the works had acted on my behalf in the past, my situation did not touch him and he would not allow a visit to the dentist. I was suffering, and the "Colonel" wanted to help. I told him he was almost as important as Hitler, that he was Hitler's substitute in the prison camp and important enough to make any decision. He gave me his word that he would live up to his authority as the second Führer and bring a religious sister who could pull the teeth.

He asked for permission from the chief of the works and was denied. Feeling his authority, he brought the sister to me in triumph, fulfilling his work of charity, not considering the norms of the discipline of the strict German school. The "Colonel" had felt the charity of Christ, who saw every type of suffering, and this simple man had elevated himself to heights unknown and otherwise inaccessible to him. Nothing like this had ever happened to the chief of the works, and his fury overflowed like a raging river. He made violent gestures. He screamed. His words were indecipherable, and he rained stiff, howling shrieks upon the "Colonel." The chief became an animal covered in saliva, frothing at the mouth like a wild horse in front of the sister, who witnessed this treatment with calm and tranquility.

Both the "Colonel" and the sister, my two heroes, remained quiet. Eventually, the chief of the works regained control of himself; his tantrum passed. He would not allow an anesthetic injection, but the sister received permission to extract my molars. Maybe the chief waited for my screams and laments as this was done, and it was hard to not yell out in pain, but I closed my fists and endured. When the sister was finished, she left us with words of gratitude and the hope of better days and nights ahead. However, it took only a week for the "Colonel" to be retired from his career as a soldier because of his brave, charitable, and – for him - foolish act. I was very grateful to the sister for helping me; I no longer had pain. I was also grateful to the "Colonel," who had endangered his own life and changed it in a negative way on my behalf.

The Kitchen Inspector

THE FOOD WAS GETTING POORER. The chief had allotted some bacon grease for the potato soup, but it was disappearing before it reached the kitchen. The cooks, who were also prisoners, but fat like good cooks, were trading with some of the vigilantes and people on the outside – bacon and grease in exchange for cigarettes and other gifts. The other prisoners were eating potato water, the same as or worse than animals.

The chief knew this was happening, but it was impossible to determine who was responsible. He named me "inspector of the kitchen." My job was to watch the food and make sure nothing disappeared. The result was like magic. We had the same potatoes, the same amount of water, but with a good portion of bacon grease and bits of meat floating around. The chief of the kitchen had been accustomed to taking out portions of meat and grease for himself and for the vigilantes with whom he traded. When I saw him start to do this again, he said that I should not deprive myself of the same benefits. I said nothing but continued watching him take away sustenance from the other prisoners, all of us having known what it felt like to be starving almost to death during our imprisonment in the past.

One day, I took all the special portions the cook had put aside. I told him that if he did not want me to denounce him, and as long as I was inspector of the kitchen, all the food would be fed to all the prisoners; it would not be lost or given away. He said, "You are going to regret this," and he and the other cooks began accusing me of various unpleasant behaviors. He said he had known me before the war and that I was a bad priest, cruel to the weak and sick. I asked him to prove it, which he could not do. I continued as inspector of the kitchen, but the cooks now hated me.

A mouse was found in the room where the chiefs ate and slept. One of the chiefs got the crazy idea of shooting it with a rifle. However, every time he aimed, the mouse ran away. We prisoners were sent to the room to fix the beds, clean everything, serve the chiefs at their table, and plug all the holes so that the mouse could not escape. The chief's greatest desire was to make the mouse come out of the room and into the patio area, where he could be a happy shooter in front of all of us.

At one point, the mouse ran out onto the patio. The chief, like a cat on the prowl, was waiting for him. With his one remaining shot, he killed the puny animal. At that moment, the chief's character changed completely. His face lost its malicious expression and he became as excited and exuberant as a boy. We could not have imagined such a transformation, from a brutal man to a happy, youthful individual who now regaled us with tales of his younger days and his extraordinary shooting abilities. He even gave us shooting lessons, which was certainly against every regulation of the camp.

Later, another soldier was heard saying, "Listen, I hear the chief has gone crazy, or at least he is missing something in his head." Maybe this statement received too much importance at the time, as we were all inclined to believe that most of the soldiers – including this one, who had accused the chief of being crazy – had more than a few screws loose themselves.

WE ARE COMRADES

AMONG THE VIGILANTE SOLDIERS WAS a man who tried to demonstrate the authenticity of his German race through his talk of cruelties. One Sunday, he was the guard while the food was being distributed. At the end of meal time, he came over to me and asked, "Is it true that you are a priest?"

"Yes, I am a priest," I responded.

"Ah, then we are comrades," he said.

I asked him, "How are we comrades? Are you a priest also?"

He replied, "Yes, I am a pastor."

I then asked him, "How is it possible that you do not follow your vocation, but instead are here with the friends of Hitler? Were you obligated to serve them?"

"No," he said, "I was not obligated but offered to serve voluntarily. I belonged to a group of missionaries, and I realized that the sacrifice was not worth it; I am much better here." A long conversation between us had begun.

He told me of his missionary adventures and tried to convince me that leaving the priesthood was the only safe way to proceed, that once the war ended, priests would no longer exist. However, his conduct with the imprisoned was more like that of a pastor than a soldier. He did not seem to enjoy making defenseless victims suffer. He tried to make it evident that he was an authentic

German soldier, but other than yells and threats, he did nothing.

He smoked big cigars but never more than half of one. Then he stamped it out with his foot so that no one else could pick it up and smoke it. Because he and I often debated about religion, other prisoners asked me to give them his unsmoked cigars, even the stubs, as they were eager for a smoke. I asked him for them, but he denied my request, telling me that he was a very advanced consumptive. That was why he always smashed his cigars; he did not want to infect anyone else.

I had seen him as an ascetic spartan and frugal, with a sunken chest. He was thin, tall, a person of somewhat advanced age, speaking very little, he eyes fixed on the ground. He lived a thoughtful, if misbegotten, life. Now I knew that he was physically sick and exhausted. I wasn't sure if he was inclined to exaggerate the seriousness of his illness or if he had known a pastoral life, which he now denied. Instead, he had chosen to live as a German soldier, in direct opposition to his ideas of Christianity, and my presence humiliated him.

He was serious and thoughtful, but his political ideas called for the abandonment of his religious ideas. One idea overrode all others: that the brilliant victory of the Führer would defeat the Christian system. He was convinced that once the war ended, the only religion remaining would be the culture of the Germans, with Hitler as their God. He was like all other German soldiers who had a blind faith in Hitler, giving Hitler the right and strength to proclaim Germany as the new religion, the authority to dismantle humanity as we knew it and to reorganize a new world. None of them could see Hitler as only a few centimeters tall, which was what he really was, or that Hitler's distorted ego and evil cruelty demonstrated a complete ignorance of Christianity and God.

THE SMALL FARMS

SOMETIMES ON SUNDAYS, DAYS WHEN we might have rested a little, we had to work on the small rural farms on the border of the forest not far away. We were to help the farmers in any way necessary. As we walked there, people along the way, as well as the farmers themselves, humiliated us. We were Polish prisoners and men who did not fit the mold of German "supermen." These people, from the smallest children all the way up to the most elderly, yelled at us, raised their fists, denounced us, and threw rocks at us. How to explain this hatred toward us? How does one little boy learn such a way of thinking and acting if not in the house of his parents? How to justify the hatred of us by the very old, who previously had hidden their hatred of the Polish in their hearts? We seemed like wretched witches rather than beings who walked quietly on an earthly pilgrimage.

Their feelings of German superiority had poisoned and separated these families from the rest of the world. From these houses, young men were being recruited into the German army. With such hatred toward other human beings, they were no longer Catholic families, or religious families of any kind. Hitler's ideas had deeply penetrated them, promising universal control and complete superiority over any individuals unlucky enough to not belong to their race of "supermen." They were being cultivated to have brutal instincts and to annul any morality other than their own splendid future of being Germans.

THE DOCTOR TO THE STICKS

DURING THE MONTHS OF JUNE and July, the farmers reneged on their contract with the chief of the work camp and sent us rotting and almost decomposed potatoes. Even before they were placed in the cooking pots, their odor was so unpleasant that the hungriest of us could not eat. Of course, with the lack of food, many prisoners got sick. I went to the chief of the works with our complaints. In my presence, he put what appeared to be the best of the food on a plate, to be given to an ugly dog. I was to feed him. I did what I was told and offered the plate of food to the dog, which fled from the rotten smell. It was a marvel how that dog would delight in eating human feces, which he found on the ground, but would not eat the disgraceful food that the cooks presented.

With more prisoners too weak and sick to work, the job of digging the channels was slowing down. No better food or medicine was available, and the whole work system was collapsing. The chief of the works resolved this problem in the German way, by yelling, "I am going to cure everyone today." He brought hard, thick sticks, went into the barracks, and hit every prisoner who looked sick. He used such strength that each man tried to get up and form a row beside his companions. Most were still too sick to work, but the chief did not pay attention to their screams. He put his boot on their bodies and smashed their throats and stomachs. They fell to the floor like cadavers, useless to him.

With their last strength, some of the prisoners tried to avoid the blows by dragging themselves to the door, where they remained lifeless. The chief became exhausted from beating with the sticks; his mouth was covered in foam. This was the way he calmed himself and held onto his manliness. It was typical for this abnormal man to use the backs and lives of the imprisoned for this purpose. I find it inexplicable that on these terrible occasions, the chief never hit me. And now an order from the Gestapo arrived, one to send me to Lodz, in Poland, to the jail on Sterling Street.

OFF TO LODZ

I ARRIVED IN LODZ, AT the jail on Sterling Street, at the beginning of 1941. The jail was a true symbol of terror, an old building of various floors, dark and fearful, a place where I was destined to remain for some time.

Lodz, the second largest city in Poland by population, was also second only to the capital of Warsaw in production of textiles. A significant percentage of the population was dedicated to commerce on a grand scale. The Gestapo had brought me there and taken me to a cell, where I waited for days with much anxiety and no idea of what was to happen to me. Almost all the prisoners there were very young and not guilty of any real crimes. Instead, they were victims of bad luck. Like many other Polish men and women, they had been picked up by the Gestapo, who were out hunting for any groups of people they could find to add to their workforce. These young prisoners were to be sent into German territory and sold to top German merchants for fifty Deutschmarks each.

One day, I was sent to the secretary of the jail. Inside that office, two officials waited for me. They seemed reasonable enough, complimenting me on my behavior while I had been in the workforce camp. Because of my good conduct there, they had decided to let me go free. However, before I could be free, I would need to sign a document changing my nationality from Polish to German. Naturally, I was not to become "the overman" in the manner of Nietzsche, a man of Nordic blood, but merely one supplement to the numbers of men who would be needed for what was to become the grand German Empire, founded on blood and death. My highly elevated status would be as part of a slave race to the "supermen."

They presented me with the document that indicated the origin of my birth as Germany. If I were to sign, I would be of German descent. I did not know what to think or say. The document listed me as a national political criminal with all kinds of frauds and immoralities to my name, but I would still be a German citizen.

Instead of feeling the happy blood of my new, proud homeland running through my veins, I felt humiliated and reduced to a state worse than slavery. The document gave me a German name similar to my own; in fact, the only thing missing was my personal identity and freedom. I said, "You have made a mistake, and I cannot sign this."

The official said, "No, it is you who has made a mistake. It is clear that you are German. Even your name, Fabisch, is a German last name. You will do me a huge favor by signing your name."

I said that I could not sign. After further coaxing, which had no effect, I was returned to my cell for three more days to reflect.

Three days to think about a document that, in one moment, would change me from Polish to German – important for the coming days and the rest of my life. The days passed and I was again brought before the officials. The same conversation occurred, with the same refusal to sign.

I said, "I was born Polish. I feel Polish. My father is Polish. No one can change these facts. I cannot sign."

The officials abandoned their somewhat courteous methods and betrayed their underlying feelings by saying, "You damned Polack. If you do not sign, you will be imprisoned for the second time. You are a Polish pig." Actually, it was my eighth imprisonment, which they didn't seem to realize. I was returned to my cell.

I reflected on the German mentality, their belief that a person could be bought with papers and threats. It was a crime to deny the possibility of becoming German. It was a crime to not sign a false document for their purposes. However, it was lawful to divide nations through political robbery, through criminal bloodletting of innocent people in Austria, Russia, and now in Poland. Perhaps what was favorable to the Germans was always moral and just, and what was unfavorable to them was immoral?

I returned to my cell with a tranquil conscience. I had been humiliated. I had felt their threats and shoves, and I had resisted them. They had not broken me down as a man. Instead, I had been persuaded that the Germans/Germany could easily become an extremely powerful force in the world, except that this would not happen through the cruel, ignorant methods they had devised. It would happen only if they could learn to live in peace and tranquility with other men and, in so doing, become truly great and superior men themselves.

A DARING STEP

IF A PRISONER HAD TO go to the bathroom, he knocked on his cell door. The guard of the hall would come and let him walk down the corridor to the bathrooms. I felt my life weakening visibly from hunger, and when I called to be let out to the bathroom, I had no intention of ever returning to my cell. I'm not sure how I came to this decision, if it was cloudy intellect or physical weakness. However, after I had been to the bathroom, I went to another floor of the jail, standing for a few minutes at the kitchen in front of the cooks.

The guard of that hall asked me, "What are you waiting for?"

I replied that I was waiting to be let into my cell, a different cell on a different floor. And just like a butterfly, the key came out and was stuck in the hole. I was in a new cell with no one's permission other than my own. It was the cooks' cell, which had beds in which to sleep rather than the usual hard cement floor. I'm not sure what I expected to happen next; I immediately fell asleep. The cooks were busy bringing their plates of puree and meat inside, and I watched them with a hunger that held no fear. I could not believe my eyes that there was still meat in the world. The foreman of the cooks asked, "What are you doing here? Who sent you? Why have you come?" My answers must have satisfied him because he then said, "You can come to work in the kitchen, but for the moment, you are too weak. You need good food and good rest. First, you eat well and rest for a few days, and then go to work in the kitchen."

I took full advantage of my situation, having plates of puree and meat, and sleeping on the mattress almost all day. These were the best days of my life in the German jails; bless them for their ignorance while I rested for one week, my best vacation.

After that, I was sent to the kitchen to peel potatoes. However, I needed a knife. The chief of the kitchen became aware of my presence. Without waiting for answers to his questions about who I was and what I was doing there, he grabbed me by the collar and pushed and shoved me along the hall, insulting me, kicking and slapping me, and installing me in a new cell. I did not care at all and did not complain of ill treatment by the chief of the kitchen; I was simply happy to have had my best vacation.

CELL 31

I COUNTED THIRTY-THREE INHABITANTS IN the new cell, which measured eight by sixteen feet and had one huge white stove, a window, and four walls. We slept on the cement floor, always in the same way, starting at the window, with the first head touching the wall. The next prisoner had his feet next to the head of his neighbor, with his feet touching the wall, and so on until the floor was full of us.

The strongest characteristic of this time was the terrible anxiety we all felt, clinging as we did to this little string of life. The Sterling Street jail had a reputation for executions, which could occur in the day or night, cleansing the streets and countryside of the Polish element. Who would they call out? Who would be next? We could hear the machine guns that took the lives of so many and transformed the remaining prisoners into frightened dolls who moved and reacted to the sound of bullets.

For all of us imprisoned on the third floor, there were only fifteen bowls for food. We received soup that consisted of nothing but water. With a loud noise, the cell door would open, and the plates were thrown violently toward us. Only seven or eight of us could be served at one time, and the liquid was at a boiling temperature. The plates were made of tin and immediately became too hot to touch, but we were to drink the liquid fast, gulping the burning fluid, hurting our mouths, throats, and fingers. We had to drink it fast or have nothing. If we did not drink quickly enough, the plate was yanked away and the liquid given to the next man. The best way to drink was to close one's eyes and tighten one's fists so that one didn't cry from the pain. We had the choice of death by consuming burning liquid or death by starvation. It was crazy, but somehow we became accustomed to this way of eating.

More Clever Than The Germans

I'M NOT SURE IF IT was because we each had only one suit of jail clothes or because the prison had no laundry, but on some Saturdays we were allowed a small packet of clean underclothes. The system went as follows. In the patio below our cell, two tables were set up. Those who received a package laid them out on tables to be checked by the prison guards. There were sticks that listed our cell numbers, and two cells at a time were called out to claim their packets. On all floors and on ladders, the soldiers watched every movement, but there was always a small amount of disorder with so many men milling around. A young Polish man took a chance and did not turn in his packet to be checked, as his mother had put a piece of dry bread inside it. Of course, one of the soldiers caught him. We thought his punishment might be to have no more packets, or perhaps the whip would be inflicted upon him, but German justice was much more severe; they cut off all the fingers on his right hand. When a dog has his tail cut, he receives medical attention. However, this young man, whose fingers were cut off with an ax, was left to bleed to death. Had it not been for the care of his companions, he would have died from his wounds.

Another prisoner was a young man of about seventeen years, slender, restless, always worried about his death or the deaths of his family members. He had been accused of belonging to an anti-German organization, and there seemed to be proof that this was true, so he expected nothing less than death. He was still receiving clean packets from his family. At this time, I received a packet too, and I took some joy in changing my filthy clothes, which I had not been able to do for months. The young man and I had an idea; we would try to write to the young man's family, asking them to put both of our clean clothes in one packet and nothing but bread in the packet addressed to me. It was dangerous, and because we had seen the other prisoner lose his fingers, our fellow cellmates said we shouldn't try. However, our hunger was immense, and our faith in God even stronger. He and the Blessed Virgin would watch over us.

Our packages arrived, and I found the one with my name. Soldiers were at the windows and at the tables. I had to take my packet and tear it as though it had already been checked, pass the second table checkpoint, and walk back into my cell. We watched every angle, our eyes trying to see everything at once while the other prisoners milled around with their packets. Thanks to the Blessed Virgin, it went very well. I did not lose my fingers as my unfortunate companion had, and we and our cellmates were amazed to taste a piece of bread. Because of our daily diet of boiling water, we no longer knew what it was like to eat something solid, and we did not have enough bread to calm the hunger we all felt. However, the effort was a success. One of the soldiers began letting us communicate with our families on the outside, and they sent us the sad and happy news of the world of which we were no longer a part.

In Search Of The Dust

EVERY SATURDAY, THE CHIEF OF the jail carried out a thorough search of the cells, trying to find any reason to justify cruelty against the defenseless prisoners. The chief would wear an immaculate white glove and go from cell to cell in search of dust particles on any object. If he found any dust, the punishment could be torture or death. We had seen how the chief used brutality to relieve his animal instincts, and we cleaned every surface so that no dust was to be found. During his visits, the chief never found one dust particle, nor one spot or piece of dirt. Our cell was cleaner than his conscience, which was covered with crimes.

A single lamp brightened our cell. It hung high above us from the ceiling. We worried about this lamp because we had no way to reach and clean it. Over many months dust had accumulated there, but it had never occurred to the Germans to run their hands over its surface. One day, after a crazy search of the cell that produced no dust, the chief called for a long ladder. He ran his hand over the lamp and found a thick crust of dust on his glove.

There was no way to make him understand the impossibility of cleaning this lamp because of its height. The chief's eyes filled with satanic glee. He called another soldier and they took us to the top of the angled ladder that connected our floor with the prison floors above. We were lined up at the top and each of us was pushed hard over the edge. One after another, we fell, crushed by the next man, yelling and walloping our heads and bodies against the floor.

This was only the beginning of the chief's preconceived theatre, which all the "supermen" witnessed. On each floor, a soldier waited to hit us with his stick and kick us forward. We crawled on our hands and knees while he thrashed us. Then we were pushed off the next ladder to fall to the floor below. That was how we traveled down twelve floors until we reached the bottom.

The soldiers enjoyed all the victims' suffering, and the chief was waiting for us at the end. His furious face made it clear that this punishment had not satisfied him. We were forced to climb back up the twelve flights, but on our elbows and knees. At the top of each landing, we received a beating. When we reached the top, the chief met us with a contorted face and screams that we had been too slow. Even though our blood covered the stairs and the floor around us, the Germans wanted more.

We were taken outside, where there was a large mound of snow. On our elbows and knees, exhausted and bleeding from the treatment on the ladders, we were to remove the snow from the patio as quickly as possible. We had no tools, but we could use our shoes and some thin reeds if we could find the energy to move. The soldiers came at us like a pack of wolves, not to devour us, but to beat us with whips, to get us moving to do the job. In the end, we could clear away only about three-quarters of the snow, but the soldiers left happy, commanded by our eminent chief.

We were then thrown into our cells, more like convulsive corpses than human beings. We remained inert for some time. We may have lost consciousness, and many were unable to recall the chain of events within the last hours, it had been so horrible.

However, after some time had passed, we began yelling, one of us, then two, then all the broken prisoners, making some sort of spectacular acting display. It was as though we were dominated by a bizarre psychosis that produced demented yelling. In truth, none of us had the least idea how to control ourselves. The behavior seems incredible, but what had happened to us was even more inconceivable. The behavior of the Germans, the extreme torture of a group of weak and innocent men, and the brutal pleasure they displayed during these acts, were for us the most astonishing. We had provided a happy diversion for them.

The Priests And The Jews

EVERY SATURDAY AT ABOUT 2:00 p.m., after our meal of a disgusting liquid, we faced another type of threat. The soldier on duty would pass through the corridors, screaming at us in his loudest voice, opening doors and treating us roughly, wanting all the priests and Jews to step out. When he entered our cell and asked if there were any priests or Jews, the prisoners answered "no."

At first, we did not understand the true reason for these events. Anyone who was taken out was forced to sing and dance and march and jump around, creating a farcical entertainment for the Germans. We finally realized they were mocking our religious beliefs in the only stupid way they could invent. Saturdays were the days we priests honored the Blessed Virgin Mary, traditionally the day to honor her through Mass and prayer. In addition, Saturday was a religious day of observance for the Jews, their Holy Sabbath. Was this good entertainment? I guess that depended upon who was judging the spectacle. For the prisoners, those days were filled with fear and humiliation, as we never knew whether we would be taken or what would happen to us outside our cell. For the Germans, those were days that were entirely appropriate and natural, days when they could enjoy the suffering of innocent men and behave exactly like who they were: first-class demons.

THE FAILURE

ANY PERSON WHO HAD THE misfortune to spend a season of his life between the walls of this jail could not ignore the two powers fighting against each other. First were the German soldiers, who put their complete support and unwavering loyalty behind the doctrine of the prison, to ensure that it was maintained. Second were the prisoners, with their great and constant need for freedom and their absurd ideas of escape and salvation. The law and the entire German system favored the vigilante soldiers, who could always count on success in any given situation. However, despite enormous odds and the immense difficulty of having no weapons or tools, and no route or help from the outside world, no lack of geniuses worked on escape projects. I did not witness this personally but will try to reconstruct the situation based on the words I heard from others in prison.

In a cell on the prison's lowest floor was a group of Polish prisoners waiting to receive their death sentences. They felt they had nothing to lose as they planned their escape, although they would face every kind of danger. Using a small spoon and a thin strip of iron, they began digging a tunnel to freedom. They would dig through the bottom of their cell, then continue digging a tunnel that would travel under the prison road and out into the world of freedom. They dug and moved about constantly like ants because time was urgent and the danger increased each day. They filled their pockets with dirt, which they took to the bathroom, dissolving it in whatever water was available. Though progress was excruciatingly slow, they never lost faith in their plan and kept digging heroically until the tunnel reached the other side of the road. Their golden dream of freedom widened their hearts and encouraged them to work even harder, like a little window of hope had opened above them.

Misfortune often seems to follow the least fortunate, those born under an unlucky star, and so it was with our heroes. By accident, they dug right into the electric cables that provided current to the jail, creating a blackout that lasted three days. The Germans responded by sending every soldier to search for the cause of the problem. In the end, they discovered the cut cable and the tunnel in the floor of the unlucky prisoners' cell. The light came on in the jail, but the following night, the young, heroic men disappeared. They died, leaving their companions to marvel at their bold, brave hearts. They never achieved the bodily freedom they had so desired, but they did escape all the cares of the earthly world as their souls left the prison and were set free.

On another day, soon after this event, my friend, whose parents had sent packets of clothes and bread, disappeared, and with him, my "good luck." Not only had I lost my friend, and not only would pieces of bread no longer arrive to help sustain our skeletal frames, but my stay in this jail was over. An order had arrived to transport me to the concentration camp at Dachau.

THE ROAD TO DACHAU

AT 11:00 P.M. ON MARCH 14, 1941, many of us boarded a train that was to distribute the prisoners to various places in Germany. Each of us received half a loaf of bread and a little piece of cheese for the journey, which was to last two days. The soldiers were to give us water somewhere along the way. Other than stops during the airplane bombings, I was taken directly to the city of Halle.

In each small train space were five people; my group consisted of three men and two women. We courteously yielded our seats to one another because not enough room was available for us all to sit down. We changed places many times during the ride, as though we were going on a happy journey to a lovely new place. Some of the people ate all their bread at once, such was their hunger, and from that point onwards, they were allowed only a drink of water now and then. Some of us were able to make the bread last for the whole trip. In this way, we did not suffer as much.

Our little group on the train was extremely fortunate when a Polish soldier became our guard. At the start of the war, he had changed his nationality so that his large family might eat. He became a *Volksdeustcher* with a German name. However, he was a Pole and a sympathizer at heart. Knowing that I was a Polish priest, he talked with us frequently in a kindly way, and when we stopped, he left the door open so we could get some air. His greatest favor was to share his bread with each of us once a day.

At our final stop, we were imprisoned in Halle, which was a central point where all the traveling prisoners were reunited to be redistributed to other places. We stayed there for a few days. By the providence of God, our jailer already knew that a priest was being held in cell No. 33. He came and presented himself, confessing that he was a Catholic. His sympathetic words gave me hope for the days ahead, when I was to be taken to Dachau. He, too, offered some solace to the prisoners, and a little gift of food, which kept us going. May God repay him for his evangelic kindness toward me at this time. May He protect that man and all his family. In the end, however, I arrived at Dachau along with the rest.

DACHAU

As the train stopped at the station in Dachau, the soldiers were waiting for us. We were immediately converted from a group of men into a group of animals. The zealous soldiers beat us and pushed us out of the train cars like rags so that we landed on one another. They injured us and slammed us into one another without compassion. We had no time to look around or ask any questions, as everything happened very quickly.

On every side of us, the soldiers were armed, and bloodcurdling screams came from their mouths. However, their weapons did not protect them from a terrible enemy such as us. We were the enemy, this inert, unarmed mass of us, and they hit us with blow after blow, not caring who they hit, raining blows everywhere, to our heads and bodies, terrorizing all these innocent people. They herded us together and pushed us along. With the fear of rabbits, we did not consider running or putting up resistance. We did not scream; we submitted to them better than sons to a father. We did anything to avoid blows to the head, and we kept moving.

All this occurred with extraordinary rapidness. Surrounded by soldiers and dogs, we crossed about three kilometers, the area that separated the train station from the Concentration Camp Dachau. Any person who did not know this situation, and who believed in those early times that Concentration Camp Dachau was only an idea, could never imagine the reality of what awaited us there.

As we walked toward the camp, we saw with true horror groups of prisoners everywhere, skeletal men, like walking corpses, doing jobs along the way. The soldiers gave us the impression that they were well-practiced in this system. They were very cruel, with real satisfaction on their lips. This was a favorable occasion for them, one on which they could demonstrate their ugly skills in front of the other soldiers and their officers. They had a naturalness and conviction, believing that this was their destiny, and a sense of superiority ran through their veins. By using every brutal technique imaginable, they would establish themselves, there at Dachau, as the rightful rulers of men and the sole rulers of the world.

Arriving at the principal gate of the concentration camp, we stopped for a moment, waiting for the doors to open to this kingdom of death. On the gate, in highly visible letters, was the comforting welcome, which could deceive no one, "*Arbeit Macht Frei*" ("Work Shall Make You Free"). The camp was called Lager Dachau because of the small neighboring town called Dachau. The camp had been constructed by a German who foresaw the disastrous plans of his new leader of state, Adolf Hitler. Any countrymen who defended Germany's original honor soon found themselves incarcerated here, in this camp that facilitated the extermination of thousands, some of them fellow countrymen, many of them other human beings brutally taken from their homes, targeted by Hitler's Nazi movement. According to the prisoners, this camp had been constructed on marshy lands in 1933 and was founded on the blood of the first victims of the new state.

I remember talking with one of the prisoners who had been

in Dachau the longest, a lawyer who was marking his eighth year in that place. He stopped to ask me, "Do you know what you should be thinking?"

I had no idea what he meant and shrugged away his question.

He continued. "You are stepping on the blood of thousands of my countrymen, those who have found eternal rest in the swamp. We were the first to arrive here in 1933 when all this was a swamp, and we were made to work for the constructors of this damned camp. Every day, dozens of my countrymen disappeared into its bowels. We sank deeper than our knees into the mud for months and months, and the corpses of our companions began serving as stairs to walk on, moving us more securely from place to place. That is what you should be thinking."

In a person's mind, the camp could be imagined as a huge place, but in terms of meters, we were trapped tightly. It is almost impossible to think of those thousands of people joined like something immense, hardly able to move around with any extra space. This space was created only by the killing of some of us, by the preordained short existence of many of the prisoners' lives.

Concentration Lager Dachau was located some eighteen kilometers from Munich. Outside the walled area destined for the imprisoned were rooms designed for the soldiers, those in charge of watching every prisoner's movement. There were rooms for officers and their families, and there were other huge buildings, which would become huge crematoriums, as well as large canisters of gas.

A two-meter-high walled fence surrounded the camp, and three watchtowers perched on top of the wall, armed guards in each of them. Along the upper part of the wall was high-tension, electrified barbed wire. Beyond the wall was a two-meter-deep cement grave that ran along the wall's entire length. The whole camp was divided by the main street, lined by poplars, and sixteen barracks sat on each side of the road. On the northern side were the gardens of the officials, as well as the young rabbits raised for their tables. On the edge of the gardens was a house where prisoners in better condition were kept; they were chosen to give carnal pleasure to the soldiers. To the south was an open area where prisoners were publicly punished. To the east was an area called Plantage, where certain prisoners wasted their lives cultivating medicinal plants. According to the rumors, this area was kept by the most prominent men, who occupied positions just beneath Goering, Himmler, and the Führer. This was where thousands of Polish priests worked, many of them dying there from inhumane treatment and terrible, inclement weather. This area was also known as the cemetery of the priests.

Beyond the open area facing south were showers for three hundred people, the kitchen, the tailoring storehouse, the shoe store, and the camp offices. Each of the sixteen barracks was divided into four sections. Each section contained a dining area and a dormitory. Every unit of two sections had one lavatory for its use. The total construction of the camp was built to house 8,000 to 10,000 prisoners. However, by the end of the war, the number of prisoners had swollen to approximately 52,000, at least 4,000 of whom came from Russia. I would estimate the whole camp inside the wall to be about two hundred and sixty square meters – perfect for raising chickens. However, these human geniuses were able to fit 52,000 starving, tortured individuals, some sick, dead, some dying, into so small a place, which even now seems unfathomable.

We were filthy in our soiled clothing and were made to strip and parade naked in front of each of the less important soldiers.

We gave up everything we carried. On a small chain, I had a medallion with the Virgin. A soldier started taking it, but I took off my shirt and it somehow became entangled; he could not find it. He cursed me and kept searching, in my hands and on my body, but it was lost, and he gave up. When the war was over, I happily found it inside the bulk of my shirt, along with some other items that the authorities had taken on the day of my arrival.

On a greenish piece of paper, they had labeled my belongings: a hat, a sack, a pair of pants, a sweater, three shirts, a t-shirt, three pair of socks, a pair of gloves, an empty money wallet, and some family pictures. The document carried the number 29697 and was signed by the S.S. RottenFührer: Handke. The document contained a red seal that said, "Burned Objects." All the inmates' objects and clothing had been stored in one of the buildings, and even though some of them had been burned, my items were still in good condition. In one of the offices, I found a letter I had written to my sister-in-law, Helen Fabisiak Kozmin, of Horleburg, dated February 13, 1945. I found two other letters which had been written to me, but which I had never seen. One of them, dated February 12, 1945, was written by my sister, Kazia, Post Mulhagen, Kreis Militsch bei Helbig. The other was from Hedwig Kulinski in Wolkwitz, uber Demmin, dated March 10, 1945. The Germans had tortured and killed thousands of prisoners, but they kept our correspondence and belongings organized and neatly labeled.

We enlightened our inspectors with our nakedness and skeletal bodies, our protruding bones that resembled leafless trees in a state of decay rather than bodies of intelligent human beings. A detail of this experience was that many of the soldiers were interested primarily in our male organs, not simply to look at them but to touch them for their entertainment. I'm not sure if this was a way to humiliate the imprisoned or if something deeper-seeded lay in those soldiers' nature, something that permitted sexual deviations and aberrations, which all of us witnessed during this time of German slavery.

They shaved our heads and any organs where God had intended us to grow hair, then poured a series of disinfectants on us. When this liquid came in contact with our skin, we twisted and turned in every direction, and our eyes filled with tears from the pain it produced. The pain made the soldiers laugh, satisfying their base instincts. After the disinfection, we were lined up under ice-cold water, its terrible pressure stinging us. Then we were dressed, still cold and damp, in prison uniforms: gray with white stripes. The sizes were all wrong. Some were much too small, so that parts of the body were exposed, while others were too large, so that walking was difficult. The shoes did not fit us. It was really tragic for prisoners trying to protect themselves from the cold, but for the soldiers it was comic entertainment. Some of the men ran like animals to huddle next to a companion for warmth, waiting for whatever bad luck was to come.

People have said that the German is a systematic man with a logical way of thinking and acting. I do not disagree that such attributes are great qualities among men. However, these admirable qualities created an elaborate system that was blindly executed, one that would torture and execute innocent men for as long as they were exposed to such a merciless nature, for as long as they were prisoners in Dachau.

QUARANTINE

I HAD BEEN DESTINED TO arrive at 13 Zuganblock Stube 1. According to the camp system, we all had to remain in quarantine, which was to be a time of transformation and vegetation, not thinking, so that we would be ready to sufficiently savor the life awaiting us there. The Stube Eltoster, the chief of the place, did everything to create the impression of absolute authority. He presented himself as the man who had executive power over sky and earth, and around whom one would not even dare to breathe freely. His face was veined, red and shiny, greasy and fat, but his body looked well-developed with muscle. He pronounced these words, which penetrated to the bone: "From this moment on, you belong to me. I am the only one to give orders. I am the man who chooses life or death for you; your fate is in my hands."

We formed lines in front of him so that he might demonstrate his furious yelling, his dictator's stick, which he used against us, his fists of a boxer, and his hard shoes to kick us. We understood his position and were therefore completely dependent upon him. We tried to silence our slightest respiration so as not to draw his attention. He told us of our new life, a life of progress, one brought about by his superior culture and education, along with good German discipline, one that would produce for us a happy life. The floor upon which we stood was the most sacred in the world, and no one must stain its surface. The religious among us realized that, by order of the Führer, another God had been born. Our catechism classes were being taught by Himmler, Goebbels, and the Führer himself, and according to Nazi philosophy, all should be ready and willing to die in servitude to such higher power.

This chief had a broad nose, thick lips, rounded cheeks, and a beard. In his previous life, he had been a simple man, one with a space between his teeth and raised eyebrows, capable of frank and easy laughter. We learned that he had been a baker in the kitchen of a small store, a white hat on his head and a big ladle in one hand, doling out soup to hungry customers. He came from a Protestant family, was the father of two boys and the husband of a pretty woman. Now he had become chief of the barracks, with an important mission in the concentration camp: the instruction and intimidation of new prisoners. We were neither his first nor his last disciples, and we hated him. He beat us all daily. He beat me so many times, I could not count them. None of us felt any of the respect he wished to instill; instead, we had only a thousand reasons to hate him.

Each prisoner had one corner of a cabinet that four individuals shared. Each prisoner also had an aluminum plate, a fork, a round knife, a spoon, and a bowl. In addition, there was a small space for any bread and a rag for cleaning utensils. We each had a bed made of the same wood as the floor, a straw mattress, and sheets. The beds were stacked one above the other. I was on the third tier. We were tightly packed together, and a small window was kept open, admitting enough fresh air to breathe. We had blankets of various colors for some warmth; all the blankets had horizontal and vertical stripes. These blankets were the torment of all the prisoners because, from the first bed to the last, whether sleeping or awake, we were to keep the stripes in a straight line traveling in both directions. We always failed. The idiocy of this task was apparent to us; that and our haste to straighten the blankets made compliance impossible. The chief would become furious, and the best way he found to express his anger was to beat us and wreck the beds. How bad our luck was with the blankets and how bad the daily beatings were depended entirely upon the chief's momentary whim.

As I have said, my bed was on the third tier. That, coupled with my short stature, created a problem. When climbing up to my bed or coming down, I had to place my feet on the bed below me, ruining the straight lines of another prisoner's blanket and creating dangerous consequences for him. Each morning, the third tier of men were to wash up first while the other prisoners straightened their middle and lower beds. When I returned, and despite my best efforts, my foot had to touch the lower and middle beds when I climbed back up to the third tier. This ruined the straight lines on the blankets. The chief would come after me, beating me with the stick, putting all his energy into his task. Of course, to free myself of his "loving gifts," I would jump or fall on him, hoping he would feel compassion when he saw me laid out at his feet or hanging from his shoulders. However, he continued beating me every day, with all his German fury, until it felt as though my bones were broken. It was unbearable, and so the next morning I unhooked the beds from one another and climbed on the wooden end pieces. This made the beds shaky and unstable but ensured that the blankets were undisturbed. When the chief entered and saw the changed situation, he was mute. I was up in the third tier, and the lines on the blankets were straight.

It took a few minutes for the blood to rush to his head. Then he exclaimed, "Ah, small priest," kind of happy, kind of mocking. With a kick to the base of the beds, he knocked the whole mess down. It broke into three parts, and I lay in the debris. He looked and laughed, but not for long. His arms instinctively began smashing me with blow after blow. Beyond all that was happening to me, I could see that this brutal energy was the reason why his superiors had given him his job. In this way, he was able to glorify the legitimate sons of the German nation; with blood and brutality, they thought to cement the future of Europe.

Every day in the afternoon, we received – pardon the expression – catechism classes. Whoever created the material for these courses must have had a brush with Catholic teaching because they began with the same fundamental question that the true religion asked: "How many Gods are there?" The chief responded to his own question with the statement, "There are three gods." (There was no other discussion of the three gods.)

One of the other prisoners, a Protestant pastor from Poland, interrupted by saying, "Now we're up to three? One would not suffice?"

The chief screamed insults at him and beat him into silence.

A trio of us seemed very close in character. There was the young Polish pastor from close to Lublin, a marvelous person; a representative of a national church recently formed in Poland (a group waiting to save Poland through their church, which was located in Plock); and myself – three of us who composed sort of a group apart. It seemed that we would form a friendship until it became clear that one of us had the same politics as the chief, asking questions about Nazism rather than touching upon issues of real faith. He had the ear of a chief, and his purpose was to discover our secret facts, anything that could be used against us and be reported back to the chief.

It has been said, *Omne Trium Perfectum* ("everything that comes in threes is perfect"), which could no longer be said of our group of three. The other two of us were disheartened, and we were wary and careful around this third "religious" prisoner.

At the end of the quarantine, we had to pass an exam. The examiner, Mr. Rakouzy, had been elected by the chief. We did not know why Mr. Rakouzy made the exam easier for us, possibly because he knew that we were religious men, but he showed careful consideration in formulating his questions to us. Any question related to our faith and our creed would have been dangerous, and our answers about our belief in one God would have required punishment. Instead, he asked us about the hierarchy of the Nazi system – easy questions that we could not miss. After passing the exam, we were free of the nightmarish threat that had hung over us. A few days later, we were transferred to different barracks blocks. My Protestant companion and I were in Barrack 28, Stube 3. Priests occupied area number 28 and were also in number 26, which contained religious men of many nationalities.

All the barracks had been built in the same manner. Each barrack had four sections, 4 or *Stuben*, numbered from 1 to 4, each divided in half into a living area with a few tables and chairs and a sleeping area. There was a window, and two stacks of beds faced each other, three tiers to a stack. There was also a common washroom with toilets and showers. Cabinets held the inmates' utensils, and the wooden floor was painted red.

A Suspicious Friendship

Strictly by luck, I was put in Stube 3; my cabinet was 61, and my bed was on the bottom tier. The Protestant pastor was put in Stube 2 and was to become my companion for some of the time we lived in Dachau. He was of medium height and had a pale face, blonde hair, and green eyes. His quiet demeanor made him handsome and captivating. The serenity of his spirit was apparent in all his external behavior. At first, he enjoyed good health and an overall sense of peace, apart from the increasing day-to-day problems in our surroundings.

We became friends, which was unusual because we differed vastly in the way we clarified the most vital points of our beliefs. The depth of our religious convictions and his perfect conformity to a way of thinking and living drew us together. He accepted that God would make of him whatever was His will, which made me admire him and abandon my intent to convert him to Catholicism. His complete respect for my religious beliefs, which in many ways opposed his own, gave me the highest respect for him as a human being.

Our friendship did not escape the notice of our companions. In particular, among the Catholic priests and Jesuits (I, of course, am a Jesuit), a rumor began that I had abandoned the Catholic faith and embraced Protestantism. This was slanderous, and my friend, who saw what was going on and that I was suffering because of him, wanted to end our friendship. However, we did continue our relationship and the sharing of our ideas, though the current of acceptance among our companions was against us for days and months, to the point that some inmates were saying our relationship was sinful. Their filthy tongues could not undo the damage done to us until an event more powerful than any other occurred, one we could not remedy and from which no one could be saved.

My friend developed soreness in his left arm. At first it bothered only his fingers. However, the swelling grew each day, as did the sharp pain of infection. When the swelling had traveled to his forearm and become too large, he went to the hospital, from which the nurses released him with practically no attention paid to his condition. He felt that his days were numbered and that death was at the threshold of his beautiful life. When his entire arm became hugely swollen, I convinced my friend to try again. This time he was admitted to the hospital, never to recover his health but to leave his bones behind, among the dead. It was far too late. Death would not separate from him, the date and time were fixed, and I did not see him again. We had said our goodbyes, embracing and kissing like true friends, and we knew we would see each other again only in the arms of the Father of all. At last, he asked if I would go to see his wife and two sons and tell them he had been tranquil. He wanted me to tell them, "I will die in plain unity with my God, in the perfect resignation to His divine will, and they should not fear anything that is to happen in their future."

The pastor died, a victim of merciless conduct by our jailers, and of pettiness and meanness among our companions, which no longer mattered. He had known how to live his life, attaining happiness and a level of peace amid days filled with pain. His union had been with God, in Whom he had confided everything about his life and his family. In my eyes, he was a saint, a hero of suffering and of forgiving. Unfortunately, I was never able to take any news or comfort to his wife or sons, who should have been very proud of him. If I had known his home address, I would have done something, even under my own dire circumstances; however, nothing outside of his beautiful life and death is now in my memory. [Regrettably, we have no mention of this pastor's name-Ed.] By placing these few words about him here, I want to pay tribute to him to recognize the value of a man who lived his life without regret – a life given freely and faithfully in service to the greatness of our God.

THE WORK OF A HORSE

ONCE INCORPORATED INTO THE NEW community, I had to submit to the laws that governed all of us who were still alive. One of the laws, "One who does not work cannot live," justified any type of working conditions, any kind of job that kept men from becoming "lazy parasites," those whom the Germans thought should not be tolerated in any human society.

One day I was told that I would be employed in the construction of roads. There were eighteen men, eighteen emaciated skeletons, and we were to drag an enormous steamroller over heavy material to level out new roads. It was an impossible job. We needed a steamroller with a motor, which could easily be designed by the Germans, or some horses to pull the steamroller along. However, it was determined that eighteen men could execute the job without incurring extra expenses. Any person would know that eighteen skeletal, weak men could not produce the same effect as well-fed, muscular workhorses, but the Germans were never wrong. They enjoyed putting our ambulant corpses to work. They took every chance to punish us, while deep down they must have known that the job could not be done.

On our part, the idea of moving that giant steamroller should have produced the response, "We cannot," but, of course, we knew we could not rebel. So, we were converted into workhorses, and the Germans, whipping us brutally across our backs, made us work beyond our own capabilities. Our sweat and blood fell, mingled together, and we carried out a small miracle, moving that defiant monster along very slowly with our will.

It took us two weeks to finish the job. Finished, we had built a good road, clean and reliable, better than horses could have done, with no irregular margins, hoof prints, or variations. This cruel, barbaric procedure, with its abuse of diverse individuals under horrendous circumstances, was our remedy against idleness and crippling fear. A brutal, intense task became a representation of our salvation while we, like so many of the European nations, waited for help from others or from God.

BAUMLAGER NO. 1

THE DAY AFTER WE FINISHED the road, there arrived (to my immense relief) orders to report to another commander of jobs. Initially, understanding the nature of the two commands was difficult, as the first was within the boundaries of the prison, appropriately named Concentration Lager. The second was outside the boundaries, an unknown place about twenty minutes away; it was called Baumlager No.1. As the name itself indicates, it was a place of work destined for building construction. Pieces of heavy cement were kept there, parts of streets and houses that had been bombed, large cement tubes or channels, all of it to be loaded or unloaded and, later, taken to places where it was needed. Seventy of us were to do the work, which meant we had to be watched closely by a captain, his aide, a secretary, and a group of soldiers, all of them armed and stationed at strategic points. The captain had full authority, and our fate – whether anyone under his command was to live or die – was in his hands. A massive brick building was being made, and I was to become a bricklayer's helper. I was, as usual, completely unskilled at the job, but necessity and the stick became great teachers.

I have read that the Egyptian slaves who built the pyramids were happy at their work. This was what the German geniuses intended – that we would be entertained or, at the very least, that our struggle to complete the work would entertain them.

The trucks could have driven right up to the construction area to be unloaded, but they were directed to stop two hundred meters from the job site. We formed a human chain, passing the bricks from hand to hand. To make the exhausted prisoners work faster, the German soldiers attacked us with their weapons, their boots, and their fists. We were not accustomed to this work, and bricks were frequently dropped, so progress was delayed. Soldiers watched for this and brutally beat us, laughing to cover their cruel gestures, mutually pleased to make any of the weak suffer even more. The rough surface of the bricks tore our hands, opening small cuts at first and then much deeper wounds, so that our hands looked like meat, raw and bleeding and extremely painful. Trucks could not be unloaded at midday or during the night, and the German soldiers were under some type of pressure to complete the work, requiring that we proceed even faster.

By order of the captain, I was sent to help prepare the mortar for bricklaying. This work was heavy and hard, but it was an actual rest from what had gone on before. Its greatest benefit was that it temporarily eliminated the threat of beatings from the guards. After I learned to make the mixture, one of the bricklayers fell ill, and his vacancy was left to me. I don't really understand why I received this job because the work captain did not like me, but in the rush of activity, he must have thought I was a trained bricklayer. I copied the movements of a knowledgeable prisoner, trying to imitate exactly what he was doing, and it was enough to do the job. I became a passive being, receiving pointers and laying bricks day after day. The building seemed firmly built, and when the principal chief examined it, he deemed it a good, strong structure. As I stood on the scaffolding, I could not help but think that one day the whole place would be destroyed, probably bombed, and brought to the ground.

I was still learning bricklaying when I was transferred again, this time to the command of Reinigungslager. The work consisted of cleaning the concentration camp's streets. We were to pick up from the ground anything that the naked eye could see. Every day we cleaned the streets and the central plaza, sometimes picking up rags or pieces of paper that had fallen and been stepped on a thousand times. This work was much easier, and it gave us a chance to approach the kitchen, whose employees were fat and "happy," having the luxury of throwing away a bone or something better, whatever did not appeal to their delicately fed stomachs. It is true that hungry and dying men will fill their bellies with anything they can reach, and a hungry wolf will eat a rotten potato; anything to eat is good. We ate everything we could find.

When winter came and a cloak of snow covered the surface of the camp, our cleaning group no longer had any value. Other than producing a large group of perfectly vacant men, we did not provide enough pain and suffering to suit our jailers. As always, the Germans demonstrated the peak of their superior intelligence. Each prisoner was told to clean the snow off the streets using the folded tips of his jacket, shifting the snow to his other hand, and then throwing it in a place the authorities chose. Every day we came and went, carrying small amounts of snow on the tips of our jackets and in our hands, from one place that was quite close to another. This system reminded me of a story I had heard of an angel who endeavored to move a whole ocean with a small spoon. Our progress bothered the work captain, as the result of all this activity wasn't very visible. Finally, we were allowed to use a machine that removed snow, one that had been sitting idle the entire time we worked, one that did the job easily and rapidly.

BAUMLAGER NO. 2

In Dachau, a prisoner cannot exist without working because any good German knows that laziness is the source of corruption and should be banished in any way possible. Therefore, once the snow was gone, I was transferred to another area of the prison called Baumlager No. 2. This was a place with a reputation of terror, known for the most refined methods of cruelty, a place where prisoners were said to be put to death. Unbelievable stories were told. For example, the camp commander sent soldiers and a work party of one hundred and seventy men out for the day, and only one hundred and fifty of them returned. It was said that no one knew who would be exterminated on any given day, that no single commander or soldier had the authority to make this decision. Instead, a chain of command was passed along. This was the reputation of Baumlager No. 2. However, during my time there, I never saw or knew of such an event occurring.

We were continuously moved from one job to the next. One day, a huge truck came, and about fifteen prisoners were chosen to load three hundred sacks of cement onto it. With the sacks over our shoulders, we had to climb a ladder to the level of the truck bed. While doing this work, men who were already exhausted lost any weight they had on their frames. So it was with me. Already exhausted at the start of the day, I was failing fast and falling behind; I could no longer walk with the cement on my shoulder. I fell to the ground and the sack was torn, its contents managing to dirty a soldier's shoes. When he saw what had happened, he reacted violently in characteristic German form, drawing his gun and pointing it at my inert body. I could see that he was filled with rage, with (he seemed to think) just and holy dignity, and he came straight toward me.

I did not know what stopped his impulse or if he perhaps lacked permission from his commander, but he did not kill me. Instead, he asked me, "Why did you do that?"

I responded to his question, "I am completely exhausted."

I'm not sure if it was because of the truth of my words or because of my cadaverous condition, but he helped me get up and softly said, "Go to your previous post."

I chose to believe that he listened to the voice of his conscience rather than comply further with German discipline and its disastrous consequences. After that day, I was never sent to do a hard job. Six Polish priests were in the group, and we were all treated in the same way.

In Baumlager No. 2 was a sub-boss who commanded a small group of us. He was a bitter man, a communist defender of Stalin, and he knew quite well that I was a priest. He was an ordinary man, vulgar like many others, and his communist orientation left roots deep in his heart and in his head, causing an anxiety that would not leave him.

This poorly educated man had arrived at a spiritual crossroads without knowing where to walk. He could find neither internal strength nor sufficient mental strength to decide which of the roads to follow. Like a good communist, he was fighting to do the best for the working class, but was this to be accomplished through all the hideous, frightening cruelties he was ordered to carry out? His head was full of such huge ideas and contradictions, and he searched for an opportunity to discuss them with me.

This man was a real communist, but he had no idea about human psychology. He began by mocking the clergy and the church, and he attributed all religious defects to me. In fact, his mocking and sarcastic affirmations made me furious. Still, I kept trying to find some iota of goodness in what he was saying so that we could have an open dialogue. He had the opportunity to say whatever he wanted, and although our conversations were largely quarrels, we were at least talking and exchanging ideas. A priest and a communist were discussing everyday problems.

At one point, he said, "Things can be discussed with you. We have large differences in our opinions, but you have never offended me. You do not talk like other priests who immediately threaten with all kinds of punishments."

I did treat him with dignity, but our opinions were so far apart we would never agree.

There was another commander, a sub-boss by the name of Strassner, who was responsible for our overall group of about one hundred and fifty prisoners. He was Austrian, small and skinny, with a dark complexion and a very thin, tight mouth and jutting chin. He had rapid, violent movements; his eyes seemed to shine and come out of their orbits. Out of his mouth flowed all kinds of insults and curses, just like a volcano that is continually spewing and erupting. His peers must have regarded him as accomplished; his services were perfect for Hitler, as he had been appointed chief of an extermination section. He was acutely observant, which meant no detail escaped his sight. He never hesitated, for one second, to take action against a prisoner, and he terrorized us all.

This small man triumphed by maintaining his "prestige" with the blood of his victims on his hands.

One day, he notified me that this would be my last day alive on earth. "Tomorrow I will finish with you, damned priest." As he spoke these dry words, he decided my destiny.

The next day, having heard the news of my imminent death, the Communist soldier came to me, utterly undone. He expected me to be filled with pain and fear, but I reacted in a way he did not understand.

"I am not afraid of dying," I told him. "I am a priest, and so I am not afraid. Besides, it would be better for my life to end instead of going on in this miserable way."

The communist tried to make me see my stupidity; he was trying to save my life.

Tired of listening to him, I asked him what I should do to free myself of my inevitable death.

He said it was a ridiculously easy thing and added, "Bring me a pack of cigarettes."

What a stupid thing to say. He told me not to refuse, and so I tried to purchase a pack of cigarettes. I can't remember where I got the marks to buy them, but the next morning, I brought a pack of cigarettes, of Yugoslavian tobacco, to where I was working. I expected my life to end under Strassner's direction. The communist presented Strassner with the cigarettes, which he said I had obtained. At first Strassner was stunned, not knowing how to react. Then he put out his hand, took the cigarettes, which must have been of enormous value to him, and stuffed them in his pocket. He began moving away from me as though he was no longer interested.

Who would be capable of thinking that something as insignificant as a pack of cigarettes could turn a wolf into a lamb? Many times I tried to understand this miracle of transformation. One pack of cigarettes protected my life from inevitable death. And Strassner, who the previous day had searched me out and planned my death, now became concerned about my physical well-being.

Later in the day, stretching out his hand and with an amiable smile, he said, "Poor man. I did not know you were in such bad health. This is not the work for you." He spoke to me sweetly, like a one-hundred-year-old grandmother, and took me to another area where the work was light. I was to move thin boards from one pile to another without leaving my chair. What an irony. My new job consisted of killing time. With a little bit of smoke, prisoners could almost win a vacation, while others still struggled and suffered. I knew that, before, my life had had no value at all to the Germans; now it was at least equivalent to a pack of cigarettes.

The result of this situation was that I felt gratitude to the wolf for sparing my life, and the wolf did not look at me with the eyes of a butcher. The old saying, "One who takes is born a slave to what he receives," was proving true. I came to realize that there was a practical side to this new appreciation of the priesthood, and if all priests offered their jailers a pack of cigarettes, their road might be easier, at least for the time being.

We heard only the smallest bits of news of life outside the camp, but lately something was changing. For the Germans, the war at the front seemed to be getting worse, though we had no idea what that meant. The political situation could only reflect badly on the lives of the imprisoned.

One day, my boss found me sabotaging the German economic system by sitting down with my arms crossed during work hours.

At one point, I was sitting with my arms crossed for a few seconds and the boss came at me in his brute, wild manner, beating me all over my body as though I were the devil and must be killed immediately. He yelled insults at me, the clergy, and the church, and dragged me like a bag of potatoes to the command secretary's office, saying that I should be publicly punished. I was very aware of the danger of this situation, but the man had made me so angry with the beatings and false accusations that I said, "Go ahead and make your denouncements and God will work against you. You know that I am a priest and I am not afraid to die. Are you content to live with how you have treated me? Inevitably, I will see you in death."

For some reason, he became quieter, as though his soul was having a gigantic reaction. He kept asking me, "What do you have against me?"

Each time, I gave him the same response. "You will see in time." I had no idea what he would see, but this seemed to worry him. After days of this ritual back and forth, he erased me from his punishment list and left me alone, as though I no longer existed.

In Search Of What I Like

THE CHIEF OF OUR BARRACKS sent me to the office to be assigned a new job. Of course, I did not feel a need to work on behalf of Hitler, but I was living under that law of the camp which stated, "One who does not work cannot live," so I asked for a job that would suit my stature and abilities.

That chief told me, "If you publicly declare the many times you have been with different women in your priestly life, I promise you a job to your liking."

I responded, "Never, I never had a closeness with a woman in my life."

My word was not enough for him. With a great laugh, he said, "All priests are the same. They use a woman and then prohibit others from doing the same thing." Then he dismissed me, leaving me small hope of an easier job.

Instead of returning to my block number 28, I stopped in front of block 24 and went through a window into the center of the dormitory. No one was there, so I got underneath one of the beds and slept. I woke up at the time when food was being dispensed, so I went back through the window into my block and got my soup. This was my new lifestyle for some days until the chief of block number 24 discovered me. I heard him coming and started dusting off the beds in a very laborious way.

He asked me, "What are you doing here?"

My response was, "I am cleaning the beds because I don't like your beds to be all dirty."

He asked me, "You don't have a scheduled job?"

"No," I said, "the office is going to assign me a new job."

Then he told me that he would put me in charge of cleaning the whole barracks. For this work, I would receive a portion of soup. However, I would still report to the office each day to be assigned a new scheduled job. Each day, I got in line where the unemployed were tended. As the line got shorter and my turn arrived to be assigned, the chief would say to me, "Go, because I do not have any work for you today."

At the time of food distribution, the soldiers would ask me, "What job do you have?"

I would say, "None." This situation went on for many days. During this time, the rumor was that Germany was losing on all fronts of the war.

The Command In Which The
Priests Could Not Work

One day, as if nothing unusual had happened before, I was sent to join a new work group. The boss made me get out of line and started noting my information: last name, number (29697, which was on my clothing), and the prison block where I lived. He was aghast, angered by the knowledge that my prison number identified me as a miserable Polish priest. This information transformed the man into something akin to a ravenous animal. He began screaming, and furious insults came out of his twisted mouth. During these moments, I did not lose hope. I remembered well the Polish saying about the cow – the one that moos a lot gives very little milk – and I waited until he was finished. The devil isn't always as terrible as they paint him.

Finally, I received a new job, which consisted of keeping the rooms of the soldiers neat and clean. It was very easy work. The soldiers always left the remains of their breakfast on the table – a little bread or cheese, something delicious to us, and we devoured everything that was not metal or bone. The work took about an hour and a half, and afterward we would stand or sit in the corner, being careful that our jailers would not discover us. We were able to smoke cigarettes, those comforting objects that many of the men wanted. We made them of a mixture of tobacco, dirty paper, and wads of dust from the floor, and they lent calm to the need of the smokers. These cigarettes were constructed with so much love but would remain completely useless unless we could procure a match. One of the soldiers had pockets in his jacket where he kept some matches and, even though he disliked priests and we were still his enemies, on certain days he would give us a match. The value of a small, broken match grew enormously because it converted the hate of that man into a form of sympathy; a moment before, he had denied that we were human.

The cigarettes were very short. One time, the match went to the youngest man, and while trying to light it, he burnt his fingers and nose. The paper was flaming; thank God he had no mustache or his whole face would have been scorched. Then, once the cigarette was lighted, there was the problem of how to smoke it and who would smoke it, as there were six smokers and only enough smoke for three puffs. The man lighting the cigarette had a puff, and as its yellowish ash was passed along, some men had to be content with the smell alone. This may seem ridiculous, but each of the men was charitable with the next, using much self-control while waiting until the next day or the day after for his smoke.

One day, I was able to help remedy this situation. I stood with the other prisoners, very serious, as though I wanted to have a talk. Then I pulled out of my pocket not just one cigarette but a whole pack. At the sight of such a treasure, everyone's eyes seemed to pop out of their sockets; their lips shivered in anticipation. When the boss saw the cigarettes, I tried to disguise my embarrassment at committing such a crime; however, he did not look at me, but only at the cigarettes. I offered him one, and he did not know how to react; he was between a rock and a hard place. Should he take the offer from the hated priest, or should he keep his hardened heart filled with fury? The cigarette won the battle; his wry smile signaled a slight change in attitude, and a shorter but easier time in our barrack.

Each day, when we cleaned the leftovers from the soldiers' rooms, we were like hungry dogs, eating the crumbs that fell from the owner's tables into our starving mouths. One day, an excellent opportunity arose to take a perfectly new belt with the S.S. initials on it, a nice pocket knife, some potatoes, and other things of lesser value. This was a triumph of treasures, which I thought I could sell on the black market. Of course, my boss had seen me take these things, but he seemed to turn a blind eye to it.

At the camp gate, an officer and a group of soldiers were waiting for us. We heard the official say, "*HANDS HIGH!*" and we knew immediately what had happened. A terrible fear ran through me like an electric current, from my hair to my toes. There was not a second to lose. There were seven of us, and thanks to my mischief, the gallows seemed close at hand. The only thing I had to lose was my life, more valuable than anything else. I raised one hand and held it up while taking objects out of my pockets and stuffing them in my waistband. My waist was so shrunken that there was plenty of room to hide things beneath my belt. I switched hands and did the same thing on the other side, making my belt quite tight. I held my breath as the officer came to me and ordered me to empty my pockets. I moved very slowly, pulling small cleaning rags and pieces of string from my pockets, trying not to move in any way that would dislodge the treasures. He yelled at me to hurry up, and I kept going with my high-pitched screams to God to distract him. He quickly tired of my antics and moved on to the others.

The last soldier asked me, "What barrack are you from?"

When I gave the number, 28, he pushed me toward the barrack and said, "Go fast, man." Many items on the floor had been dropped by other prisoners, and it seemed a waste to leave them behind, so as I ran toward the barrack, I scooped them into my hat and kept going. I was well-loaded with objects, and when the boss of the barracks saw me come in, he said, "Some time ago, I heard you were a devil, and now I see you are worse than a devil." But he had to smile at my plunder, and he put his arm around me and let me pass.

TOOTH FOR TOOTH

A STORY WAS TOLD REPEATEDLY in Dachau, and it is worth re-telling because in this terrible place it gave everyone a laugh. Our soldiers had a Gypsy who served them hot coffee in the kitchen. Naturally, the Gypsy was stereotyped for being a Gypsy. His duty was to serve coffee and do nothing else. The poor man performed his duty with punctuality and fidelity and never deserved a word of reproach, but the soldiers made him a daily joke, a mockery. Some of them were malicious in the way they tormented him and enjoyed this as a happy sport. The Gypsy had no way to react other than as Christ would have done, quietly accepting anything they said or did to him. Each day brought new humiliations, and even the soldiers themselves noticed the Gypsy's humble conduct and quiet patience. At some point, they lost interest in this activity and announced to the Gypsy that they had the best news he could ever hope to hear. As a prize for his admirable conduct, serving the coffee satisfactorily and putting up with all their in-conveniences, they would no longer torment him daily.

He was gracious and modestly thanked them for their gesture of peace. Because he was a Gypsy, he wanted to give them better proof of his gratitude and noble heritage. He said to them that, as of the next day, with all humiliation and courtesy, he would also provide a gesture: he would no longer pee in their coffee cups every morning, as he had been doing for a long time.

This news dropped like a bomb. Some of the soldiers were filled with fury, hitting, pushing, and kicking him. Others were laughing so hard they could do nothing. Eventually, after calming down, some reacted by asking him the reason for his actions.

He responded with, "It was very natural. Every morning you offered me insults, shoves, and kicks, and I could do nothing against you. I could not hit you or even mock any of you, so I invented this way of dealing with you. I observed that you savored the coffee more each day after I started peeing in the pitcher, and I did not want to deprive you. I have continued to pee in the pitcher until today."

Amazingly, this story does not end with the expelling of the Gypsy or his transfer to another job because it must have seemed there was no reason to do so. The lessons were that we must all have needed a little laughter and that Gypsies are not as foolish as they appear to be. Personally, I would not want that Gypsy in my kitchen.

This story of the Gypsy reminds me of one told to me by a comrade in Dachau, a young priest who recently had been in a large parish under the tutelage of a very respected Monsignor. A woman worked as their cook, and she was very dedicated to her job.

The Monsignor, wanting to avoid future problems, gave his new assistant a warning: "If you want to argue with me over an issue, you can do it to your liking. You will never be treated poorly because I understand religious life and try in the best possible way to have peaceful interaction with my associates. *But* do not try to disagree with our kitchen lady because you will never be sure of the price you might pay. When she gets mad at you, she will not say one bad word to you; I assure you, she will treat you with more attention than before. However, she will stick her dirty finger somewhere. Instead of removing things from the soup with a spoon, she will use her dirty hands."

I laughed a little and, of course, could not believe this could be true, but it was enough to always make me a very courteous and respectful person to the lady in the kitchen. I'm not sure what similarity there is between the lady cook and the Gypsy, but I was always a real gentleman with both of them, just in case.

THE SICK ONES

AFTER ALL THE DIFFICULT PHYSICAL labor and all my maneuvers pretending to work, I had another idea. I thought I would pretend to be sick so I could stay in the infirmary. Under the norms that governed Dachau, a priest could not work while gravely ill. Because I was still a somewhat healthy individual, the whole idea was foolish and unrealistic. However, the idea of defying the regulation of the camp, one that stated a prisoner must work every minute of the day, was very appealing, so I decided to go ahead with my plan. They say that every crazy person still has one idea, and I had mine.

I needed two things: a certificate of my profession as a priest and a serious illness so that I would be admitted to the camp hospital. The first thing was no problem, and the second was made easier through an unexpected source of assistance: a nurse who offered to help.

I arrived at the hospital with a priest certificate, prepared by a competent person, and presented myself to the nurse, Tony Zagier, a young man willing to help me with my idea. We were both well-aware that a person on the sick list without an illness was a very dangerous situation. However, in my chart he listed a "Harmful Fever" that didn't exist. When the doctors visited, I appeared sick and was listed with a high fever, which lasted for many days. The doctors did not bother to investigate my case and left with the recommendation that the nurse Tony continue observing this phenomenon and keep them informed.

My situation as a person pretending to be sick could not last too long because of the danger of discovery. Therefore, following Tony's advice, I got out of bed and soon became an assistant to the sick. I was dedicated to the room's cleanliness, and with a broom and a rag cleaned all the patient areas and corners of the room. One week of this and I took another step, advancing to become a helper to the sick. You can imagine the surprise among the sick patients when I no longer had a broom, but instead a coat with thermometers and other medical tools. Such insanity could occur only in this bizarre place, where nothing good and reasonable existed. I went from bed to bed, taking pulses, noting fevers, and distributing remedies and injections, to the great amazement of the other nurses.

A Russian lawyer, one of my better friends among the patients, exclaimed, "Man, it scares people to be around you. You are wily and we never know what you will be tomorrow."

I said to him, "Don't be too frightened because I am not yet in the service of the Gestapo. My idea was to pretend to be a sick person, and then I had a chance to help the sick." After a week of training from my friend Tony in how to give injections, which was not so difficult, I began giving them. He helped me with whatever I needed to learn to do this job.

Tony was the son of a forest guard educated in the shadowing of wild animals. However, he did not follow his father's footsteps in overseeing the legitimate hunters and the criminals of the woods. When he was a little boy, he learned to hold a rifle better than anyone, but he did not use it. He was as thin as a tender tree and seemed to not leave a shadow where he passed. He was not aggressive, and he did not take satisfaction in talking about himself. He was a patient listener when others spoke of the past and present. He was not one of those people who are pleased with sweet, effeminate comments; instead, he preferred to hear expressive appreciation from any patients around him.

"Tony, you are a true iconoclast."

"The devil himself could not measure up to you."

I knew that phrases like these would make him feel proud and vigorous, even though Tony had no devilment in him. He was admirable, with pure intentions, while living in an environment of filth and hatred. Under his direction, I grew up, gaining not only in age but in the necessary skills for my new position. Once, he saw me hesitate to give a patient an injection, a man whose body was a bunch of bones connected to the skin. "Chester," he exclaimed. "Don't be frightened. The patient does not have the energy to protest." Encouraged by his words, I stuck the needle with strength. The patient did not cry out, although tears rolled down his face due to his sad condition.

In a few days, Tony arranged for me to oversee the sick room. He said, "Chester, you didn't kill anyone and have demonstrated good qualities with the sick prisoners. Starting tomorrow, you will be in charge of this room."

Tony was very kind. None of the officers found out who put a Polish priest in charge of sick people, or of anything else – an act that was directly against the rules of the concentration camp.

THE INFIRMARY

My sick room contained forty-seven people. Almost all of them were victims of the bombardments, and they were Polish, Russian, Czech, a young Greek man, a Hungarian Jew, and a Yugoslav. All were neglected by incompetent doctors who could not provide a correct diagnosis. A Jewish doctor from Moscow took charge of important matters. This doctor was known for his admirable calm and well-proven charity among the sick. He had extraordinary experience in his profession and deserved all the confidence and respect he received from those in the room.

One day, a sick prisoner from another room arrived. He was sent to us because no one could help him and because he screamed so loudly in pain that the other sick individuals in the room had no peace. He had been given X-rays, but no diagnosis could be found.

The Jewish doctor stood by quietly and said to me in a soft voice, "X-rays have not shown anything, but not everything can be seen on an X-ray." He began examining the patient without an instrument, palpating only with his fingers. He recognized what was wrong. Indicating with his finger, he said, "Here is the cause of pain. We need to operate."

The operation effectively confirmed the doctor's diagnosis. Because of his skill and excellent hearing, the doctor found and removed a harmful lung tumor, the size of an apple, underneath the ribs of the patient's right back. Everyone, including the surgeon, had to move away from the sick patient because of the tumor's terribly strong odor. However, this poor, sick man had been successfully operated on; he had undergone a rare type of surgery. Sadly, due to the advanced infection and his dehydrated condition, the patient died despite the successful surgery.

Among the sick, a Yugoslavian prisoner awaited his fate as so many others did. The time had come for his bones to be laid down in the crematorium. He no longer spiritually or physically resisted death, and the doctor, as well as everyone else in the room, had given him up for lost. All efforts at diagnosis had failed. He was terrified of death and yelled and constantly lamented, "Nurse, save me, save me."

Knowing my ignorance in these matters, I could do nothing. We all wished he was dead so that his suffering would end. He was making life impossible for all the other sick prisoners, yelling day and night. To be honest, we were losing our patience with him. I gave him a full glass of water with some added drops of liquid I had found. I said, "Drink this, and if it doesn't help, then there is no other remedy that can help you."

The poor man drank it down immediately with full faith. He was like the skeptical ones around Jesus Christ, not necessarily believing in the man but wanting to believe in the power of what was offered.

When night came, the room was silent as a tomb; except for some snoring, nothing could be heard. The man had stopped yelling and had gone to sleep after drinking the mixture. I had no idea what was in the bottle I had given the sick patient (I had also taken a couple drops for my ailing frame), so I approached the doctor and asked what it was.

The doctor responded, "Be careful. This is a potent poison. Never make a mistake because this could kill a sick patient." I told him that I had already done it, that I had given some of the liquid to the Yugoslavian patient. In those moments, I wished I had taken all the liquid myself, because I had killed a man. I ran to the man's bed, put my ear to his chest, and frantically took his pulse, then calmed down somewhat when I discovered that he was still alive.

The doctor told me to wait until the following morning. "You have killed without wanting to. However, you have done the patient more good than harm, as the better solution was death."

Before I tried to sleep, I returned to my victim, whose death I awaited at any moment. I worried about him like a mother for a son, wanting to tear him out of the arms of death, checking on him every hour, looking for signs of life. Each time it was the same situation – he was sleeping tranquilly without any struggle.

In the morning I expected to find a cadaver, and I didn't dare take his pulse. Then he opened his eyes and said, "Nurse, I am dead, dead hungry. Give me something to eat."

To be dead from hunger is far different from being dead. The doctor was surprised and thoughtful. I asked him, "What is the answer to this mystery? How could the patient not be healed by professionals, but improved through an ignorant man's dose of a killer remedy?"

The doctor responded, "You are a doctor of ignorance and have saved this man. We are people of science, which is sometimes worth nothing. We must be satisfied with the outcome."

Among The Communists

WHEN I WAS INITIALLY INCARCERATED, I was named a thief and spy. Because of these supposed actions, I had been accused and sentenced, but nothing had ever been proven. This was also written on my hospital chart. In truth, while among the sick, I won some respect from my companions for these supposed crimes.

A significant number of young Russian communists were in our group of prisoners, each of them in the flower of their lives, recruited from all social classes, angry and passionate in their beliefs. From time to time, a German journal fell into my hands. In those magazines, it was not difficult to find explosive writings against communism. I wanted to hear the opinions of the Russians, especially the professional lawyer with whom I was friendly. I asked them to read one of the journals and discuss communism with me.

The lawyer said, "To be able to discuss communism, I would need at least five hours for the introduction."

I answered, "I will give you not only five hours, but five days or more if needed so that I might understand a defense of your belief."

He took the journal but never glanced at it. He asked, "And why does communism interest you so much?"

I answered, "I only want to form a straight and just idea of communism and not lean on the opinions of a journal. What is your profession?"

The Russian said, "If you want to know my profession, go and read my chart." His chart said that he was a spy and a thief. "I am not only a thief," he said, "I am a spy also, and that changes things a lot."

I asked him, "What kind of thief are you? I mean to say, what is your specialty?"

He said, "My specialty is watches."

I said, "Oh, how rare. A thief specializing in watches who is a communist?"

He said, "The communism has nothing to do with the watches, but espionage has everything to do with watches. To be a good communist, you must have a watch of excellent punctuality, but if you are late, it is not a sin. However, if you are a spy, you must always arrive on time. You, as a thief and a spy, should know these things."

Other discussions followed. I admired these young men, full of enthusiasm, who defended their communist ideals. Their philosophy coincided perfectly with that of Pope Pius XII, who said that communism was a force that would dominate the entire world. They appeared to think that only one solution existed for the world and that was universal communism.

I could not remember hearing a priest speak about Jesus Christ with as much persuasiveness and fervor as they spoke about the founder of their social movement. From the start, I noticed that they were far more interested in religion as a problem than in actual social or political issues. They attacked the church for being responsible for the workers' plight, depicting the Vatican as the richest bank in the world, more fabulous than Solomon's mines. They felt that the clergy was the biggest enemy of prosperity for the working class (while we Polish men had identified Hitler as the greatest threat to independent life), and yet one surprising fact became clear during all these talks. The existence of God was more evident to them than it was, at this time, to me.

In these difficult years, my faith had been called into question on many occasions, although I continued to fundamentally believe in God the Father. These young men, entirely educated in the atheist school, the school of militant communism, were more ardent believers than I. The existence of God was so evident to them, they never experienced any doubt. When I discussed my own doubts and fears, they were completely surprised at my thinking.

They asked, "And you are not certain about God? Why not? God has hurt no one. God has killed no one. It is man."

I battled their incredulity as well as my own embarrassment about any doubts I had related about the existence of God. These men did not have a philosophical education other than their communist training, and that was a problem in terms of any discussions about the immortality and spirituality of the soul. My ignorance of Russian, as well as their limited German, contributed to our differences, even though we had the best of intentions when we began any discussion. At length, we overcame our disagreements because we liked one another, despite our inability to reach any level of agreement.

Some of the sick Russian prisoners in the room yelled and cursed their injuries, suffering greatly. Almost all of them also cried out, "Oh God, Oh God of mine, help me."

After so many years of fighting God within Russia, after years of being educated in atheistic ideas, no one could tear God from the hearts of these young men or keep them from asking Him for consolation.

One young Russian prisoner had been confined to his sick-bed for eleven months. His knees and legs bore nails and other shrapnel, and he was unable to move them in any way. His face was pale, but otherwise he showed no visible signs of pain. He lay quietly among us, seemingly content.

We never heard him complain once. Walking through the room one day, I stopped to check on him. I asked him, "How do you feel?"

"Very well," he answered briefly with a smile on his lips.

Not completely satisfied with his response, I asked him, "Really, you are not suffering?"

And he responded, "Oh no, I am suffering. I can hardly stand the pain."

I asked him, "But, you are a man like all the rest. Why don't you scream like all the rest?"

His response was, "I have a terrible urge to scream like the rest. I suffer a lot. But I do not want to yell and make the suffering of my companions worse."

I did not have any comment. His response spoke for itself and did not need explanation. His was heroism of the true kind, so human, so clean that no comment was good enough to make. This young communist, constantly in pain, was motivated solely by pure and human compassion; he knew how to climb to the heights of heroism that few ever achieve.

The condition of my patients was worthy of sincere compassion. They had miserable food, barely enough to warm the throat and stomach, but not conducive to regaining one's lost health.

The prisoners who distributed the food were most concerned with serving themselves the best and most food. Sometimes, the others received only water. When I was personally in charge of the distribution, I did everything possible to see that each received his portion.

The authorities did not supply any of the medicines my patients needed. We relied on Tony, who had access to the pharmacy, to send it to us whenever possible or if especially needed. The authorities did not care about the health or suffering of any of the prisoners. Tony was not the chief of the pharmacy, but he often entered where the devil could not, stealing what the chiefs would not take out for the sick. Tony was a good organizer, and he stole for us, knowing he would be severely punished if caught. We tried to make of ourselves an organization, passing food among everyone and using medicine in a moral way. Our "organization" had no negative aspect but was instead a symbol of man's ability to overcome that which had been taken from us as prisoners, our health and our freedom, that which was taken by the very first German representative of Hitler.

The English Spy

A CAPTAIN OF THE ENGLISH Army was being held in Barrack 15. Denounced by one of his collaborators, a man of French origin, he had fallen into the Gestapo's hands. The captain was of medium height and was not very heavy. He had fine lips and a copious amount of black hair and thick eyebrows. He expressed himself very slowly, as if thinking ten times before uttering a single word. He had a darker side to his personality, but overall he was a pleasant man.

He said, "I'm not sure why they don't go ahead and execute me. They have all my data and an abundant amount of material against me." When the Gestapo had questioned him about why he was in France, he had sarcastically answered, "I surely have not come to smoke French cigars."

The Gestapo had his notebook, which listed all his encounters with anti-Hitler collaborators, the exact times and places of those meetings, and many of the surnames of men the Germans wished to capture. The captain often spoke about the ineptitude and clumsiness of the Gestapo, that collaborators were usually notified an hour and a half before the Gestapo arrived to arrest them. This was partially due to the Gestapo's "To-Be-Picked-Up" list, which announced whom they were looking for and was circulated time and again to prevent capture.

The captain waited in Barrack 15 for his death. He was able to move around and engage in conversation. Whenever I visited him, he had the same temperament: cool, unworried, ready to talk and discuss. We often talked about historic themes, the England of years past. He said, "We Englishmen will never fight for any other nation unless there is a direct threat to our own interests. And we are capable of selling the souls of our mothers to make a good business transaction."

I never knew many Englishmen and never would have come to such a conclusion on my own. I wondered if it was just this particular individual who had such a cynical view or if it was truly the opinion of his countrymen.

One day, as I was having lunch with him, he was taken away. We were conversing as usual, and in the middle of his lunch, the Gestapo arrived. As they took him, he said, with a tranquil smile, "Goodbye, my Polish friend. We will see each other again in the other world." He disappeared from my eyes forever, but his words rang in my ears every day. I continue to expect the fulfillment of his words, that we will see each other in the next life.

THE BOY WHO SNORED

I REMEMBER A SMALL YOUNG man, a native of Poland, who occupied the top bed above me in one of the barracks. He was delicate and funny and knew how to adapt to different people of different ages, with respect for each nationality. During the day, he was the delight of the room. However, at night, he was a torture for us. While the whole world tried to sleep, he began playing his musical instrument with huge phlegmatic bursts; even the deaf covered their ears to get away from his unpleasantness, his constant snoring. No one in the room could sleep. The yelling of his companions would not wake him, nor would the light slapping of his face, the tugging of his nose and ears, or any other remedy his companions devised. The room developed an unpleasant enmity that we wanted to avoid at any cost.

A magnificent idea occurred to us. When a young boy cries or makes a noise, the young mother puts something in his mouth to quiet him. So, we sprinkled into his mouth (with love) a small amount of asphalt, which he then swallowed. He woke up with a bad, sour taste and a rolling stomach, and he began to vomit. This poured down over the side of the bed and onto my face, waking me from my sweet sleep. He did not know what to say or whom to suspect; he was determined to look in every direction and stay awake to find out who was trying to kill him. However, sleep overtook him and immediately the orchestra began; his enormous snores occupied every corner of the room. The next night, our reaction was not so cruel, but we were ready with another remedy, a piece of candy. This woke him up. He was grateful for something sweet on his tongue; he ate the candy, then went back to sleep, immediately snoring so loudly that all of us were ready to do something even more dramatic. But what?

We made a black drink of some type of lotion we had found and slowly poured it into his open mouth. When he awoke, his throat telegraphed his stomach, and he again started vomiting, though he suffered no truly dangerous consequences. However, now this young man no longer trusted his neighbors; he secured himself in bed in such a way that he was not on his back with his mouth open. Therefore, we all had some completely quiet and tranquil nights of sleep. He said that he felt much better sleeping in this position and woke up feeling fresher and more rested. Of course, the rest of us felt the same way. We confessed our guilt to him and asked forgiveness for our part in trying to cure the snoring. He laughed and said he did not hold any resentment in his heart. We continued to have a good friendship, maybe better than before because everyone was able to get some rest at night.

The Jewish Prisoner
Who Was Saved

Along with some of the difficulties that Hitler and the Germans faced in the war outside the camp, some of the prisoners experienced a slightly improved condition. Among them was a sick Jewish prisoner from Hungary who was transferred from another sick room. He had been hated in his previous sick room for being Jewish and needed a blood transfusion to save his life; no one had been willing to give him their blood. In our room, several German prisoners refused to give him their blood, so I offered to give my blood for analysis to see if we were a match. The exam revealed that the Hungarian Jew and the Christian priest shared the same kind of blood. He received the transfusion and the following day seemed to be feeling somewhat better.

From that moment on, I treated him as though we were brothers by blood. When I visited him, I called him brother. It seemed to bother him greatly. He asked, "Why do you call me brother when I am not your brother?"

I said to him, "You being a Jew and me a Polish man does not mean we are not brothers."

"No, no," he yelled at me, "I do not want to be your brother. I am Jewish, and I want to be only Jewish."

I told him, "You know that your life was saved by Polish blood, which is also Christian blood."

When he heard those words, he screamed at me, "No, I don't want that. I want only to be Jewish and of pure blood. I would prefer to die than be a Christian. I hate the Christians. I hate them with all my being."

At the time I was grossly offended. I did not understand his way of thinking because I did not understand what had been happening to all the Jews in Germany.

THE THIEF

IN THE NEIGHBORING ROOM WAS a young Czech nurse who moved among the sick. Every time he walked past the Jewish patient, he lost some item from the food tray. Such was the extent of his hunger, every bit of food the patient could reach disappeared into his thin form. His clothing hung on his body like rags over his stick-like arms.

The nurse was going crazy trying to correct this situation, to stop this patient from stealing the food meant for others. The patient was sent to my room. The nurse told me, "He steals from everyone in the room, anything and everything he sees."

I said to the Jewish patient, "You have been a thief, stealing bread from the hungry, those who need food every bit as much as you," and I slapped him in the German way. I don't know if it was the right thing to do, to slap a starving man who was suffering, or if it was terrible impatience and frustration on my part. However, it seemed to awaken his conscience. From that day forward, he was almost an idol among the others.

The Jewish thief was no longer a thief. He was a man who became very interested in his companions and offered his helpful services to everyone. On the surface, he did not appear very attractive, with his tiny eyes, sunken, yellow cheeks, and long, pointed chin that resembled a lost promontory in the ocean. However, something extraordinary beat inside his skeleton, a heart with so much spirit and kindness, the heart of a man full of rich stories and jokes, and he became most cherished among us. He gave each patient lavish attention; he could genuinely empathize with their suffering. A room of pain became a room of smiles. When he moved among the sick, the shadows of sadness seemed to leave the room.

The thief's abrupt and mysterious change had me very thoughtful for a long time. Sharing a moment of his humor, I approached him with the intention of exploring the source of his transformation. I asked, "How do you explain such a positive change in yourself? You went from being a bothersome and disliked thief to the most admired person in the room."

He laughed and said, "Look, since the first blow you gave me, I knew I could not survive here in the way I was going. It is preferable to laugh than to cry and better to make good relations between people than to be hated by everyone." A man who had been a thief and who had stolen from the sick, who was covered in dirt and injured by the pain of war, was able to find in himself a cloak of good and kind human virtues and to promote and participate in the common goodwill of all.

The Young Greek Man

Among the sick in my room was a victim of the Germans' relentless bombardments, a young Greek man who had been in naval service to his country, captured, and later transferred to Dachau. He was very young; his life counted only eighteen Aprils before a bomb had shattered his leg. The German chief who admitted him to the camp hospital gave an immediate order that his leg was to be amputated. The order was given to a Polish doctor from Warsaw who, along with another doctor, had once worked in a Warsaw hospital on Hoza Street. The young man's age and plight touched Dr. Gzarnkowski. To make a young man an invalid for the rest of his life would be a terrible cruelty if any chance existed of saving his leg. The doctor was willing to disobey a direct order from the chief and perform an operation, not an amputation.

The poor Greek yelled and begged for his leg to be cut off, or for the doctor to let him die because the pain was so fierce. He had heard the word "cholera" pronounced by the doctor many times, and he repeated it to me when I asked, "Do you know any words in Polish?"

He said, "Oh yes, I know Polish: cholera, *piorunie*."

Afterward, for months, I would change his bandages and he would cry and say, "*Piorunie*, kill me. I prefer to die than to suffer so much."

However, months passed, and finally he understood that his pain would end and that he would walk again. I have no idea how the doctor fixed his leg, but after eleven months in bed, the Greek man started walking on both legs.

Then he would say with satisfaction, "Thanks to cholera, *piorunie*, and the *psiakrew* of Dr. Gzarnkowski, I will be able to return to my country, healed and complete." Indeed, if and when the war ended, he would return to his country of Helenos, telling his story with compliments to Polish cholera, which not always kills, but heals.

THE JUBILEE OF
TEN YEARS IN DACHAU

IN BARRACK 7, ROOM 2 was a sick man, a citizen of Germany, one of the first to fall into the Gestapo's hands. A lawyer by profession and a descendant of a Bavarian region, he had shown courage by declaring his personal freedom from Nazism. At this time, he had been in Lager Dachau for ten years. He was of an advanced age but remembered a thousand miracles and the smallest details of his life in this somber place. This man wrote in a plain, realistic style, and he dreamed of writing a book about the cruel course of Hitlerism. However, he could not write it in this place, and who would help him? His three sons had been in the Wehrmacht, and apparently they had opposed the State; they had all lost their lives to Russian bullets. Before they were killed, they had never once intervened with the government on behalf of their father, who had vegetated for a decade there in Dachau. It was ridiculous that the government should fear a broken, elderly, Catholic man who had hardly the energy to live.

While the man's three sons rested forever in Russian lands, this sweet, kind man tended to the sick with all the feelings of a mother. After ten years in Dachau, he did not believe that anyone might be interested in his life. It was not the Gestapo or even the German government that showed such interest but his miserable skeletal companions who had the bad luck of being fellow prisoners. They were organizing, studying, and preparing to celebrate the day of his ten-year jubilee.

Naturally, there would be no pretty presents because there was nothing to give him. Their gifts were from the heart and worth more than any material thing. Those who worked in the factory offered him a piece of metal engraved with a decade of years. Those who worked outside the camp said they would try for a good cigar or candy, though what we really needed was a bottle of champagne and a bouquet of flowers, things too dangerous and difficult to procure. All his gifts came in the form of proclamations, the sincerest feelings of the other prisoners in verse, prose, and song. On that day, not one person did not express his intimate feelings. Stories, poetry, jokes, and compassion were voiced in German, Polish, Czech, Russian, Hungarian, and Yugoslavian. They offered him the intensity of their pain only in its opposite, wishing him days and weeks of great happiness and freedom from the sorrow with which they struggled every day. The Russian communists said they wished that God would permit him to return to live the rest of his life under his own roof in the company of his loving wife, who would prolong his days with tender kisses. There were visible tears and expressions of great affection. This poor, elderly man was touched to the core of his being, and he let the tears run in abundance, like precious pearls, down his cheeks.

He said, "I have lost the love of my sons but have won the love of my brothers in pain." His eyes overflowed, and he kept reaching into his pockets as though looking for something to give the men in return. All assured him that they wanted nothing but to honor him and share in his sorrow and happiness.

This was surely the only day of celebration in his ten years in Dachau. Supporters of the Hitler State hated him. Those who loved and encouraged him were hated as well; great injustices had been done to them, and they had terrible fear for the days ahead. However, nothing was powerful enough to take from these men their love of rectitude. Somehow, their hearts remained alive and unbroken.

ZBYSZEK

Among the sick was a young boy, torn brutally from his mother's arms. He was taken to Dachau for being "dangerous" to the great Germans. Maybe because of his tender age, or maybe because he had no family to nurture him, he held a special place in the prison. His name was Zbyszek. He was the son of a Polish captain who, if my memory is correct, was from a small town. He had no formal education, having been schooled at home. His mother was devoted to him, writing many letters, trying to instill in him the principles and norms of the Catholic Church. I had the luck of reading two or three of her letters, which she ended with these significant words: "My only son Zbyszku, I ask God that you return home as innocent and good as the day you left."

Sadly, he was no longer that ignorant, innocent boy. From the time of his arrival at Dachau, he had known only the roughest cruelties, and so he had begun changing himself so that he could adapt to his circumstances and survive. Very quickly, he went to the other extreme, becoming a renegade with the foulest mouth, spewing obscenities, and even worse, becoming a willing killer of some of his companions. If we had compiled a list of the worst and most dangerous men in the prison, other than the German soldiers, Zbyszek would have occupied the first position.

He received brief instruction as a "nurse," and he knew he

must blindly obey orders from his superiors. Disobeying orders meant death. For Zbyszek, it was very clear that, to live, he must kill other prisoners. He was to give lethal injections to the very sick. He would give those injections to prisoners who sought relief, doing so without looking at them, with all brutality. His actions pleased his cretinous superiors and guaranteed their confidence in him. If a prisoner became ill, his life or death was determined by which nurse attended him.

Zbyszek became undone when a sick prisoner arrived from block No. 28, the priests' barracks, as he seemed to hate priests most of all. He became devoid of all human feelings, insulting them wildly. He actually became the terror of the Polish priests. Consequently, they were all afraid that they might encounter him if they showed too much pain or illness. They tried living with their suffering, never once asking for help from the nurses and never going to the hospital. And still, the loving letters from Zbyszek's mother kept arriving with the words, "I beg God you will return to me as innocent as when you left."

For these words, the door had already closed; nothing could reach his lost conscience. At his young age, Zbyszek became very experienced at killing. It was impossible to find a person of any nationality, other than the Germans themselves, who had so much responsibility for the lives or deaths of others.

Once, a terrible typhus-like illness struck the inhabitants of Dachau. Although Zbyszek was to attend to the sick prisoners, he fell victim to the sickness almost immediately. It attacked his brain, and the doctors said his days were numbered. To be rid of him, the Germans sent him to my sick room. There he fell into my hands – the hands of a priest, the type of individual he hated so much. I made him reflect on his past, saying I would give him an injection in the same way he had killed many people. I would take away his swinish life, stained with the blood of innocents; I would finish him once and for all. Of course, I would not do this. However, he began remembering his past, his religious life, his beliefs.

Finally, he cried, "For the love of God, I beg you, don't kill me!"

I am not on the side of those who commit terrible acts and then pretend they are innocent; however, I would defend pure innocence and the desire to change one's life whenever possible. We men condemn other men, but God asks the question, "Who of us is without sin?" There are many reasons to defend this young man. He was taken from his family at an incredibly young age and imprisoned for no reason. He had the terrible fortune to be interned in Dachau, the most brutal of places. Most importantly, he no longer had his life or future or any hope whatsoever. My greatest wish for him was to recognize his failures and begin again. However, this would not be his path. His illness passed, and God saved Zbyszek. Instead of being thankful for his life, Zbyszek did not have remorse for his actions; he did not change.

One day, it was Zbyszek's turn to "treat" a young Italian man who anxiously waited for help with his illness. It was the afternoon of an ordinary day like any other. Zbyszek approached the bed of the sick one, carrying a syringe that would be fatal to the young man. Zbyszek acted naturally, calmly, and because it was his position as a nurse to give injections, no one paid much attention. The young Italian had blind confidence in his healer who, in cold blood, unloaded the syringe into his veins. He expressed his gratitude in German with "Danke Schoen" and fell right to sleep. However, he soon awoke again, screaming in pain. He called to his mother, who was so far away on the other side of the Alps and who could not know that her son was dying. "Mama, mama mia," he screamed.

These words reached Zbyszek's conscience like nothing else had done, like the blood of Abel before God's throne. When he heard these words from this last victim, Zbyszek stood up, petrified, unable to move forward or backward. All the prisoners he had executed paraded through his conscience, and he heard his own mother's words, again and again: "I ask God that you return home as innocent as when you left." Under the illuminating light of God's purity, Zbyszek clearly saw his own wickedness. He knew what he had done.

The young Italian man would never see his mother again. A sad but true confession came quietly from Zbyszek's lips: "I also have a mother."

This one confession was not a phrase that could erase the past or the insupportable acts he had done, nor could it fill the silence that surrounded him. However, I believe it carried to the depth of his soul, making him see another way in which to act and live. "God, what do you want me to do?" Saul asked this question, and Zbyszek asked himself the same. "What do I have to do to clean up the blood of so many innocent beings that I have spilled?"

It was possible that Zbyszek had killed a thousand patients, although I could never confirm any number among the imprisoned. He did not defend himself or show any remorse on his face. It was possible that he had no conscience at all because of how he had been forced to live. He placed no value on human life, had no time or reason to his own so that he could no longer feel anything. However, we had glimpsed something deep inside him. Pale and unbalanced and walking like a lunatic, Zbyszek started going back to his work, but then left the room and disappeared from our lives. After his disappearance, there were no more syringe killings by his hands. It has been said that the blood of the innocent clamors in the heavens for revenge. In this case, the blood of an innocent young Italian man brought Zbyszek to the mercy of God and to his forgiveness – and perhaps, on his day of rebirth, to His eternal pardon.

Hampel Edek

A FEW YOUNG MEN IN Dachau had the name Hampel. Even though they had identical names, they were very different from one another. They worked at the hospital but in separate areas and were known for the different ways in which they treated sick people. One of them passed through life without writing his history. He made no mark, and no one knew anything about him. The other man was lovingly called Edek, and the best experts in psychology could not have explained why this ordinary man of medium height, thin and plain, enjoyed the utmost esteem from everyone around him. He came to work in the hospital treating the sick; like a dentist in Dachau, he certainly did not have much healing work to do, considering the German system.

Wherever Edek appeared, the most downcast felt a drop of happiness in their hearts. When any of the prisoners spoke with Edek, each man took something good into his innermost being, something that only this most insignificant man seemed able to give. Edek was imprisoned like the rest of us and had supported the burden of thousands of others in Dachau obligated to live under the brutal conditions of the State of Hitler. While most prisoners' hearts perceived only the sadness, the misery, the discouragement, the defeated spirit, Edek's heart always found the light of God, some tiny star of happiness inside himself, and the satisfaction of being alive. Men died in pain and shame every day, yet breaking through all that, through all our hatred and curses toward the Germans, Edek's warmth and understanding flowed. His lips were for the service of God's good, to instill a breath of hope for better days that were hidden from view. He was persistently busy, helping and lending services to people who sought him out and who gained the benefits of the mysterious encouragement and strength that emanated from his heart.

The Dachau authorities used Edek for their purposes too, sending him to the private homes of their chiefs and higher officials. He attended to prisoners and dignitaries alike. During one of these trips, while he traveled to aid the wife of one of the Gestapo, a crash took his life. The soldier who was driving informed us that a piece of iron had gone through Edek's skull, leaving him instantly lifeless. Blood covered his body and he was sent to the crematorium, as were so many other living bodies made to disappear there.

News of the accident traveled from mouth to mouth and had a profound resonance in the hearts of all the men who knew him. The hearts of those still living felt a stab of pain. The prisoners' focus crystallized around Edek's death. Prisoners did not sleep, more able to believe in the end of the world than in their idol. Edek's death united imprisoned men from all nations. A crazy idea pervaded and empowered everyone: to give Edek a proper burial, to not see him vanish into the crematorium.

The prisoners implored the authorities to go against Dachau's ruling custom and allow a burial worthy of the esteem in which the victim had been held. This way, we might recover from the tragic end of an extraordinary life that had been in full flower. It is the only instance I can recall for which an exception was made.

We received permission to prepare a Christian grave – a coffin, crucifix, and candelabra, and a place where Edek's body could be viewed for three days. A dark room was converted into a stifling chapel, but any prisoner was free to walk past the tomb of his companion and say goodbye in a respectful, Christian way. With tears in their eyes and immense pain in their hearts, they made fervent prayers to God for peace and eternal happiness for one who had suffered and given so much love to others. Some men fell to their knees in reverence, and the line of prisoners stalled for as long as it took each man to pray. Prisoners waited patiently and in homage. On the third day, no flames consumed Edek. Rather, our mother earth received her beloved young son and sacred writings were read above him: "From earth, you have come, and to the earth, you will return."

This young man who had lived to serve us all during his short and difficult life had said goodbye. Our pain at losing him was profound – as profound as our living confidence that we would see him again in times to come.

JULIO

THIS NAME SOUNDED STRANGE IN a land of Polish people, and anyone would have thought that Julio was a Spanish man of pure blood, like those purebred lines of Arabian horses. When asked about his origin, he said that the devil knew nothing of the name Julio. He came to Dachau in a state of physical and moral agony. Julio had been chief of a railroad station close to Lublin and was accused of sabotage. The Gestapo took him and passed him from hand to hand while they tortured him, trying to make him confess secrets of any diversionary group that worked against the Germans. He was a young man of twenty-six years, but his body had become truly skeletal, and his mind was incapable of formulating a sentence.

In those days, I was working in a common area called *Curtenwerberei*, where we wound dirty rags into a fat rope for use in the maritime ports. On the first day of his new job, Julio was placed next to me and I must admit, I felt a certain repugnance for him. This was because of his thinness, because he looked already dead, a miserable bunch of bones sticking out on all sides. Injuries and sores covered him, creating the appearance of leprosy. His head hung down, and he could not answer even the simplest of questions. Each of us tried to get him to talk, but he would not lift his eyes or open his mouth. Other prisoners felt a certain distrust of him, unsure of his mental stability and competence. To encourage Julio, I told him I was a Catholic priest and that he could have confidence in talking about anything with me.

He looked up slightly and answered very slowly, "You are all the same."

The days passed, and Julio and I were unable to communicate with each other. When the chief of the work area came to observe us, he was immediately furious that Julio was not doing his job, and he began to strike him. I intervened, saying that he was a new man and had not learned the job yet. In this way, Julio was spared one more beating. The chief lost interest and walked away.

This insignificant act changed Julio's demeanor toward me. He asked, "Why did you do that? You could see that the chief would strike me, and he could have struck you as well."

I answered him truthfully. "I wanted to save you from suffering because it seems you have suffered enough."

"It is so," he said. "I have suffered barbarity, but until today, no one ever stood up for me or defended me against the brutal Germans."

I told him to not place too much importance on such a small circumstance. However, this event was the start of a friendship. Little by little, Julio's heart opened, and we understood each other more every day.

In Dachau, it was well-known that transports of prisoners sometimes went somewhere else, to other places of perdition, never to return. We would be called to the central plaza to await selection, and one day, Julio was called. He would receive his last bowl of soup at Dachau and then be taken by truck for transport.

I knew his fate was in my hands. I snuck into the clothes barrack and asked for a new uniform because mine was badly torn.

This uniform was not the same as the one Julio was wearing for transport, so I ran to where he was and begged him to put it on. He was too frightened and refused to change his clothes, knowing that if we were caught, we would suffer terrible consequences. I insisted. Finally, he changed his uniform and moved away from the group getting ready for transport. That time, Julio remained with us and was not taken to his almost certain death. In the following weeks, his spirits revived.

On another occasion, he was again chosen for transport. I pushed him to the ground; the overseer passed by and did not see Julio among the group of prisoners who had gathered. A third time, Julio was chosen for transportation to the quarries, from which he would certainly not return.

An edict stated that no priests were to be chosen for this work. When Julio was selected, I yelled out, "Priest, he's a priest," and shoved him aside.

In this way, the director of a small railroad in Poland became a priest, and he became a friend like few others. He was convinced that priests were somehow above the human masses because they exposed themselves to grave dangers to save the lives of their brothers. Julio was intelligent and well-educated, without pretensions, and he wanted to lead a helpful, attentive life, bringing heartfelt expressiveness and an admirable humor to his fellow men. The horrible cruelties he had suffered and the harsh life he was living, trapped in Dachau, did not have any moral influence on his religious life. I was happy to call this young man a friend.

JASIU

AT THIS TIME, OUR GROUP gained one more companion, whose name was Jasiu. He was a brutal young man with a filthy mouth, very vulgar and violent in his ways. From the beginning, he did not blend in with us. Some of us received food packets from different parts of Europe; we shared them with Jasiu, and soon he began regaining his physical strength.

He disliked any of us commenting on his language or behavior and always gave the defense, "I'll have enough time to be penitent when I am old. Now is the time to enjoy myself and have fun."

My efforts were like a bit of smoke in the air; Jasiu persisted with his violent ways as though a thousand years were ahead of him. He was assigned to Barrack No. 21, and some young Russian communists were in his group. They were very interested in my relationship with Jasiu and in the priestly profession. They watched and listened intently to all our encounters.

It was a Monday, and Jasiu and I had conversed for a long time. He said goodbye in the same joking tone: "I am young and have plenty of time to be penitent." He laughed and left me for the last time.

I did have a chance to ask him, "And who has promised you sufficient time to change your life and be repentant?" Jasiu gave no sign of any illness, though death was knocking on his front door and already coming through the windows.

The following Wednesday, I went to visit Jasiu. Some of the Russians began yelling, "*Bachka, bachka,* your friend has died."

I asked them, "Who has died? How is it possible that it could be Jasiu? I left him only a few days ago in good health."

They described what they had witnessed. With all his strength, Jasiu began screaming that the devil was taking him, and a thick foam came from his mouth. Then, without warning, he died. I could not determine whether this had been a rare case of epilepsy or some superior intervention, but this never-before-seen phenomenon terrified the Russians, who fully believed that the devil had taken Jasiu.

What will be, will be, and only God will know. I do not think that Jasiu was a truly specious and hollow man, although he enjoyed boasting of all the bad things he had done. He wanted to be a bad hero, posturing in front of others to impress them, as if he never knew the value of being morally good or accomplishing anything positive. May God forgive him for everything and have mercy on him for all eternity.

One Day In Dachau

I CANNOT EASILY DESCRIBE A day in Lager Dachau with exactness, as to truly understand, a person must have lived inside its walls. Twins could not describe its reality accurately, as each man would have a different view and set of experiences. Typically, the day began at 5:00 a.m. with the chief yelling, *"All RISE!"* At this time, those who were still alive started moving, jumping from their beds as if flames were burning them from underneath. Only the dead in their sad vegetation, those who had passed away in the night, had the privilege of peace.

We were then to go to the main plaza and line up in formation. We were to drag our dead companions behind us so that they, too, were in line. The authorities were not interested in who was alive or dead; they were concerned only that the numbers of men that day matched the number from the previous day. It was not human but numeric, and prisoners could not be worried about bringing the dead to the plaza or saddened by their terrible presence. The numbers had to match.

The living were then directed to the *"WASCHRAUM!"* (washroom), where three hundred of us pushed into a space made for ten men. We were to have a bowel movement, whether or not it was needed; we either "sat well" or were "not able anymore," which gave the soldiers their morning jokes and laughter. Time was not measured by wristwatches but by how quickly each man could evacuate, then get up and move on, while the next man jumped onto the seat and received his only opportunity of the day to relieve himself. There was yelling, pushing, and so much chaos; the air was foul-smelling, and a silent observer would have had to laugh at this strange performance although it was not at all funny.

Cold showers were next. We had to move so quickly, some prisoners were able to wet only the tips of their fingers before they had to move on. Then we made the beds, supervised by the soldiers, who were on the lookout for *"SIDE DIRECTION!"* – a twisted curve or uneven edge in the bedding. It was an offense that resulted in a beating. This was only the beginning of a day; furious tantrums by the chiefs, early morning suffering from the subordinates, and much more punishment awaited us all.

Coffee distribution followed – or let us say, the prisoners received excessively hot, blackish water made from sour-tasting roots that the cooks had picked from God knows where. Brazilians and Colombians would probably be offended that this drink was called coffee, yet men were in charge of carrying the tubs of liquid to the barracks. The weight of the buckets and the weakness of the bearers determined the time it took to accomplish this task. The chiefs became angry if it wasn't done fast enough or if one drop of liquid was spilled on the floor. The carriers were struck or beaten, and if a coffee carrier became tired or distracted, he was severely punished. We held out our mugs for this precious beverage, emptying every one of those buckets to fill the emptiness in our stomachs. After this, each prisoner washed his mug and put it away in a cabinet. Everything had to shine like crystal. Our biggest worry was that the inspectors would find a speck of dust or dirtiness with their penetrating eyes and we would receive another beating. The total time we received for these morning rituals – the washroom, fixing the beds, the breakfast, the cleaning and storing of utensils – was one-half hour.

As I said, every morning the whistles of the Block Alterers sounded the call for us all to line up in the principal plaza. The Block Alterers and the S.S. were responsible for counting the prisoners, the sick men leaning on the arms of their companions, the dead dragged like dogs, each man lined up – dead or alive – and counted. When the results of the count were different from the day before, the problems began. Some days it was a simple error in adding the groups, an error not difficult to discover and correct. It was much worse when any among the imprisoned were missing from the plaza. On such occasions, the Block Alterers and the S.S. went off to find them while we stood and waited. They did not need long to find an individual because Dachau offered no places to hide. The risk of hiding was not worth the terrible consequences.

Sometimes during the night, a prisoner became so desperate that he ran to the electrified fence surrounding the prisoners' area. To even graze those sharp wires would kill a person instantly. These men did not intend to escape; they were planning to end their lives. I cannot condemn them or judge them, as dark desperation had overtaken their minds. A person living without human dignity, in constant pain and suffering, could not choose that which was lawful or unlawful because there was no law; some men moved blindly forward to their deaths. These instances were few, especially compared to the vast majority of prisoners dedicated to holding on, even to the thinnest string of their utterly miserable lives.

After the formation in the principal plaza, the lines of men broke up and went to their destined jobs under the supervision of strong, armed guards. Passing out of the prison gate, we were to show our happiness for our work by singing loudly. Prisoners sang and yelled in different languages and keys, and the whole effect was madness.

Upon arriving at our workstations, we were commanded to begin *"jogging,"* a diabolical system that exhausted any physical reserve a man had remaining. Constant movement was required, working and moving, and the foremen were as absolute demi-gods, abusing the prisoners in every cruel way, with no fear of reprisal from superiors. Work times were the worst, with the sufferings and deaths of the men enhancing the reputation, stature, and confidence of the brutal foremen. At 10:00 a.m. we were allowed ten minutes of rest as *"bread time"* was called and we received a small portion of bread. Often, bread was withheld from prisoners or from Polish priests, all at the foremen's whim.

During the autumn and winter months, thick fog covered the regions surrounding the concentration camp. This fog covered the areas where we worked and gave some prisoners the hope of escape. An attempt to escape was exceptionally dangerous for the fugitive; when it did happen, the prisoner was caught not far from his place of departure.

A fellow prisoner of Belgian origin, an admirable young man, formerly a private boat captain and owner of plantations in the Congo, tried more than once to flee Dachau. Once, he was already in Switzerland, happy, planning a new life, when the neutral Swiss turned him in to the authorities. His escape failed, and he suffered the loss of his liberty. He had rather feminine features, and we suggested that he try to obtain a woman's clothing, transforming himself into the other sex to get away. He did escape in this way, and when he was completely and undoubtedly safe, he sent me a note using an entirely different name. He was very lucky to have survived. The Germans were strong in the air, on land, and at sea, and they were cruel and had no sympathy for anyone who tried to escape. For each refugee who fled from an individual barrack or work group, ten innocent prisoners were made to pay; the lives of ten would sometimes be taken for the rescue of one.

Generally, work continued until 11:30 a.m., at which time we returned to the barracks. This was a moment of elation for everyone, as the abominable work was done, and we all began thinking with golden imaginings about what food we might receive for lunch that day. These were but illusions, as the prisoners often had no food. The priests in block No. 28 were starved most often. Men lost their priestly equilibrium, and their hearts filled with a frightening hatred of the Germans.

Then the inspectors arrived to look for pretexts for punishment, anything to make the defenseless suffer, any small spot or tiny mark on a utensil or cabinet. When they found an excuse, they threw everything out of the cabinets, all the utensils onto the ground. It all had to be washed and the floor spotlessly cleaned, leaving no time for prisoners to wolf down hot water adorned with a greasy bone, known as soup, even when it was offered. The priests in Barrack No. 28 did not receive soup, but the problem of the hungry Polish priests and the pain they felt from hunger bothered no one.

We were again called to form lines and return to work; we had conquered half the day, and the other half – including its violence and foreboding – was still to come. During the rainy months, prisoners looked for ways to cover themselves, holding pieces of paper or empty cement bags over their heads. To the soldiers, this was a crime, as it was against the economy of the Reich. Any man found trying to shield himself from freezing rain was made to remove all his clothes, then was beaten badly enough that he would never try such an act again.

Smoking during work hours was forbidden. Some prisoners found actual cigarettes when the soldiers threw them on the ground. Because they were hard to get, these cigarettes had social value among the men. To share a few puffs of a cigarette with others, no matter how vulgar the gesture, made the men stand out like deer in headlights. If one of the smokers found not only a piece of a cigarette but a whole pack, that man's status and esteem among the other smokers instantly skyrocketed. Smoking was punishable by beating, so there was also the aspect of heroism and self-sacrifice in the finding and sharing of a smoke.

The exact hour of the end-of-the-afternoon jobs varied. Some commands returned to camp and others remained for extra hours, enduring long marches before they could rest. It was not only a glimpse of hot water or prepared food that brought them back with lighter hearts, but also the conversation among friends, which unburdened their spirits, and the thought of lying down at night to rest. Tired of this dirty world, the priests broke strict laws prohibiting prayer in Dachau, taking advantage of long periods of waiting to vocalize in prayer. They moved their lips as if they knew of no other way to pray. The soldiers would see this and became enraged. They did not spare the lashings of the stubborn priests, whose desire to speak with God in this damned, condemned place was so intense. The priests mocked the jealous soldiers by praying, and they were beaten for it, their tears and pain flowing openly. It was as if God were saying through them, "You do not allow me to reign in Dachau, but I will always reign in the brave hearts of my faithful priests." And God continued to reign because the priests continued to pray.

THE PUNISHMENTS

THIS CHAPTER IS A CONTINUATION of the previous section, *"One Day in Dachau,"* because the punishments to be described were part of daily life in the camp.

The same plaza where we lined up each morning was the setting for another type of public punishment that took place daily. For anyone who committed an error, a special table was prepared. The prisoner's arms and legs were spread and tied to each table leg so that the guilty one could not move. This left the most vulnerable and sensitive part of a man exposed to every strike, with only his thin pants modestly covering the front of his body. Two soldiers would line up with their lashing instrument, a whip made of dried mule skin, which lent magnificent service to those German hands of justice. It was a terrible instrument, and the pain it caused is impossible to describe. The instrument was brutal, the man using it was a brute, the chief determining each punishment was another brute, and the punishment was more cruel than any mistake that could ever be made.

Crossing the plaza at a slow pace was strictly prohibited. Prisoners were to run, never looking at the principal chief's office, which was next to the prison gate. Moving too slowly was sufficient reason to give a prisoner twenty-five lashings. The minimum punishment for any infraction was twenty-five lashings.

Any other mistake could mean more lashings – fifty, seventy-five, or more. While he was being whipped, the prisoner who made a mistake had to beg forgiveness and not make a sound, or he would receive more lashings. Any sign of rebellion against the whip, any crying or screaming, and the lashes multiplied. The executioners' fury did not abate out of any feelings of compassion; the lashings continued until a prisoner fainted from the brutality of the beatings or from the loss of blood. Hitler's supermen fell upon a prisoner until his bloody body looked like something at a meat market, as though he were an inert mass. They never showed signs of remorse or humanity.

One brave young boy decided he would not surrender before his executioners. He did not cry or yell as they lashed him mercilessly. His pants were torn apart, and he bled profusely, beaten so badly that once he was untied, he fell to the ground like an old rag. He was in such terrible condition that he was taken to the hospital. However, the German doctor who saw him said that the boy did not need medical attention because it was too late. The martyred boy could never be accused of weakness. He had not cried out or yelled or made a sound. He had never surrendered to the soldiers who beat him. He was dead.

Once the daily lashings were carried out, one would think that a prisoner would be allowed to return to his barracks, but this was not the case. According to the whim of the principal chief (the *Lagerführer* or the *Rapportführer*), prisoners who had been beaten were to remain standing on the plaza while their companions returned to their barracks. The German chiefs and the soldiers who beat us may have had some humanity in their private lives, but they became inhuman beasts in the presence of the imprisoned, who in fact were no longer treated like living men, but only numbers.

On many cold days in autumn and winter, the sky unloaded torrents of freezing rain. By order of our superiors, prisoners stood motionless for long hours in the rain. This new genius of an invention for punishment was often aimed at prisoners in Barrack No. 28, punishment for the unforgivable crime of prayer. Priests being called to Christ had to pay severely for their holy crimes and for their love of God. "Oh God of mine, help us," was our fervent prayer as men fell without further strength and their dead bodies were dragged to the crematorium to be converted into a small pile of ashes.

Although I never saw this, some of the prisoners said that before 1941, the punishments had been milder. German soldiers had been armed with lashing instruments, but the beatings had been less cruel, and a band of musicians had played and sung songs, happy pieces, during the beatings. Within Dachau, prisoners passed along these stories from one new group of inmates to the next. A German saying comes to mind: "The crueller a German is, the more authentically German he is." Logically, it would have been against German psychology to beat or kill defenseless victims and feel some type of "degrading" compassion at the same time. A band of music accompanying abominable acts would have changed the atmosphere and, in a diabolical way, might have allowed the soldiers to experience happiness and contentment for proceeding toward the great German ideal of perfection. The first years of the war were more routine, while later, the viciousness and killing escalated. Happy music was no longer necessary to encourage the Germans to enjoy their work.

THE SHOWERS

PRISONERS FROM ALL OVER EUROPE entered Dachau through the camp's main gate. To the right of the gate were the showers. This area formed a large part of a building that also held the kitchen and a room where money was kept. The shower area was divided into two sections. On one side, we left our clothes when entering. On the other, we endured frigid water and a quick, violent scrubbing of the body. This was where the last possible bit of heat remaining in our skeletal frames was taken away. Every two weeks, each prisoner had to have a shower.

There was a system made famous by the German priest, Dr. Kneipp. He believed that a quick spray of cold water could cure many diseases, even incurable diseases, by changing the patient's internal temperature, making it the same as the external temperature of the air. The priest applied a spray of water to the patient in the hopes of improving the patient's circulation, and a red spot formed on the skin where the water had made contact. However, Dr. Kneipp did not require the patient to stand under freezing water for over two minutes. Instead of experiencing a positive effect on blood circulation, the prisoners in Dachau who stood under the harsh pressure of freezing water for as long as it entertained their captors – sometimes for many minutes – began freezing to death.

Ordinarily, once the shower was over, those who could move went to dry off and get dressed, trying to regain some body heat by rubbing themselves briskly. Some prisoners collapsed and never moved again. Sometimes, when the chief officer in charge of the showers gave the order, *"ALL OUT!"* we were ordered to run naked, barefoot and wet, outside into the snow and the severity of winter. There, we formed lines and stood at attention. If we moved at all, we were beaten. Some prisoners, knowing they were freezing to death where they stood, chose to be beaten because they knew that if they did not die from the beatings, their blood would be warmed in the areas where their bodies were punched and hit. Some prisoners froze to death where they stood.

Throughout the freezing showers, lice clung to us. Some of it was washed away, only to return when we reformed as a group or returned to our barracks. A disease called "the itch" invaded Dachau, and those who became ill were sent to the cold showers, then out into the snow and ice until they died. Once the carriers of this disease had passed away, "the itch" was eradicated from the camp. Some of the prisoners valiantly resisted death; in those cases, the men were made to stand outside for hours or as long as it took for them to collapse and freeze to death.

THE CREMATORIUM

WHEN THE JUDGE AT THE Nuremberg trials asked Hermann
Wilhelm Goering to stand and be accused, he refuted the accusations against him by saying that his only motive during the war
had been to protect his love of country, his personal liberty, and
his life. Hermann Goering was not the only one of Hitler's followers to deny his war crimes, though he and others had planned
the construction of the gas chambers and crematoria.

At first, Dachau had only a small crematorium and no gas chamber. Many years passed before the Germans felt the need to build a
new instrument of death and generate years of blood and moaning
that glorified their nation – a nation that claimed the title of a superior culture. Who knows what vast plan of destruction, toward people and other countries, caused the rebuilding of those crematoria.

Much before the first new stone was laid in Dachau, many
rumors circulated, some bringing fear and others happiness.
However, none of the prisoners knew that a new building meant
the total destruction of the minds and bodies of thousands of
prisoners. One day a new command was formed whose project
name told us nothing. Barrack X was to be built close to the site
where all the prisoners were held. It was separated from us by a
yard of moat and a highly charged electrical wire fence, as well
as by a wall that enclosed us and obstructed our view of the new

building. An area was chosen for the structure, destined to become a new crematorium and gas chamber, in the shadow of the trees. This place received no name, and prisoners could not have imagined its future purpose. In this way, priests and other prisoners worked on a construction project as they would on any other, with total indifference; it was simply the building of another barrack. Barrack X was to provide more showers to accommodate the hundreds of prisoners who were still arriving. It was not until the construction was almost complete that, despite German cleverness, its real purpose became known to any who had worked on Barrack X. Soon, the new showers became a gas chamber, and the crematorium beckoned to the dead.

A time arrived when the gas chamber was finished and awaited its first victims. Who would be taken first? That very afternoon, just past 4:00, a group of young men from Barrack No. 7 formed two lines. Their demeanor and tranquil behavior indicated that they had no idea of their fate. The soldier guarding them made a few jokes, and fellow prisoner Tony Zagier and I stood by, horrified and unable to speak the truth. An officer appeared and told the prisoners a lovely tale about how privileged they were to inaugurate the new showers, which had been built for the good of all prisoners. He said that they should be proud because their names would be written into the history of Dachau. Each of the condemned received a towel and a cup of soup.

When one of those young men was asked why he had a towel and a cup of soup, he responded with all sincerity, "Don't you see that we are going to inaugurate the new showers?"

This boy firmly believed the Germans. He asked childish questions about the officers' watch, and the conversation back and forth became so friendly that the entire group laughed and joked together.

My friend Tony said to me, prophetically, "Chester, I'm telling you, within an hour their clothes are coming back to the barracks empty. The poor fools have been tricked." We were told to leave the place where twenty men were destined to be gassed.

Some prisoners witnessed this first execution. By climbing onto the roof and looking through a type of window, they could observe the effects of the shameful gasses. Those scenes could move not only the hearts of men but those of any dumb beast. Most prisoners who witnessed such hellish scenes were frozen in fear, as though they had been transformed into granite. Germans who observed those deaths showed no signs of compassion. Even if they had human feelings, to display them would be treason.

The doors to the gas chamber were opened completely, as if an amiable invitation were being extended to enjoy the delicacies that the German supermen had prepared. The first of the prisoners, ignoring reality entirely, ran happily forward. Naked and ready to enjoy the benefits of warm water, these poor souls stood in front of the faucets. However, water did not fall from above as it usually did. Instead, the faucets were turned on from below, and the air became increasingly dense and heavy. The condemned looked around in distrust, then realized what was happening to them. There were voices of desperation, terrified screams, prisoners begging for their salvation, but it was too late. Their deaths were the first in a long chain of murders to come. No one came to their rescue, and there was no salvation.

Foam came from the mouths of the young men; their eyes bulged and they lost their equilibrium. They fell over each other, trying to stand, screaming and crying. The stronger the prisoner's resistance, the longer his torment lasted. Some men took almost one-half hour to die. I do not pretend that my description of these events can ever represent the full extent of their horror and suffering. It is based solely on living prisoners' testimonies and the few words here and there that were overheard from the soldiers. This horrendous and deadly German invention worked perfectly; once the deaths were verified, the bodies were dragged to the next terrible place, the crematorium. Lethal gas took away their lives, and electricity reduced them to dust. The sacred scriptures say that man is made of dust and to dust he will return, but these people were denied the natural progression of life and death. They were murdered.

While the bodies of those executed were still in the hands of their murderers, their souls were rising toward the Christ who, with open arms, said to them, "Come to me, blessed, and take the rooms prepared by my Father." It is impossible to say how many men were put to death.

Group after the group was chosen for experimentation with gas. These events remind me of when the Germans first used gas against the Russian troops during World War I. In those earlier experiments, hundreds of cadavers littered the ground. I remember reading an article about this, in which the inventor of the gas was interviewed. After he had seen the fields covered with the dead, his sad impression accurately reflected the Teutonic spirit when he said, "It is cruel, but what can we do?" I wondered what he would have said if the gas had been directed at him. Would he have been able to pronounce the same phrase? "It is cruel, but what can you do? Go right ahead and kill me. In these times, we need to execute people with gas. What else would we do with these people, even though they are innocent? They are in the way. Their presence bothers us. They are not part of our superior race of supermen. We must exterminate these men who otherwise would live with liberty, with purpose, and with joy. The only men who have a right to live are Germans."

Days later, the chief of the concentration camp at Dachau received the order to take all the Polish priests into the gas chamber. Small groups of priests were made to stand in formation, and among the first men chosen were my closest comrades. All the Polish priests knew we were destined to walk into that darkened gas chamber at some time. We knew this with certainty. However, not one among us could know the exact day chosen for his death. We also knew with certainty that the Lord held the destiny of men's lives, and when my group was selected, we stood and waited to go through the doors of the gas chamber. Then something changed the order. The same authority that, a few days earlier, had ordered the annihilation of all the priests, gave the order that we should turn around and return to our barracks.

Some of the priests who had been so close to death were saddened because they had awaited the crown of martyrs and an escape from this terrible life. Other priests regained a desperate hope, being among the men chosen to continue living. I do not know what God thought or did in those moments, but it is possible that we were not destined for the glory of martyrdom. It is also possible that an old proverb – "Bad weeds never die" – applied to us. In the manner of bad weeds, perhaps we remained there because we were capable of living, of continuing to grow our roots in any soil, even the poisoned soil of Dachau. More beautiful and delicate flowers could not exist, and God had taken those men into his Glory.

A story was told about the crematorium, a grand adventure carried out by a group of prisoners who suffered the ultimate punishment. It is a story that deserves mention. Each of the barracks in Dachau had a group of soldiers who watched over us. They were not like angels who protected us; they were more like bad guardians. One command boss was among the worst; he was cruel and vicious to everyone in his charge, and the prisoners, as well as the other guards, hated him. Everyone knew that men sent to their deaths in the gas chamber and crematorium would often stand as if trying to say goodbye. Then they would quickly fall back down to be consumed by fumes and electricity.

One group of prisoners thought, "Why are the dead the only fine and courteous ones struggling to stand and speak to us in their final moments? Why not the Germans?" And they threw the bad command boss, still alive, into the electrical oven. He was so shocked that he could not scream or cry out, and he did not stand or wave goodbye. He disappeared into the hot oven and was never seen again.

However, this genius plan did not include an important aspect to ensure success. The prisoners had not taken the time to remove the boss's weapon. Immediately, bullets exploded and created an infernal noise. The German soldiers rushed to the crematorium, knowing what had happened but unable to bring back the boss. The soldiers started grabbing whoever was close and throwing those men into the crematorium, the same oven through which their comrade had just passed. It was "an eye for an eye," except that many prisoners were taken for one terrible boss. Some German soldiers felt pleasure about the command boss's death. This was evident even though they tried to pretend that a great injustice had been done.

THE SACRIFICE OF
JEWISH FAMILIES

THE INTERIOR OF THE GAS chamber and the crematorium had born scenes of a terrible witness, and remembering them makes my blood boil. Those places were used for major executions. One of the biggest and most resonant events took place in our vicinity when many, many Jewish families arrived, taken from regions threatened by the invasion of the Allied forces. War had reached the terrain of Sicily and the doorstep of Mussolini, and these Jewish families were told that they were being taken into German protection. The Jews had objected that the Allies were not their enemies, but they had been shown the necessity of a forced march and of being transported out of the fierce battle zone and to a safer place. These people were innocent, and a terrible trick was being played. They were told to take all their provisions, especially gold and silver and jewels, because their new land would be a place of peace and tranquility, one that would require provisions for trade.

By this time, the fate of the Jews in the Warsaw Ghetto – who were taken from their homes as prisoners and who never returned – was well-known to every child. However, these Jewish families had not learned that lesson thoroughly; they trusted the German words and their pretty promises. Carrying all their valuables and food, some with halves of pigs on their backs, they arrived in

Dachau feeling safe and happy. Children and elderly people arrived, and their manner of speaking and dress showed them to be genteel and well-educated. However, as soon as they encountered the other prisoners, they were made aware of the German treachery, and horror and fear filled them.

In reality, no place was "safer" than a concentration camp, where the Allies did not land, and where the Gestapo protected you with all they had – until the day they took you into the gas chamber. The Jewish families were brought in from diverse Balkan regions, and they did not look like those of us who were already vulgar prisoners. On the contrary, they could have been our special, horrific guests at Dachau, bringing their rich provisions and elegant manners to the table. The first abuse came when the women and children were taken away from the men. This tearing apart of families had a devastating effect on all of them and on all of us. The second act was to give each of them a well-prepared meal, their last one on this earth. Afterward, they were to turn over to the Gestapo any items of value.

They had no time to hide their treasures, and many of them swallowed everything they could, even the largest items, anything that would go down the throat. Others tried to throw their items as far from where they stood as possible. This meant that many precious objects littered the ground. I, myself, found some well-sculpted and engraved silver objects, which the Gestapo confiscated along with every item that had been discarded. All the families were interrogated for hours so that they were certain to relinquish any remaining possessions. The Jews were clever, but the Germans were relentless.

Prisoners were then taken for X-rays so that the Gestapo could be certain they had confiscated every piece of metal in existence.

Those who had swallowed anything received huge doses of laxative which produced violent fits of diarrhea. If there was any question of remaining treasure, more laxatives were given. The Germans did not seem to care that their main purpose had become picking through feces, the smell, the mess surrounding them becoming desirable to them, as though they were nothing but pigs.

Once this process was complete, the Jews had no more value to the German nation. From that moment on, they were useless, and the fastest, cheapest, surest way to eliminate the large number of them was the gas chamber. The Jews were separated and destined for the second act of a well-premeditated tragedy. Dispossessed of all their belongings and riches, they stopped being men and became Jewish dogs. If their origin had been like that of the German Shepherd, they would have had more value to the German nation. However, now they were in the way and had to be eliminated. Once the victims were dead, they stayed very silent and never told their terrible stories or sad secrets. They had endured cruel vandalism and beastly savagery to their bodies; after only the shortest of stays, they disappeared from our sight. We were left with a short, sad, somber memory of their brief time filled with angelic illusions.

In the days that followed, prisoners who worked at the crematorium recounted the perverse and cruel deaths of those innocent creatures, those innocent families, in which a son disappeared into the crematorium a few moments before his father. They told of a fantastically beautiful and precious child, about four years of age, who was killed disgracefully, his death more cruel, in a way, than the deaths of his parents. The poor boy did not endure the deadly gasses of the gas chamber. Instead, a soldier carried him in his arms. At first sight, the prisoners who observed him were consoled, thinking, "Look, what a good man this soldier is, saving the life of a lovely child." At that moment, everything seemed right and magnificent, unexpected in the lives of these savages.

However, the soldier was not a savior; he was a lion looking for blood. The arms carrying this child were not the arms of his father, nor was it the chest of a loving father to which the boy was pressed. This soldier wore a mask and was nothing but a hungry beast ready to devour his prey. He carried the child in his arms to the crematorium, the place where bodies were converted into dust. Although the child had indeed seen skeletons there before, he did not understand their meaning. He wasn't afraid because he believed in human affection, especially that of the man who gently carried him toward the fire.

The prisoner in charge of the ovens received the order to open the door; he did not realize that his act of obedience made him a complicit criminal. The child moved by instinct, with both of his hands strongly holding the soldier's neck; he would not let go. The soldier pulled the boy's tiny body away, trying to separate the boy from his chest and neck. The child let out a cry painful enough to reach the sky where his dead mother, already converted to ashes, could have heard him and awakened. However, it did nothing to awaken the strong man who carried him, drowned in misery and rottenness, nothing to arouse the slightest spontaneously human feeling toward protecting a child, a beautiful, innocent treasure of life. The soldier could not conquer his hatred of the child's Jewish roots and threw that child into the fire.

This act, with its profound indifference toward human life, went far beyond race or religion. I could not think of an act in history that would prove it to the contrary. How can one understand this act? Even if we say that the soldier was abnormal, there is no answer to this saddest of questions. One could search in the formation of Hitler youth at a very young age. One could overhear soldiers' talk that said authentic Germans did not demonstrate feelings of compassion, that such feelings were visible signs of weakness and inferiority. Hitlerian rules dictated brutality and unbreakable cruelty as a demonstration and affirmation of German loyalty and authenticity. The superman was in complete opposition to the path and doctrine of the most perfect man, Jesus. When Jesus shed tears, he did not feel humiliated or that his manhood was lessened. He was a perfect man, and his tears were a noble response to human misery. The Germans were enemies of compassion and searched for ways to exhibit their virility and their manhood, like vicious beatings and killings, their cold hearts expanding with the pain of other human beings.

The property adjacent to the gas chamber and crematorium was a place not only for Jewish executions but for the killing of many different people. The number of gas chamber desirables grew according to the situation at the military fronts. Allied bombers were not even considering visiting the towns neighboring Camp Dachau, and close to 15,000 inhabitants of those towns eventually became victims of nightly executions.

A group of Russian soldiers shared the bad luck of being brought to the camp. They numbered perhaps ninety-nine, all of them flourishing with life. The first to arrive were soldiers, privates, and then a few days later, the officers. The Germans kept the Russians separate. Russian officers received marks on their backs, crosses that looked like famous crosses from an earlier time. Although we were separated from them, we had ways of communicating. It was clear that although they were communists, raised as complete atheists, many of them prayed daily.

They had come from a place where there was no God, and they had fallen into a place where believing in God and praying to Him were not allowed; God's entrance into this area was prohibited. I distrusted their belief in God and asked some of them what they had asked of Him. They said they had prayed to be allowed to return to their country after the war. Their prayers were quite fervent and united us as people with a desire to return and share the liberty of our native lands. In this way, there was a compromising of ideas among the men, to unite with Russia and other nations in a prayer for the freedom of us all.

The effects of our prayers may have been good for a communist country, but they were not so good for its inhabitants in the prison. The Russian officers, along with having red crosses painted on their backs and the sides of their pants, were sent to the barbers. The barbers were ordered to shave hair crosses on their heads so that the officers could easily be recognized from a distance. Therefore, they would never try to escape. This was strange and made everyone wonder about their future.

We did not have long to wait because the Germans, pretending to observe international legal rules for prisoners, had already judged and condemned these prisoners to death. They would never be called to trial, and would never have a word said in their defense. The German penal code stated that officers were to be granted ninety days before any death sentence, and for some unknown reason, in this instance the penal law was enforced. The Russian officers were notified of their death sentence and received ninety days before the execution. Until that time arrived, they were guarded with particular vigilance. On the ninetieth day, they were taken to the property next to the gas chamber and ordered to dig a ditch for their eternal rest. Those prisoners watching wondered at the remarkable calm with which the Russian officers dug. United in a sort of religious pietism, they knelt in front of the hole as they were told, inclining slightly so their bodies would fall quickly into the hole. They waited in this way for a gun at the back of their heads, which cut them down one by one, without the least resistance, like the automatic machine cutting of trees. As officers, international law was to defend and protect them, but no one remembered them. They have all disappeared, submerged in profound silence, and today no one thinks about their murder or of any of the Germans' abysmal long list of criminal acts.

KATYN

BEFORE HE WAS SHOT, I spoke with one of the Russian officers about the events in Katyn and the horrors that the Russians committed against the Polish. He asked the surprising question, "Is it true that four hundred Polish were killed?" I told him the high number was more like 12,000 killed, and he made no comment.

It is a wonder that such barbarity could occur, and many people were inclined to doubt the Germans, saying they may have used an excellent opportunity to create suspicion and propaganda against the Russians. Once the war was over, special commissions would be formed to investigate these events. However, despite their best efforts, they never discovered who was responsible for the killings at Katyn.

When some of the exhumations were done, the body of a German colonel who had been a German prisoner was found in an area where the Russians had never gone. Who can explain this mystery, as well as many others? Did the Russians capture that colonel from German custody, then kill him? Did the colonel escape and run toward his death? Is it possible that the suspicions of the Russians in Dachau were true, that the Germans were responsible for the massacre in Katyn? The Russians accused Colonel Friedrick Akreus, a German officer, of ordering the massacre of Polish officers in a camp at Katyn, but no definitive proof of this exists. I do not consider myself an enemy of the Germans, nor a particular friend of the Russians, but a doubt persists about the events at Katyn that still bothers me today.

ELEGANT JUNG

AT THE TOP OF EXECUTIVE power in Dachau was a relatively quiet young man with the last name of Jung. His stature was thin and tall, and in the outside world, he would have been considered full of masculine charm. He was always clean and well-dressed, his uniform immaculately fixed, ironed, and without stains. His hands looked elegant in his gloves, which made him appear more like a salon manager than a sector officer. Overall, he was naturally extremely attractive. In addition, it was as though his mouth were hermetically sealed, guarding with passion the secrets of so many souls "stained by lustful intent."

Judging him by his exterior, no one had the slightest idea or suspicion about his activities. He seemed courteous and full of grace, and prisoners held him in high esteem. Compared to other German officers who had high rank and responsibility in the concentration camp's organization, he was someone from another world and deserved respect.

A boss of the execution command, Jung had personal contact not only with male prisoners destined for the afterlife, but also with many women who passed through his hands. Those women faced the same execution as the rest. However, his true persona was profoundly occult, deeply hidden, and the women represented special attractive value for his strong feelings. In the presence of a woman, Jung forgot his charming appearance and stopped being a man who could command respect. Instead, he became a vile thief in unimaginable ways. Women who were destined to die by his hands first had to perform "delicate acts" – sexual acts for Jung. I never witnessed this, but many prisoners saw his actions repeated time and again. It was generally known that Jung abused all the women. It seemed as though he felt it would be a shame to waste a single opportunity for fornication or other forced sexual acts with any woman who crossed his path. After he committed his sadistic acts, and while looking as attractive and charming as ever, he sent each woman to her death.

Most of the men condemned him for what he was, but some defended as reasonable his need for the women. I was in complete awe of what had happened. Many times, I asked myself how a man so apparently elegant, with an unlined face, strong lips, and gloves without a stain, one who appeared to be a gentleman, could also be an abominable monster. It was an aberration, but the facts do not lie.

Some Nationalities At Dachau

IT IS LIKELY THAT WHEN Dachau was first built, no one knew what its achievements would become in front of the entire world. Judging by its original small dimensions, it is hard to believe that anyone had planned for a day when ample room would exist for the sons and daughters of so many nations.

Dachau's first builders and inhabitants were from the newly born Reich. Their sweat and blood kneaded muddy dough over which they slowly built the buildings destined to torment so many lives. Those buildings were responsible for their own moral death, and the immoral death, without compassion or remorse, of all those who followed. The influences of the powerful and merciless swastika reached further and further, but so did the number of its adversaries. Bombers flew overhead, and every time a plane could be heard flying past us, as though we did not exist, prisoners in the camp were tortured and killed.

Concentration camp Dachau was built in March of 1933 and had the potential to hold 8,000 to 10,000 inmates. As far as I know, the first Polish prisoner was marched through its doors in 1940, and the first contingent from the Balkans in 1941. They were quickly followed by the first transport of Russians. The first Italians appeared in Dachau in 1943.

After Anschluss in Austria, the charming and cosmopolitan

Viennese and people from other parts of Austria began occupying the barracks. Receiving the Führer so warmly into their arms had not served them well at all. They had fallen to the ground, taken as prisoners like the rest of us, with distrust in their minds and hearts, and with a growing hatred for the broken cross and its abominable leader, Adolf Hitler. They had no choice but to accept Hitler's politics or, as they did in Schuschnigg Kurt, to speak out and pay the extremely high price of imprisonment at Dachau. There were now Austrians, Czechs, Jews, Poles, Hungarians, Belgians, Hollanders, Lithuanians, Italians, Yugoslavs, Luxembourgers, French, Spanish, Russians, Chinese, and some black people. We tried to make a count, and among the prisoners there appeared to be thirty-two nationalities, although I cannot be certain.

I met only four Spanish men in Dachau. Few prisoners were from Luxemburg. Those men called themselves the sons of Free Luxemburg. They were well-developed physically and were admirably organized, united even though they were few. They enjoyed much influence among the prisoners. They were strong in the kitchen and in the plantations, and were lucky in the prison, able to endure their period of suffering without too much lessening of their physical and moral strength. They kept meat on their bones and were cleanly dressed.

I do not know what the other prisoners thought of the Yugoslavs, but those men had a very moral character, which they demonstrated throughout their time in Dachau. They had a strong spirit of solidarity and worked intently to help their compatriots. This was pleasing to see. A few medical men were from their nation, and they did not distinguish between secular or non-secular patients, treating all prisoners, no matter what their religion or profession might be. Dr. Arco, a figure of high standing at the hospital, was faithful to his conscience first and then to his countrymen, despite the dangers that threatened him.

In contrast to other nations, Mussolini's Italy began by sending its women instead of its men. Four Roman beauties had the distinction of being the first to represent their nation. From the moment of their arrival, they grabbed the attention of inmates and the Gestapo alike. These were proud women who found themselves surrounded by their persecutors. One had the impression that the spirit of Roman women in the time of Nero animated their hearts, so magnificent was their carriage and air of self-confidence. We knew nothing about the Gestapo's conduct toward them on their journey from Rome to Dachau, but it seemed obvious that they would always defend their dignity and their Roman nobility, and above all, their Catholic faith, which shone in their eyes. The Gestapo's arrogance and beastly instincts were transparent, and their weakness to satisfy their desires was consistently evident. Though the Roman women knew that the Gestapo could take their lives, a slap in the face for those who dared force a shameful act showed the women to be of unbreakable Christian conscience. This was a courageous act and became a protection for these women, who were generally known among the inmates and the Gestapo as unapproachable.

Among the Italian colony was a boy who had not yet seen fifteen springs, a boy known for his linguistics. He had come to Dachau early and had been allowed to live. The boy had managed to learn different languages, to communicate with others and to be understood well by them.

The German armed forces who had operated on Italian ground and found themselves obligated by the Allies to retreat were not content with the systematic destruction of everything in their path. They transported significant quantities of stolen

MEMORIES OF A DEVIL

objects from ransacked houses, markets, and stores, taking everything from the Rubicon River to Germany. I had often witnessed our captors' insatiable appetite in every possible way. Materially, they were not content with stolen liquor or savory bottles of wine, valuable art, jewels, or other objects. They wanted torn laces, old shoes, worn kitchen utensils, clothing with holes, like a band of poor housewives trying to prepare a family breakfast "feast." They threw themselves over other people's goods and their misery as if they were dying of hunger and thirst.

I remember, at this time, the Lager Führer Redwitz – a barrack boss who was somewhat kind and who watched over us – holding some of these useless objects in his hands and saying, "What the hell is this for?"

On another occasion, this same boss's eyes lit upon various enticing liquor bottles, and he exclaimed with profound sincerity, "Oh, Heiliger Fascismus!" He crossed his arms over his chest in an expression of gratitude to Mussolini for these gifts to the tastebuds. None of us held it against him that he took some of the bottles for his personal use. Redwitz was condemned in the second Nuremberg trial – condemned and executed. He had been born a man of heart, and the party had not achieved a complete transformation with him; he had not become an absolute monster.

This had been his style in dealing with some of us: "My son, do not compromise me. Do you not realize that with your conduct, you obligate me, against my will, to yell at you…excuse my brutalities. If I turn into a brute, it is you who have turned me into a brute. You do not understand that being a brute torments me."

May God take into account the paternal gestures he manifested toward the prisoners during diverse periods in Dachau.

May God keep him in His merciful hands.

THE GERMANS

Among Hitler's subjects, the first imprisoned group was made up of Germans whom the Gestapo had taken from their homes and brought to the area to work. Some of these men formed the first crews to construct Concentration Camp Dachau. They told sad stories about the building of the camp, when fellow workers had sunk into the mud and remained there forever. The terrain was deep mud, and the men who sank could not be rescued. Screams for help did nothing, and the other men, who had now become prisoners, were beaten and forced to work, with no time to think or in any way help save their mates. The only thing they could think of was that they would be beaten to death if they did not continue working.

When night fell, darkness engulfed the men trapped in the mud, who could be seen only by the whiteness of their teeth and their fixed and brilliant eyes, begging for help that never arrived. Those men caught in the mud remained there until they died. Conditions worsened each day as the living men were forced to stand on the dead bodies of their fellow inmates so that they would not sink. Like people who try to cross a stream by jumping from rock to rock, men jumped from cadaver to cadaver to move from one side of the mud field to the other. To comprehend this scene, one must consider the fact that Hitlerian ideals were carried out by fanatics – cruel German fanatics.

Many prisoners told stories such as this, and an elder German soldier, a man of some integrity and kindness, rare in those times, confirmed that they were true. He had a good education, and perhaps because he loved his country, he did not elaborate on the subjects related to that horrible time. However, he had witnessed it all and said it was pure truth, that we now lived on top of a cemetery. We could see that his words gave him a great deal of pain. Perhaps because he did not want to dishonor his country any further, he became silent. No one dared continue talking about this most inhumane event.

The largest group of German prisoners were members of the Communist Party. Because of their ideas, which were contrary to those of the Führer, they found themselves in the camp, slaves separated from the free world. In the outside world, these men threatened Hitler's nationalism, but inside the prison, they posed no real threat. They received organizational positions in the prison population, some of them as prison cops, recruited first from the lower social classes. These prisoners had violent instincts; they were brutal people with little moral conscience. They had a lot of power and became the horror of those who depended upon them for work orders. Any type of boss such as this could kill at will, and they always found a reason to do so; they were forced to commit crimes and atrocities without number. There was no legal authority over any boss, and these prisoners in privileged positions knew how to show their own loyalty, drowning their souls in the blood of their mates. The proved their loyalty to the German authorities over and over again, and it is no exaggeration to say that they led 100% better lives in Dachau than they had in their homes, receiving rewards for every abuse. They washed their hands of all their acts like Pontius Pilate symbolically washing his hands of responsibility for Jesus Christ.

The cops were the true owners of our lives until the arrival of Principal Chief Weiss, who changed the situation and the prisoners' living conditions. His motive for seeking to prohibit all sorts of punishments by the cops was not known, and often, he could not stop them. However, he helped us, though his stay at Dachau was short. He was soon transferred to another concentration camp away from the arbitrary, violent acts of the cop bosses.

THE MARTYRS OF POLAND

THERE IS NO DOUBT THAT the largest number of prisoners in the camp were sons of the Polish flag. The hunt for them began as soon as the troops of the Black Eagle stepped onto Polish terrain, where citizens were arrested for threatening national liberty. On September 23, 1939, when I was arrested in Poznan and taken to the prison on Mlynska Road, the cells of that prison were already full of Polish citizens.

Polish martyrdom began in our own land, inside the jails and prisons, and continued during our exile in concentration camps in Germany and Poland. The Germans knew that there was no better way to ensure German triumph than to imprison non-Germans, as well as many of their countrymen of whom they did not approve, and put them to work in the prisons and extermination camps, whose gates were never likely to rust because they opened with such frequency. Poles from every area made their entrance, miles and miles of them, the best sons and daughters of Catholic Poland. Boys and girls were ripped from their mothers' arms, and husbands from their wives. Mothers, defeated by pain and cruelty but fortified by the prayers of the living faith, cried in their homes, losing the people they loved. All the flowers of the feminine and masculine youth of Poland were forced to say goodbye to their families and their land and begin walking the long road to places of torture. There, they would leave their bones, converted into piles of ashes. This was the ill fortune of the nation, some of them preferring to fight until the last soldier had died, until the last drop of blood had been spilled over their loyalty altar before giving up voluntarily to the invaders' brutality.

The "Hymn to the German God" firmly and clearly expressed the feelings of our German enemies. The fact that the Protecting Association of the Superior Silesia published it does not require special comment.

The "Hymn to the German God," edited in 1939 by the Vereinigung zum Schutze Oberschlesiens (the Protecting Association of the Superior Silesia), goes like this:

The Lord paralyze the legs and hands of the Polish.

Make them crippled, send blindness to their eyes.

Punish the men and women with deafness and insanity.

May the Polish people be converted into ashes.

That the children and women be sold like slaves,

And that our hard feet, their gardens trample.

Give us the pleasure, Almighty, to kill the adults and children.

Allow us to sink our swords in their defenseless bodies.

Make the Polish country sink in a sea of blood and fire,

That the heart of the Germans does not soften,

That instead of peace, war will decide the luck of the two states,

That even when I'm preparing to go to fight to the death,

Even dying I shout, "Lord, change Poland into a desert."

Polish prisoners were in Dachau in large numbers. Each wore a red triangle with the letter "P" on his or her chest so that everyone would know their odious origin. Concentration camp Dachau had international cadavers, but the largest number of inhabitants by far were Polish. The loathed Pole came from all social classes, and we were reunited behind the camp fence to purge our unforgivable crime – which was, of course, being Polish. At one time in the United States of America, the black man was the most hated because he was black. The Germans hated the Polish. And, of course, not all Poles were heroes and sincere patriots. Some achieved "important" positions in Dachau and were loyal to their enemies rather than to their countrymen and brothers.

More often, we found among the Polish a firm union and solidarity, with the goal of helping one another, such as was evident among the Slavs and prisoners from Luxemburg. The vast majority of Polish prisoners were Catholic and, because of that, not trusted by the bosses. It is impossible to present the moral and religious spirit the Polish maintained, but once the war was over, many of them made public boasts of how their faith had saved them, through graces received from the Sacred Heart of the Blessed Mother and especially from St. Joseph. This seemed to indicate that their religion, although silenced, had not died in the hearts of those saddened and suffering people.

Among the Polish were prisoners difficult to classify, those in prison for "political crimes." Many others were kids between fourteen and sixteen years old, taken by force to Germany for the price of fifty marks paid to their families. They were employed for agricultural tasks, filling in, for the German husbands sent to the front, in the cultivation of the land and care of the cattle, and for sexual matters, fulfillment of marital rights. Many of these boys were ignorant about sex, and did not cooperate. They were embarrassed and fearful and refused to copulate with the German women. In doing so, they denounced German authority and were brought as prisoners to Dachau. I tell this because I saw these boys and listened to their stories, which they told me personally.

Another, more mature Polish man had been employed in the construction of German subways. He was completely blind, but for him, this was an advantage in two ways. The entire time he had been working on the subway tunnel, he had been underground, inside a mountain in total darkness, and this posed no difficulty for him. Once the job was finished, he was the only man left alive. Because he was blind, he had not witnessed the execution of all the other workers after construction was complete; he was allowed to live. Workers such as this man were brought to the prison during the night.

As a nurse, I attended those Poles arriving at Dachau who, due to the rigors of winter and their miserable footwear, came with feet covered in blood and sores. Some men had lost their toes and had never received medical treatment. After working for the benefit of the Reich and having their bodies converted into a mass of sores, they received the treatment of dangerous criminals and became prisoners of the concentration camp.

The Germans hated the Poles, but they used them whenever they could. To be hated or loved? We, the Polish, had many reasons to be proud of being the most hated culture, hated by those who considered themselves far superior. I do not think they were superior by nature, only by propaganda, born of the insanity of some of their philosophers. It seemed that to hate us so much, they must have truly feared us. We were defeated by numbers and brute force, by treason from our neighbors to the east and indolence from those to the west. However, our personal and national spirit remained intact. Despite our inhumane sufferings, we held our Polish dignity high. The sons of Poland could be beaten and mistreated, our bodies destroyed, but we could never be fully killed. The Polish were not weakened. We became more vigorous and more Polish during our persecution. We were lovers of our country and our freedom, and no man could take away the nobility and greatness of the Polish spirit.

The Sacred Scriptures say that the world is filled with the dumb and stupid, and this is so. The world would not dare tell the truth, the historical truth, which was that German brutality caused all of Europe's misfortunes during the war and that it should have been punished without compassion. The world should have been finished forever with the perverse nation that killed countless numbers of people.

Instead, the dumb world turned its head and said, "Look at what they do." It did not raise a single finger to protest German actions; it did nothing concrete to face the nation that had spilled so much innocent blood. When Poles made a mistake or committed a small injustice, especially toward the Germans, the whole ignorant world screamed in protest, calling for the vengeance of the sky and the fury of God. If only the entire world traveled the same road of justice, honesty, and truth.

Perhaps Poland would have been treated with more respect in the world if it were not Catholic and if it believed in atheism like so many other nations. Evil hates anything good, and the weak are pulled by those who are more powerful, even if their origins are evil. This is the fate and nature of a vile world without Christ's principles. Throughout history, we can see so many against Christ. In the war, some neighboring countries aligned themselves with Germany, despite its terrible nature and brutality.

THE REDS

WHILE HITLER'S TANKS ADVANCED TOWARD Moscow, Russian soldiers fell into their hands like fish in the nets of fraudulent fishermen. They did not attract much attention from the other camp prisoners, appearing to have been educated in communist ideology and to share the same communistic heart. They presented themselves as big men, well-developed, without any signs of physical weakening, as though their system had provided good nutrition before and during the war.

They entered Dachau on a boastful wind, ignoring the reality of what awaited them. Maybe their trust in Russia's military strength was so strong that they had no fearful thoughts, no panic about their future. They talked openly about their communist ideas, and they had sympathizers among the prisoners of other nationalities and even among the soldiers.

Once the initial wave of enthusiasm had passed, dark clouds entered, one after another. Hunger and the inability to find sufficient food were the first to arrive. I heard that the Russian prisoners were driven to fight over a piece of potato. One instance, in particular, was a furious fight among themselves, which happened in front of the kitchen, over a completely rotten potato. There were communists among German prisoners and soldiers, but the Russians were careful to stay together on the margin of concentration camp life.

The Russians ignored my profession. When in a group, they expressed love and enthusiasm for communism in a greater way than I was ever able to speak about the love of Christ. However, only a few minutes later, when one of the same Russian men was separated from his group, everything changed; his statements were charged with hatred for communism. I thought this must be due to his suffering and disillusionment while in prison, and the misery in which he was forced to live – the only possible reasons for such a striking contradiction. Then it became clear that while these communists were in a group, the commandment was, "Thou shall love communism with all your heart." When they spoke individually, it became, "Thou shall hate communism with your entire mind, with all your heart, and all your strength." The explanation that one of the Russians gave to me was entirely accurate: "You should know that no real communist is going to speak badly in the presence of another communist, no matter how intimate they are. If one is arrested and his friend has spoken against communism, it is his duty to denounce his friend, and it is possible that the government has already overheard their conversation. If neither friend has anything to declare, they are both much safer. Do you understand?" I did understand, then, their way of speaking in a group to protect themselves, no matter what they believed. Speaking as individuals, they could be more truthful. Denial of oneself and one's own morality exposed communism's frightening strength.

Once, I asked a group of them about the reason for the recent war between Poland and the Bolsheviks, which took place in 1919 and 1920. The answer was a complete lie but deserves to be told here. The Russians said they were obligated to attack Poland for the cruelties the Polish had committed against the Russian people. They knew that Poles had hanged Russians from every tree along the road from Kiev to Warsaw. When I asked where and how the Poles had captured all those Russians, they said the answer was quite simple. The Russians who occupied Polish territory had been captured and killed. I objected that this was a pure communist lie; if it had been true, the entire world would have known, and Poland would have been punished. They responded that they knew it as the truth and had learned this history in their schools. They said my Polish teachers had taught lies, and the world had not punished Poland because Poland was capitalist like the rest of the world. The Russians had learned these lies about Poland, lies ingrained so deeply in their thinking that there was no way to convince them otherwise.

Among the Russian prisoners, big, boasting words were heard with much frequency – words that did not harmonize with their intelligence or education. These words did not offend me because they were not said in an evil way, but in a way to affirm manliness. They were like the Americans, who did not feel that prideful boasts were shameful. The difference seemed to be that Russians said these boastful things when they were agitated and bad-tempered, and the Americans said them when they were satisfied and felt that they had done something grand.

The Russians, as their days, months, and years accumulated in the concentration camp, never again achieved the sympathy or enthusiasm with which communism was first accepted. They began seeing their own convictions defrauded, and they learned from many prisoners of different cultures about the falseness of their government and its system. When this occurred, they did not hesitate to publicly acknowledge their own loss of belief in the communist ideology. They became quite fearful during any atheistic speech or act and developed a true religious belief that seemed deep in their hearts. They began praying every day, and they asked me to teach them prayers in Polish. With burning fervor, they discussed religious subjects, such as the existence of the spirituality of the soul and the afterlife.

When the camp allowed us to receive packages, the Russians saw that many were arriving for the Polish prisoners. Though Poland was a country dying of hunger and misery and being destroyed by the Germans, there was an abundance of goods, enough to send to their own people in concentration camps. These products were not sold for capitalist purposes but were being sent freely out of kindness and love. The packages were a small event, but large enough to demonstrate another communist lie about the capitalist nature of Polish culture. This proved that everything was not sold for capitalist gain. Communism was nothing more than a group of advantage-takers living like emperors, relying on the backs of their poor and ignorant people.

My description of the Russian prisoners at Dachau must now include the terrible deterioration of the inmates. Except for Polish priests, no other group was so severely punished in the concentration camp. They lacked large-enough barracks and did not receive any of the packages with nourishing contents that arrived continuously from the east. Their barrack was originally built to house four hundred prisoners but, instead, four thousand Russian people were crammed into Block No.7. It stopped being a single cell block and became a huge hive in which the poor Russians piled up like old rags.

Once I received an order to go to that barrack and attend

some of the men who were ill. When I approached, I saw a pile of skeletons. I asked, "Where can I find the sick men?"

There was a clamor of noise and a string of insults came from their lips. They shouted at me, "Everyone is either sick or dead."

Amid the yelling and the whistles, I tried to move among them. It was very difficult, and before I could go far, a door hit me in the face. Of course, I forgot my mission and returned to the authorities who had sent me. I said to them, "There are no more living people in the Russian block, only ambulant skeletons, and the floor is covered with cadavers. You cannot walk a step forward or backward without stepping on the dead or hearing the moans of the dying."

The German officer said, "I know it well, but what are we going to do? Too many people for such a narrow place." That was his sole impotent reaction, and nothing changed.

A strange thing happened at the end of the war when the bear devoured the guts of the black eagle of Nazism. The Russian sons who had pulverized the doors of the German capital with their canons should have been insane with happiness and enthusiasm at the defeat of the enemy. Instead, just as with the Russian prisoners, a great unknown seemed to present itself before their eyes. I remember well being filled with happiness and joy for having survived all the days of such a terrible calamity. My excitement was almost childish when I saw my group of Russians. I congratulated them on their victory and expressed my wishes for a prompt and happy return to their country. Then I stopped, almost frozen, because their faces were unhappy and their anxiety was palpable. I said to them, "How can you not be joyful in your victory? Your military has entered Berlin, and already Germany is on its knees, begging for mercy like the worst sinner in Europe, which it is."

Instead of being enthusiastic, they answered with an extremely sad and uncertain question: "But where are we going to go? Where can we go?"

"I prefer to die than to return to my country," broke out one of them. None of the others opposed him. In their silence, filled with bitterness, they all seemed to agree with their comrade.

Another one extended his arm and said something I would never have expected: "This is my firm and irrevocable decision. I prefer to open my veins rather than return to Russia." No further argument against communism was needed. There was a non-existent promise of paradise, and this Russian son had said it more eloquently than anyone else. What does our stupid world need with all those idiots who want to introduce communism into their countries? People love communism because they do not have any concrete idea about its reality. Communist propaganda does a good job until a person tries to live under its rules as a simple Russian citizen.

One of my friends, an excellent man who had responded to my religious instruction, cried like a child and asked me for advice about his future, which was totally unknown. He asked me, "Where am I going to go? I cannot return to Russia. I do not want to. You do not know what communism is, but I know it well."

I told him of the possibility of going to France, along with a Russian-Jewish doctor whom I knew. In the end, that is what both of them did. May God keep them in His hands and guide them toward happiness.

THE FRENCH

ONE DAY IN JULY OF 1943, at the hour of 12:30 p.m., the French arrived *en masse* at the vineyard of the Germans, Dachau. If no mistake is made in the gospel, certainly the French made a serious one. They came into the camp as the sick would go to a medic, looking for a place that would make them feel better. Entering the terrain behind the walls separating liberty and slavery, personal dignity and bestiality, they found nothing in common with the proper customs they had known in previous years. The high chiefs of the camp accompanied them, and instead of seeing them as henchmen armed with weapons and dogs, the French went to their barracks with an air of dignity and superiority.

The formalities were completed on the plaza, under the blue sky and within everyone's sight. On one side sat the writers, taking information vigorously but observing etiquette and delicacy while waiting for answers. On the other side, sitting comfortably by rank and in a dignified group, were the French. Among them were priests and an older general, already over eighty years of age, worthy of compassion because of his physical state. Of course, he was still a dangerous man to the Teutonic Empire. His white head looked like a dove, and he had a pale complexion covered with thick wrinkles. I was his interpreter. He told me he had committed absolutely no crime other than being ranked high in the military. Nevertheless, the Germans did not leave him in peace as he deserved.

This French general confessed to me that his greatest suffering was due to his age, primarily that he could no longer take advantage of the delicacies of intimacy with women. I asked him to reflect a bit and told him that considering his age and circumstances, he might want to think of something more serious, such as his death and the account he must give to God. However, he was not confused about priorities like someone as dumb as a priest. Saturated in sexual thoughts, he could not see an afterlife, only a living world of delight, one in which God could not find a door where he might enter. He reproached me deeply as being ignorant of the delights of the flesh, saying I was not qualified to advise him because of my lack of information about this vital subject. I left him alone with his burning aspirations of unsatisfied flesh, his hands shaking like autumn leaves.

The French were thin rather than fat, with a lively character, and they passed the days in Dachau without knowing the true reality of the concentration camp. They were not given the experimental joys of what desperate hunger felt like and did not feel the ferocious discipline of the brutal German system directed against them. Compared to us, their presence in Dachau was like an out-of-season stay on the Riviera.

We couldn't help but notice their aversion to water. Everyone else fought madly against the plague of lice, imposing strict hygiene as much as possible under the circumstances. The French, however, ran from the frigid water more than from the lice. Instead of washing their entire bodies, they were content with putting a finger in the water and passing it superficially over their eyes. Looking at the French in the concentration camp, we did not know if this group was an exception, having nothing in common with the true Frenchman. Understanding the French culture a bit and the influence of that great nation on the formation of many nations, I prefer to think this group was unusual. I cannot imagine that the French nation prefers to be dirty or that its countrymen would put such a stain on the glorious history of France. This group in Dachau should not have been brought to the camp at midday. They should have been brought at 5:00 a.m. so they would learn to work, suffer, and take better care of themselves and their country.

THE PRIESTS

It is generally believed that the number of incarcerated priests in Dachau was approximately 2,700, composed of twenty European nations, including the Germans, Polish, Czechs, Dutch, Belgians, Lithuanians, Slovenians, Hungarians, and, at the end of the war, the French. The priests did not form the largest group; from the beginning, we were mixed in with the rest of the inmates and disappeared in the masses. However, the authorities quickly realized the spiritual current that flowed through the lives of this group. For this, the bad root was cut out, separating the spiritual element from most of the prisoners. Polish priests went to block 28, and the rest of the priests to block 26. We never knew the reason for this separation, but we came to understand that all the Polish priests were destined for extermination. According to the bosses' plans, the camp would attempt to liberate itself from the most dangerous element, the Polish clergy, after which everything would be much easier.

The priests in block 26 had better treatment, somewhat easier jobs, and slightly better food. Every day, Mass was held in one of their rooms. They took turns saying Mass and could approach a table for Communion without punishment. German authorities, as well as many of the German priests, were collaborators in this way, openly opposing Polish priests, preventing them from participating in any religious observance simply because they were Polish.

Among the Polish priests, a famous German saying referring to Communion was well known: "*Fur die Polen fibs es nicht.*" ("It is not for the Poles.") What a great ministry. Was it their way of showing their infinite love for Jesus by protecting Him from the vulgar Polish pigs and dogs who were being denied Communion? Or was it the inexplicable hatred for those same Polish individuals? The first I cannot accept, and the second I do not want to touch because I do not want to say that the hearts of some of the priests from Germany were so rotten and filled with hate that they had no room for understanding, a bit of respect, or human love. For my part, every time I wanted to receive Communion, I did so from the hands of the Jesuits or the Dutch, often through a window. They never said I was a dog or pig or that I could not partake of the precious Host.

This abominable behavior was applied not only to Polish priests but to other Poles as well. I remember that one of my former professors of religion, an inmate at the prison, told me a story just before he died. It was a story that shed a bad light on German priests filled with Hitlerian spirit.

This professor was in the last hours of his life. He made his confession and wished to receive Communion before embarking on his journey to the next life. None of the Polish priests had the materials to give him Communion, so he reached out to a German priest, explaining his need to the other man. The German priest was insulted, offended that a Polish priest would ask such a thing of him. The request was denied. My professor asked another German, who had more influence among his colleagues, to help him take Communion. He was punched, kicked, and thrown out of the room for making this suggestion. May God judge us all in this matter. Also, I do not intend to commit an act of injustice by saying that all Germans were the same, without any redeeming aspects. Many Germans were excellent priests.

A good example was a German priest who was the founder of a religious order. I would later meet him again in Uruguay. He was a good German and an excellent priest, and I don't say this simply because he helped me during the harsh times at Dachau. In Dachau, he procured bread for me every time he had any left over, not as an exception but in a charitable way, as often as possible. He chose to help me, the son of his enemies, and demonstrated his truthful human and Catholic feelings.

Many years later, the same priest was paying a visit to his spiritual daughters in Montevideo. I listened to a speech he delivered to a small crowd about his life in Dachau. He made a tremendous mistake. He talked ultimately about himself, how comfortable his life had been in prison (and we have to wonder how that could have been), not considering any of the tremendous sufferings of others. He remained fat before, during, and after his incarceration as an inmate, and he spoke of Dachau as a good life, one of physical comfort. He said he could have lived there for another thirty years.

The great question of why this priest did not speak about the thousands who died of hunger or the other sufferings and deaths in the camp is unanswerable. He presented a false reality about Dachau while thousands of other prisoners raised their voices against all the injustices there. By speaking in this way, he defended the cruelty of the German regime and the quality of his life, which was somehow favored while he was in Dachau. I hope that I am a good priest and a good Pole, but I cannot remain in accordance with him, nor do I begin to understand him.

In the mornings, at the time when everyone awoke, those in charge took pleasure in screaming at us and using any excuse to fall upon us like birds of prey, covering us with hits, wounds, blood, and bruises. These madmen insisted that everything be in perfect order while they created complete chaos. The most sacred part of the barrack was the floor; without exaggeration, it shined like a mirror. Everyone had to clean the floor, washing and scrubbing and using cans full of wax. Inmates spent hour after hour on their knees, trying to remove the most minimal stain.

Along with the floor, the priests spent hours on Sundays and many other days cleaning closets, according to the disposition of the chief. Out in nature, some of the smallest clouds caused the biggest storms, and some of the smallest spots caused heavy beatings of the priests from block 28. The rationing of food and the sad prohibition of daily meals were also used as tools to cause the starving men more pain and discomfort.

In the streets of the camp, moving from one end to the other was permitted, but we were strictly prohibited from sitting on the rocks that lined the streets. Sitting was a daring act brought on by exhaustion, and the inmates were tormented if they were caught doing so. If anyone could have observed the tactics of the Germans with the Polish priests, they would have seen that we were never allowed to rest and that the most dangerous jobs, those that made our execution easier, were given to us.

From the beginning in Dachau, the jobs in the planting terrain were given to Polish priests and other priests. These jobs were terrible. This terrain was designated for growing plants and for the brutal treatment of prisoners. In freezing rain or during the most furious storms, with no coat or covering, we were forced to continue working. For entire days, the few calories within our bodies disappeared through our soaked clothing, which hung over our bones. Under such conditions, it was natural that a few unfortunate prisoners would die during the work day or would be so frozen as to fall, unable to walk farther. The remaining priests used their last strength to drag cadavers from the planting area, toward the center of the camp, while trying not to succumb to death themselves.

A Polish proverb says, "When someone wants to hit a dog, he will find a stick." When the Germans wished to entertain themselves at the cost of the Polish priests, they always found a reason to justify their ways. Not long before the end of the war, their brothel was functioning well and with great success. Suddenly, the priests were accused of proving their virility with those ladies who were conquering the hearts of our chiefs. The order was given that on midday on a Sunday, all the priests, except the Poles, would be taken into the plaza, where their genitalia would be publicly whipped. We shameless Polish priests would await our turn and would receive a special amount of punishment. Before the whippings began, an announcement was made over the loudspeaker that no enemy planes were near the Reich territory. Therefore, the priests and German soldiers lined up in the plaza. The chiefs were excited to begin. However, as they prepared for their task, Allied planes appeared, coming directly at the plaza. Everyone ran, scattering and trying to find cover. None of the punishments could take place.

There was never any evidence that indicated the priests had looked for loving consolation in the arms of prostitutes. They denied all the allegations and, when tested for hygiene, did not show any positive results for diseases. Although we were called to serve our God through celibacy, it might have been understandable in Dachau to find a priest in the arms of a young, warm-blooded girl who could provide some comfort. However, there was no indication that such acts had occurred. We priests felt that the Germans envied our celibate lives and would have done anything to degrade us, knowing quite well that we had committed no real or actual sins. Instead, by punishing us to exhaustion, they succeeded in completely removing any physical or psychological temptation the priests may have had.

As I mentioned earlier, when the Polish clergy were put in Barrack 28, they were separated from the rest of the clergy, who were put in Barrack 26. St. Peter's advice was well-followed: Support one another. Among the Polish priests were men who were superior spiritual examples, and great friendships seldom seen in such an atmosphere were formed. There were other religious men, for example, Bishop Kozal, whom some of the priests hated from the beginning. He performed special tasks for the German chiefs, following their orders, but it was also clear to me that he felt the spirit of Christ very deeply. Similarly, a bishop of the National Polish Church, Father Kowalski, worked on behalf of the Germans but also had an unyielding faith. The two men were distanced from each other by their jobs in the prison, but they were united in mutual comprehension by their faith. Both left their bones in Dachau.

I cannot say that we Polish priests were angels without faults or conflicts among us. We were men exposed to many tribulations, and even in our religious formation, we had faults like any humans. More than a few times, harsh words filled our daily language, and our troubles strained the ties of any type of fraternal unity. Each man was firmly attached to his life, and to save it, he was often capable of acts unworthy of praise.

Such a man, called Franciszek, held the post of secretary. He was an ally to his enemies and the enemies of his incarcerated friends. To save his life and position, he left his own people in many bad situations. At the end of the war, he paid very heavily for these acts. When the Allies arrived at the concentration camp, I saw him walking the halls of the hospital, having lost his mind completely. He had saved his own life during the reign of the Germans, but by the time of liberation, he was lost to himself, with no remaining mental ability or awareness. Some of his comrades attributed this to his guilty conscience, but who, besides God, can know for sure?

We improvised prayers, and one of the few good things the priests could share was their sense of humor. No one was better than the priests at remembering good times and trying to find comic situations, and none among the priests were better at this than the Jesuits and Capuchins. We did not hold back from telling jokes, and there was always some type of competition that involved joking with one another and making the others laugh. I shared my storage space with an older priest who was young in spirit. He was of Lithuanian origin and did not speak much; when he did, we would laugh very hard. He was a font of jokes and comical stories. This small man was crushed by his sufferings but he felt triumphant and happy when his tales incited laughter and applause among his friends.

During our imprisonment in Dachau, the priests went through every phase of abuse, and no one raised a voice in our defense. The underground radio was filled with horrible news that traveled across the German borders and around the world. For example, the events in Warsaw were well-known, and war news with brutal details was broadcast every day. The German clergy did nothing within their own country to help the other prisoners or us. The bishops of the Third Reich completely ignored our situation. I know perfectly well that Father Coning searched among the bishops, beginning with the apostolic ones, making our situation clear and insisting that the German government intervene on our behalf. They not only ignored this plea, but some made fun of him for his efforts. Cardinal Faulhaber tried to convince Father Koning that this was a grave error, that the alarming news about Dachau was entirely false, and that the priests interned there were treated like children, enjoying themselves in the gardens. The reluctance to enter such a terrible mess was somewhat understandable, but why the cardinal would say such a thing is impossible to explain.

THE WINE

THE PRIESTS WHO HAD BEEN in Dachau before my arrival talked about another humiliation that had been forced upon them, a form of punishment that some of them actually appreciated. Once a day, around 10 a.m., all the priests, armed with aluminum cups, were to gather in a hall. They were made to stand in straight lines, and their cups were filled with something that must have seemed like celestial ambrosia, wine that even the gods of Olympus might envy.

The German officer of the hall would yell, "*Achtung*!," and everyone would come to attention. The cups were quite large and filled to the brim, and at the officer's command, they were to be emptied in three gulps. If any prisoner could not perform this feat, the cup was filled again, and it was to be emptied in one gulp. Most of the priests choked on the wine and spat it back out all over themselves, the soldiers, and anyone else nearby. This is what the soldiers were waiting for. If anyone spat out or choked on the wine, he was insulted, punched, kicked, and beaten with sticks, the soldiers laughing derisively and enjoying this routine every day. To some of the priests, this was not a punishment, only a happy delirium. Some of them had a lot of experience drinking, not only wine, but Polish vodka and other liquor, and they had no problem draining their cups in one gulp. And because the soldiers kept filling their cups, hoping the priests would spit and choke, they kept drinking steadily until the bottles were empty.

Through well-organized propaganda, the outside world was convinced that the Germans were acting as true gentlemen in their treatment of the abominable Polish priests, giving them a cup of wine at no cost, similar to what St. Paul had given his disciples. Among the people who believed these lies was Cardinal Faulhaber. Responding to communications from P. Konig, he had the audacity to affirm, "It is evident to me that the priests do nothing at Dachau except garden and drink wine." To the Germans, serving wine to the priests – followed by punches and beatings – was not malicious behavior, but an elegant way of entertaining the priests, as well as themselves. I did not have the pleasure of participating in the drunkenness of wine, or in this form of elegant German entertainment.

Neutral Zone

In the outside world, to prevent a fight between two enemies, an area of neutrality is sometimes created. In the early days inside Dachau, when there was no reason to have such an area inside the concentration camp, the Germans, with their superior knowledge, marked off terrain between the prison camp street and a ditch (which was later converted into a cultivated area). This was intended to impede any attempted escape. No prisoner could step into the neutral area, and guards were placed in the watchtowers with the mandate to shoot any prisoner who dared. Touching this terrain was the same thing as trying to escape, and the internal rule book of the camp said it was an act worthy of immediate death. In fact, some prisoners chose to end their lives by stepping into the neutral terrain, where they were shot to death. To the Germans, such a barbaric act was nothing other than a simple display of military discipline. Some soldiers saved prisoners' lives by shooting into the air as a warning, but we all know that a good soldier never proves his machine gun accuracy by shooting empty air.

From time to time, the soldiers and officers allowed themselves a form of entertainment that gave them pleasure, one that could have rivaled any that Nero invented. It was entertainment that came at the cost of great suffering. This "game" took the lives of innocent people, men who happened to be living in a grossly abnormal situation, one that permitted unconscionable behavior.

The entertainment went like this. A soldier took an inmate's hat and put it inside the neutral terrain. The inmate was to go into the neutral terrain to retrieve his hat, at which time he would be shot. If the inmate refused to go inside the terrain, he would be severely beaten. In many cases, the prisoner had no idea about the "game" being played, refused to step inside the neutral terrain, and was then beaten almost to death. Thankfully, this was not our daily bread, but it did sometimes occur and was responsible for the fast disposal of innocent people. Imagine these Germans, who aspired to be the rulers of the world, and the inhumanity they would have created. However, thanks to God, who knows how to defeat poverty within nations, Christian virtues can flower over barren lands and manifest their own superiority.

A Bit Of "Revier"

When I first arrived in Dachau, I saw three barracks that had no numbers but were labeled with the name "Revier." Inside those barracks were ill prisoners, the operation room, the pharmacy, and the area where the dead were kept until the gold could be removed from their mouths. This place inspired horror. We knew it was a place where killing was done by lethal injection, thereby alleviating Dachau's budget and general economy. The inhabitants changed daily, without speech or movement, on their way to another world. By order of the authorities, the gold hunters searched each cadaver, pulling any form of that metal from their mouths. The Germans considered it an economic loss for any gold to enter the crematorium.

In 1942, a delicate layer of snow covered the camp, and I was walking next to the hospital on one side, where the morgue was located. Between 2:30 and 3:00 p.m. arrived a large vehicle, destined to move the cadavers to the crematorium. The fence doors were opened, and nurses were walking about, dragging things over the snow. They laughed and talked and seemed to be enjoying themselves tremendously, pushing one another so that some of them fell against the bundles, increasing their laughter even more. They were dragging things onto the truck and then going back into the building. I realized they were loading the cadavers and throwing them into piles in the truck. They threw the cadavers by their extremities, making them jerk and dance in the air, the dead landing in the truck amid all the nurses' laughter and light-heartedness.

It was said that the hospital in Dachau was one of the best of its kind, with an X-ray machine, surgeons performing operations, a storage of rich and abundant pharmaceuticals, and medics and nurses in white hats and coats. Everything was clean and shiny, and anyone inspecting Dachau would have been impressed with the facilities. Unfortunately, everything that is clean and shiny is not golden. A large part of the medical care was entrusted to the inmate nurses, who had worked at various professions before the war and who most often had no clue about the care of a human being. Every day, a line of prisoners stood in front of the revier, patiently awaiting their turn to be seen by one of the nurses, who had the power of life and death.

One nurse had been a baker, and one had been a meat market butcher who learned very well how to kill living men. He carried this out marvelously in Dachau. The German bosses chose him, and he decided whether a fellow inmate was useful. As did many Germans, he felt that little difference existed between men and mules. It was understandable that a butcher was considered a good killing professional.

What experiments could a butcher conduct on a human body? Being a simple butcher, he knew only how to cut up an animal. Accustomed to cutting the meat of pigs and cattle, he could do the same with human beings, his bosses thought. He did things with a brutality that no medical person would dare employ, presiding over the operating table, opening the skull, taking out and cutting the brain into pieces, and then putting it back in place, as though a man's life could be returned to him.

The inmates told a story about the wife of one of the chiefs of Dachau; she took a sentimental liking to a young prisoner. She asked to have his skull for the top of her desk, in this way seeing him whenever she wished. The butcher chose to please the chief's wife rather than respect the life of an inmate, and the young man was sacrificed to satisfy her feelings.

Among the inmate doctors, two eminent men actually healed people with excellent skill, even in the circumstances of Dachau. They were Doctors Czarnkowski and Arko. The first came from Warsaw, and he accomplished some operations that seemed beyond human hope. One of his famous cases involved a young Greek man who came to Dachau with a leg broken in eleven places. He would have been executed, or certainly had his leg amputated, except for the efforts of Dr. Czarnkowski, whose surgery left the poor man hanging over the bed like a log. Months passed until the man could stand again, but in the end he regained the use of his leg, whole and healthy.

Dr. Arko, from Lublana, was wonderful to me personally when the medics recommended the amputation of all my toes due to serious infection. The procedure was very advanced, but thanks to Dr. Arko's wise and prudent intervention and surgery, my feet were not mutilated and I am able to walk today.

Dr. Jan Piatkowski came from Paris and quickly became known for his inventions on behalf of the ill inmates. Optics was under the direction of Dr. Antonowski, and dentistry was elevated by the presence of the most beloved young man of all, Edek Hampel. There was a doctor from Lwow, Tadeusz Sznider, whose reputation went beyond the camp; physicians from Munich sent him their X-rays and presented case studies for his opinion. Under life's ordinary conditions, these supermen would have been destined for great humanitarian acts, but their aspirations were imprisoned in Dachau.

The Experiments

THE CONCENTRATION CAMP AT DACHAU was famous for its experiments on the inmate population, who were their guinea pigs. Dr. Klaus Karl Schilling had the appearance of a better man than those brutal other butchers, and his work had a scientific appearance toward the goals he pretended to accomplish. He appeared to have noble aspirations, performing experiments for the betterment of the entire nation of Germany. If people around him believed his intentions, they were blind, because he was an evil man.

The first experiment Dr. Schilling conducted was with malaria. He had the mosquitoes, whose value rose above that of any man in the prison. Imagine an inmate obligated to feed the *muckenfuttern* mosquitoes with his own blood. The poor man, seeing the bug stuck to his body, knew it was sucking out the last of his blood reserves, knew that it bore and was depositing its disease and that in a short time he would be in torment without hope of being healed. Some prisoners volunteered themselves, for the betterment of other humans and because they had no hope whatsoever for a future life. What was one fewer life within the prison? The doctor was angered by the attitude of the priests, who did not volunteer to sacrifice their lives on behalf of his noble experiment, his great vision, the progress of science and humanity.

About 2,000 prisoners became part of the malaria experiments. That group included Jews and Polish priests. At first, it seemed as though nothing was wrong. The first germ was injected into the quadriceps muscle, then a second injection followed. If the sick person survived, a third injection was given in the arm at gunpoint. After twenty-four hours, the injection site became a dark mark and the disease spread quickly throughout the body. The inmates were in so much pain, they all screamed as loud as their lungs and mouths would allow.

Once malaria had fully infected an inmate's body, the next step was taken. An operation was performed in which the infected site was cut open and the doctor went further, injecting more of the disease germs directly into the open wound, without the individual's consent. There was never a need for consent, only the insane doctor's grave necessity to fulfill his gruesome requirements.

A good friend of mine, a well-known man who should have had a splendid future, Father Czeslaw Sejbuk, was among those who died. The doctor injected him with those lethal liquids and kept experimenting on him for a long time, until Father Sejbuk's body became one big, rotten wound. He was one of those who suffered the most, his body giving off a terrible smell and beginning to decompose while he was still alive. He died, like so many others, in this horrific way.

There is no way to understand the diabolical perversity of Dr. Klaus Schilling, the mental state that allowed him to carry out those experiments on human beings. Perhaps he was a man gifted with the skill of a wizard, who believed that a superior race benefits from whatever use is made of an inferior race. It would be logical, then, that an inferior race (such as the Polish were considered to be) should benefit greatly by means of experimenting on the so-called superior German race. If the Polish people were to conduct experiments on the Germans, no one would come out alive.

The fourth room in block 5 stopped being a gathering place for the ill and was converted into another location for experiments. These were carried out by a nurse and were done to help German soldiers exposed to the dangers of the sea. This experiment consisted submerging a prisoner into a tub or water tank filled with cold water. A cable was connected to his chest and another to his nose so that his heart palpitations and the amount of oxygen he was receiving could be recorded. Following that, the water was frozen, and the man was kept under the ice until he was as close to death as possible. At the signal, the ice was broken and the frozen victim removed. Often, he was already dead. If he was still alive, he was placed on top of a bed and covered with blankets to see what the results would be.

Another idea occurred to our doctor, taken from the story of David in the Scriptures. When David could not heat his own body, young and beautiful women lay on either side of him until he received enough heat to live for a few more days. For the Polish priests, if the blankets were not enough, the prostitutes were brought in to try to animate the man's frozen body. For one of the priests, the warmth of their bodies saved his life.

We also heard about the altitude experiments performed at S.S. Ahnenerbe, where Jews were chosen as the victims. They were placed inside a cylinder in which the air pressure corresponded to an altitude of between 5,000 and 8,000 meters. Then the pressure was dropped at a terrible speed to the altitude of sea level. The quick change in pressure was to simulate the rapid fall of skydivers. An Austrian assistant who scrupulously kept notes wrote these words of observation: "They went crazy and ripped their hair out with all their strength to alleviate the pressure. They dug their heads and faces with their fingernails until their lungs exploded." No account exists of anyone coming out of those experiments alive.

THE FOOD

In the German language, two words describe the natural maintenance of physical strength for human beings: *essen* and *fressen* (both meaning "to eat"). Cultured people use the first one when referring to man, and the second when referring to animals. The first word involves the chewing of food, not simply gobbling as a dog might, and drinking, or *trinken*. When the Germans announced mealtimes, they used the expression *fressen* as the supermen called us dogs to our meals.

For a short time, we received a potato in our soup, an unbelievable luxury so that we could work like animals. The imprisoned characterized this as enough not to die, but insufficient to live. Soon the dark clouds arrived and anything solid in the soup was removed permanently. As I mentioned in previous chapter, we also had a blackened liquid the Germans beautifully called *der kaffee* (coffee), the daily drink of the incarcerated. This was a disgusting, sour drink, made from the bitter roots of herbs picked from the concentration camp fields. German generosity knew no limits.

The Germans loved to call themselves *Kulturtragers*, the "culture bearers," and the concentration camp served them magnificently, establishing their culture as creators of hunger and all sorts of other barbarities. The system implemented in their camps produced satisfactory results, complying with the sayings of Goebbels himself: "Twelve million slaves could easily cover the national work necessities, being fed very little food, costing a very low price."

The fact that these slaves died in huge numbers like poisoned flies did not bother the *kulturtragers* because, to them, a prisoner was nothing more than a cheap, disposable product.

One must not forget that most of those human beings put into the fire of the crematorium were in terrible physical condition, and on the day of their departure from this earth, they had little skin on their bones. However, other prisoners died from accidents while working or from being brutalized, and sometimes from a medical ailment such as a heart attack. Those offered something more to the Germans, something contemptuous.

Human cadavers quickly became disgusting and smelly. However, the cooks knew how to make these atrocities into something attractive to those who were starving to death. I was invited one day to sit at a table that held plates of specially prepared human flesh. I could not eat it, but others ate freely, trying to satisfy their hunger in this way. Looking down from heaven, the dead men may have felt some pride for, with their bodies, helping calm the hunger and fending off the deaths of many prisoners. God reward them with eternal peace for this charity.

THE INVESTIGATIONS

THE SOLDIERS IN CHARGE OF guarding the prisoners in the camp were experts in creating ways to make us suffer. It was a system of control over every person, improvising ways to avoid moments of peace and tranquility. Inside the barracks, these controls were carried out by one military individual or a group of them, soldiers of any rank. They would enter a barrack and it was as if a devastating swarm of locusts had passed through, ruining everything and leaving a barren field behind. The soldiers destroyed everything. Sheets, pillows, clothing and anything else they could find flew out the window and into the streets. If it happened to be a rainy day and mud covered the street, then everything was soaked in mud. Prisoners, of course, were responsible for the condition of their belongings, and the Germans enjoyed the sight of everything destroyed, the mud, the prisoners sweating blood, trying to put it all back in perfect order, never able to satisfy those brutes who had no human feelings.

Anyone who is familiar with prison life knows that it does not exist without a secret or black market. Such a market cannot exist without theft. The inmates of Dachau did not want to steal because it imitated the Germans' behavior and was against one of God's commandments. However, thefts were committed with agility and dexterity, though they were not called thefts; they were called the organization.

Stealing did not enjoy any prestige among the prisoners, but the bigger and better the organization, the higher the prisoner's esteem. An internal market was developed, built upon this system. It followed a rule that a small thief (a prisoner) could steal only from a big thief (Germans, who had stolen everything from every nation) and not from another prisoner. Prisoners did not try to steal everything. They were more select, stealing only leather, shoes, and, a few times, liquor. Shoes that prisoners made for the internal market were marvelous, double- soled with double lining, the love for their prison brothers imposing a serious obligation upon them to do their most elaborate work with extraordinary perfection. The inmates were to receive the best items and the Germans the worst. Of course, the Germans saw these good objects in the hands of the prisoners, and the only way to learn how this was occurring was to investigate.

During the last years of the war, rooms in block No. 28 had been converted into workrooms for the shoemakers. The Germans decided that invading that barrack would reveal rich treasures. They arrived quietly on bicycles, which they rested against the wall. Then they entered silently to surprise the prisoners. Unfortunately for them, the biggest surprise was that they failed to find the objects in question, and they lost their bicycles, which they had left outside. One of the Germans also lost his gloves, which he had taken off and laid on a table, the better to proceed with his inquiry. The bicycles were taken apart, and they and the gloves were buried in holes on the grounds of the concentration camp, never to be found. The soldiers' rage aside, they could not hide their admiration for the lowly prisoners and their ability to hide objects with no hiding places in sight. We were victorious in our escapades.

This event can only be compared to the "organization" of the famous gangsters of America, burying things in plain sight of the authorities. The German chief officers tried different tactics to discover what had happened to their stolen items, joking as though the whole episode had no meaning to them, severely questioning and then threatening the group of prisoners involved, but nothing worked. Incarcerated prisoners were making a mockery of them and the soldiers' threats evolved into severe punishments. However, no prisoner revealed a word.

This was a most curious event in Dachau, one in which the absolute owners of the situation and our lives, the Germans, could not overcome us. The theft was not committed with bad intentions or to achieve great wealth. Instead, it was a perfectly executed act of defiance on the smallest scale, one that made us feel grand. One can imagine that future generations, upon discovering our buried treasure, will apply the fluoride or Carbon-14 dating method to decipher its meaning within the context of the Holocaust. Lovers of antiques will place the rusted bicycle parts with great piety among their valued archaic objects.

With some frequency, searches continued for the missing bicycles throughout the concentration camp, all the way to the entrance. They always failed, so attention was turned to searching for shoes that the internal market had distributed. Among the prisoners, myself included, were those who wore the shoes that their shoemaker friends had made from leather belonging to the Gestapo. One of the victims of this search was a distinguished Polish man from Lodz. He was wearing shoes, and there was no time or way to remove or change them when the German officials arrived.

At the sight of the Gestapo's leather shoes on the prisoner

from Lodz, one of the principal chiefs screamed, "Those shoes are made from the body of the Gestapo."

This statement had a double interpretation, and the Pole replied courteously and craftily, "Excuse me, sir, but these shoes are not yet made from the skin of any Gestapo." The boss was a bit dim, but he caught the meaning and had to agree with the remark because it was true.

Searches continued, and prisoners also continued their internal commerce, not for money, but because it benefited the poor lives of those inmates who survived in the camp. Not all the bosses were against the organization. Some gained some wealth for themselves and their families by selling items outside Dachau on the black market. In this way, a strange arrangement continued, with the prisoners organizing and the German officers stealthily confiscating goods and selling them for their own profit.

THE INSEPARABLE

MEN HAVE GIFTED THE DOG with the noblest title of "man's best friend." Dogs are loyal and devoted, and it seems nothing can separate them from their owner. However, other creatures, with no nobility, attach themselves to humans and never let go. They are called lice.

Lice found excellent conditions for growing and multiplying in the concentration camp, where human misery and skeletal flesh favored it well. The hair and folds of the lips and ears, and the skin of the prisoners made a natural nest for the bugs. There, they deposited their eggs and bred constantly. The Germans made sure the barracks were clean, and inmates changed their underwear once a week and had a shower every two weeks, but the lice remained. Men were obligated to scratch everywhere while the lice invaded the entire body, causing constant movement and irritation. Lice were on a man's lips while he ate, mixed with human saliva, on the cheeks and ears and between the toes. The lice were satisfied with the smallest amount of blood the starving and dying men had to offer. Prisoners who were already reduced to complete misery felt the presence and biting of the lice, and it was unpleasant. However, in Dachau, with its eternal suffering, lice were merely an annoyance.

Unexpectedly, those lice were a definite benefit to some of the inmates during critical moments of life and death. More than a few times, when inmates had been exposed to terrible weather for many hours, their blood was almost frozen in their veins. The lice could not tolerate the cold either, so they would group together, covering a man's entire body, trying to find a warm place. The man kept moving to get away from the bites and, by doing so, kept his own blood circulating. This elevated his blood and body temperature by some degrees. In this way, the lice prevented the man from freezing.

I remember a similar story that my uncle told me when I was a child, something he had seen during the First World War. When a soldier was found on top of the snow, one whose comrades had left behind, the first thing his rescuers did was check his nostrils. If lice filled them, the man was still alive. If the nose was empty, the man was dead. The prisoners tolerated the lice unwillingly, but perhaps they provided a service to us and were not as bad as we judged them to be.

Entertainment

Historically, it is well known that fathers who have been quite inhumane with their sons try to change memory and perception as the days of their existence come to an end. They seek to leave behind the memory not of an abominable person, but of a person who is more paternal and comprehensible. Something similar took place in Dachau. With the prognosis being fatal for the Hitlerian Empire, the German bosses began feeling that they might be held responsible for their acts of brutality toward the prisoners. Thus, they opted for a change in tactics. To enhance their image and, in this manner, cleanse their hands of the blood of innocents, they introduced sports and entertainment into the prisoner's lives. This way, the concentration camp became not just a place where the Nazi regime exterminated undesirable elements, but something better, something one did not expect to find behind a strongly electrified fence. From inside the clouds appeared a star that changed the panorama of our sad, vegetating routine.

Instead of enjoying the prisoners' sufferings, the bosses had to tolerate, with simulated smiles, their victims' happiness. The arrival of Officer Weiss, whom I mentioned earlier in this account, changed the melancholic atmosphere in Dachau, as though the tiniest breath of freedom was permitted. First, soccer was permitted on the property adjacent to the prisoners' barracks, close to the hospital. Some Sundays, once food was finished at noon, we could participate in this rare spectacle, which the inmates quite appreciated. We played not only to pass the time and to have some type of distraction, but also to organize rivalries among the teams representing diverse nations. Frequently, some of the bosses could be observed among the spectators. They were temporarily able to set aside their beastly attitudes toward the inmates and watch their enemies play. The prisoners enjoyed the game of soccer, and although they played for competing nations, they set aside political ideologies and united fraternally inside the rivalry of the sport. The farther the bullets were from us, the more the soccer ball united us. We gained some level of happiness over all the hatred.

Along with sport, we were allowed to cultivate a higher art. The construction of a platform could be seen taking place beside the kitchen and the laundry, and French, German, Italian, and Polish prisoners were to represent their nations by doing something worthy of their flags: acting on top of a stage. The actors could always count on a big audience, with significant support from the prisoners, even more than during the games of soccer. The German authorities did not spare their own support for the construction of the stage, its decoration, and the preparation of costumes. We did not know from whence came the elegant fabrics, which were quite luxurious, or the elaborate stage decorations that the chiefs of the camp provided. Some of the German soldiers also acted, with the top chiefs themselves participating.

Public opinion among the prisoners was that the French won the "most hated" category for the acts they presented. There were whistles and boos at them because their acts were so morally low and censurable. I remember one night when the inmates in the audience were completely hostile and adverse to the entire production. The Italians received enthusiastic applause, as they had quite a number of good singers. They organized a singing group of four voices that received very favorable comments and response. I could imagine that the Germans awaited something better, and when they performed, they were effective in their visual acting. However, their play did not deserve any awards because their singing was terrible. They were unable to prepare anything worthy of their nation and did not deserve any applause (nor did they get it).

The last group to perform consisted of the lovers of scenic art, the Polish. We won applause for the beauty and elegance of our costumes. When I first saw the fine costumes, I thought they must have been a result of theft from the Germans, but I was wrong. They were due to the generosity of Officer Weiss, who gave the Germans permission to provide whatever we needed. The theatrical acts were presented in Polish, and many of the spectators ignored the content because they could not understand the words. Therefore, a good summary of each story was delivered in different languages before the beginning of every act. The choir wore national costumes representing remote times, reminding me of the sad events in history when three ruling bodies divided Poland. These stories won the sympathy of the inmate audience and prolonged applause. The melody of one piece, "*Oto dzis dzien krwi i chwaly*" ("This is the day of blood and victory"), was repeated from the past but represented prisoners who had been in Dachau from the first moment. Though the play's principal ideas disparaged the rapacious Germans, everyone became insane with enthusiasm and collective happiness.

Among the spectators was a group of German officials, not including Officer Weiss, who came in at the finale, hearing only part of the last song. Moved by the applause and the emotion in the audience, Weiss exchanged words with the other officials, then gave the order for the song to be repeated. I'm not sure if it was his lack of understanding of all the words or if the music simply moved him, but he let himself be taken up in the moment and applauded the choir.

During the song, I sat with the German priests, who did not make a single comment. However, once they heard the beauty of the song and the great enthusiasm of the audience, they were filled with animosity and exclaimed, "Oh, this must certainly be a German song because the Polish are unable to compose such a piece. They have presented a German song as their own music."

According to this theory, everything lovely and grand was German. Every author of every artistic work in the world, maybe even the creations of God, borrowed his talent from Germany. This made me think of some other claims when the Germans came to my city of Poznan. Seeing the beauty and artistic design of some of the buildings, they said it all had to be the work of German architects, the only people capable of creating such splendor. Germans created the entire universe. It would have been more effective for them to stick their noses in the asses of the cities before pronouncing such ridiculous sentences.

In the middle of the plaza, a metal pole was raised, and from time to time it transmitted musical pieces and political news from the front lines. The music was a welcome reminder of another world, one that still held liberty and beauty. Sometimes music was played during rest periods on Sundays. In those moments, we felt a thin bit of family life, being able to converse with other inmates who were also friends; we felt a little more like intelligent human beings.

We were especially interested in war news. When the radio announced, "At the front," everyone would stop talking and listen, trying not to miss a single word. We all knew that news unfavorable to the Germans had a two-week delay, and our happiness would increase when we heard of any frontline catastrophe. I guess we should thank our oppressors for knowing how to boost our spirits in this way, allowing us thoughts of German defeat and our liberation. If only a tenth of what we heard was true, the Allies had surrendered three years before the German defeat, and the Germans owned the entire world without knowing it themselves. Neither the chief officers nor the simple German soldiers ever acknowledged any falsehoods.

A historic event, one that brought out German emotions of rage and revenge, was the news of the fall of Monte Cassino. While the Allies kept attacking that mountain fortress, bombing and flattening the mountains that blocked the passage to Rome, the Germans were sure of their triumph. When luck changed and the Allies overtook the impregnable, inaccessible caves, with Polish General Anders raising the white and red flag of victory at the top of one of the mountain caves, our chief officers became angry bulls, roaring their disgust against the Polish. The yell "The pigs, the Polish" resounded everywhere as their German military brothers were made to leave the caves, just as hunting dogs make rats come out of canals. We had committed the fault of valiantly defending our country and demonstrating our heroism by winning Monte Casino with the Allies, and, for this fault, we wanted to sing with happiness, "Oh happy fault taking Monte Casino from the Germans." The soldiers who conquered Monte Casino covered themselves in immortal glory. At the same time, they gave us at least one battle to celebrate in which our enemies, the supermen invincible and superior to all other nations, were defeated. The justice of this victory converted our daily pain into a well of happiness.

FRIENDS ARE COMING

AT THE BEGINNING OF 1941, when I left the Polish city of Lodz, known by the Germans as Litzmannstadt, I waited a long time at the train station because of approaching enemy planes. The sirens sounded as planes cut through the sky in search of something to devour, and more than a few times our transport had to pass through open fields with their frightening presence overhead.

One night, the city of Munich awoke to the terrible voices of sirens announcing the arrival of the Nazis' enemy. Anyone close enough to see it, even from afar, would never forget it. It was a night of splendor because it held redemption, while both sides illuminated the skies. The Germans did not sleep, and their defense preparations were excellent. Their *Fluegzeugi-Abwehr-Kanonenbatterie*, called "flak," was continuously shot into the sky against the powerful hum of the Allied bombs. Lights from reflectors traced the air and crossed the foggy night in search of planes, and the heavy bombers made every effort to evade the light rays. There was tremendous noise from the detonations of flak and the exploding projectiles. Anyone seeing this phenomenon forgot about the cold and the danger bursting over his head, and stared in amazement at the spectacle.

The first night attacks that we heard happened over Munich on February 12 and 13, 1943, while we slept. No one suspected that on that holy night, such luminous guests would arrive. When the bombs began falling, the tanks shot fire upward, illuminating a celestial horizon. The noise and light carried eighteen kilometers to those inmates imprisoned in the hands of the Germans. Everyone awoke, and despite some level of fear, there was a yell of happiness. The inmates got to their feet and threw themselves into the camp streets. They forgot the cold and their fears and felt a sense of hope that made them run from one end of the camp to the other, shouting, "Friends, bombings, bombings," as if the day of our salvation might truly arrive. The inmates did not feel hatred for the innocent Germans whose houses fell upon them in ruins; they felt hatred only for the destruction that Nazi Germany had caused – thousands of destroyed families and the deaths of millions of innocent people.

Day and night, the bombings increased in strength and intensity, over diverse cities. Some of the planes were hit and caught fire, their pilots jumping out and falling not far from the camp. The Germans pointed their machine guns at the soldiers suspended in the air by their parachutes, then yelled, "*Ein grosser sief*," happy if they could hit and kill any of them. I personally saw a plane going down in flames, and the pilot made enormous efforts so that it would not fall into the concentration camp.

Sometimes, the Americans allowed themselves a small joke against Hitler, dropping signs to tell us of their presence: "Adolf, We're Coming Soon. The Flyers of the USA."

One day, I read a German news journal that was quite ironic. The Allies considered their path of flight in high-altitude airspace as not belonging to any country. The German government appealed to Switzerland to stop these flights from crossing their land. To appease the Germans, the Swiss filed an angry protest against the Americans regarding the violation of their neutral airspace. The Germans said nothing about their own firing against the Allies above the territory of Switzerland.

If an absurd dialogue had taken place between the Swiss and the Allied pilots, it might have sounded something like this:

"You realize you are above Swiss ground?"

"We are perfectly aware of this."

"And do you know that you are violating international law?"

"We are perfectly aware of this."

"Do you know that we are obligated to fire against you?"

"We are perfectly aware of this."

"Attention, attention, we are going to open fire!"

"And do you know that you are firing 1,000 feet below where you can hit us?"

"Naturally, we know this well."

The Swiss placated the German government by firing upon the Allied planes, knowing full well the planes were flying many meters beyond their reach. The Allied planes flew high above the Swiss shootings, without interference directly toward their targets.

The pilots knew the concentration camp location perfectly. At night, when they dropped their bombs, they shone a brilliant light over the four points of the camp, illuminating us as though it were daytime, protecting us so that no bomb would fall near us. The lights generally shone for twenty minutes, and after one was extinguished, another was lighted. It was a marvel of ingenuity, and there was much discussion within the camp as to how this was accomplished. We were certain this was a well-kept military secret. Finally, rumors were later confirmed that the lights were somehow being reflected from a mountainous area, quite a distance from the camp.

The Liberation

THERE IS NO DOUBT THAT the prisoners of Dachau had become well-informed about the military movements on all the wartime fronts. The radio station in the plaza and the dissemination of news throughout the camp functioned marvelously. We had learned that the days of the German occupation were numbered, but we did not have any reason to believe we would be released from prison, nor did we have any tangible hope for the future.

At the end of 1944, the Allied planes gave signals of fearlessness and flew close to the ground, the best signal that they may have already dominated the sky over German territory. Hitler's words, given to his people at the beginning of the war, had been an open failure. He had built a wall around his country, forged by the power of his party, but he had forgotten something equally important. He had failed to build a roof that would protect Germany from invaders in the air.

Although an end to the war on the European continent appeared to be arriving, the issue of what would happen to prisoners under a totalitarian power remained a threat. The Germans may have lost strength before a powerful adversary, but they had not lost their audacity and brutality toward weak and miserable human beings. While we lived between the anvil and the hammer, time passed in an excruciatingly slow way as we awaited either our death or salvation.

One day, we looked into the sky and caught our collective breath as four dots against the sun kept getting bigger. At incredible velocity, planes were flying directly toward our barracks. We were very frightened because we knew that those birds heading at us could also create our tomb. We closed our eyes and heard the explosions, and where the dots had been, only smoke and debris remained. Their destructive work evident, the Allied planes returned and flew low to the ground again. It seemed as though they were already the masters of the sky. Those planes' performance was important, not only in combat but in the minds of the imprisoned, where hope appeared inside our downcast hearts. We all prayed that our days of suffering were coming to an end.

Suddenly, word spread from mouth to mouth that the top chief, Weiss, had received the order to make us disappear in a single day. We were to be shot. This news was cruel, and we believed that nothing was impossible for these men, our would-be executioners. Rumors multiplied and grew, and prisoners took various positions regarding their own lives. It seemed impossible to us that with one shot, we would lose our lives after having survived so many terrible years in Dachau. I immediately got in contact with my friend Tony Zagier, and we were determined to defend ourselves at all costs. We got kitchen knives, quite like the machetes used by the people of South America, and although our plan was stupid and imprudent, we were determined to fight.

The exact text of the telegram that Himmler sent to the chief of the concentration camp at Dachau verified the truth that we were to be killed. It said, "*Golfried Weiss Die Ubergabe Kommt nicht in frage; das lager is sofort zu earlier; kein Haftling darf icben-*

dig in die Hande des Feindes Kommen. Die Haftling haven sich gru-
enhaftt gegen die Zivilbevolkerung bekommen." ("The surrender of
the enemy camp is out of the question. The entire camp must be
immediately eradicated. Not a single prisoner must fall alive into
the power of the Americans. The inmates have behaved horribly
with the citizens, H. Himmler.")

Weiss was responsible for following the execution order from
his superior. He left the open order on his desk so that the prisoner cleaning the furniture could easily see it. We did not know
if his position was to follow orders and massacre us or to follow
his conscience. Overall, upon hearing this news, the prisoners
showed no special degree of anxiety, having had their lives threatened many times before. They had no energy to start a revolution.

The Germans' plan and the only way to liberty had been
Esgibt einen weg zur Freheit (the practice of the following virtues): *Gehorsaam* (obedience), *Sanberkeit* (cleanliness), *Fleiss* (as-
siduousness), and *Nutzliekucit* (utility). Living through that were
15,000 prisoners united in their desire to be saved from Dachau
by the Allied troops. On April 14, 1945, General Eisenhower's
headquarters had confirmed the news that they were coming.
Chief Weiss' noble feelings were in our favor; he would not follow the massacre order. However, against his will, his S.S. comrades, under the leadership of S.S. Wikig, a German known for
his cruelty, decided to obey the order for our execution. Wikig
had joined the first International Division of the S.S., which had
been formed in 1940, and was made up of the worst individuals
from Norway, Finland, Denmark, and Holland.

It was a Sunday filled with light, the day destined for the
execution of all the prisoners. However, the famous saying "man
proposes, but God disposes" applies here because it became the

day we were saved. On the order of Chief Weiss, the number of survivors shrank as the executions were carried out.

The Polish priests began begging for celestial help through prayers to the adoptive father of the Savior, St. Joseph. "Just as you saved the life of Jesus from the evil hands of Herod, also save our lives from another Herod, this man Himmler."

All was quiet, and we had no sign that our prayers were answered as we remained on our knees, fervently praying. And then came Divine intervention so clear that even the hardest communist and the most atheistic German had no other explanation. It was April 29, 1945, a day of glory for God and for the thousands of prisoners waiting to die at any moment. We had been praying when the Allies arrived at the entrance of Dachau. The Allies' first bullets broke through the blue sky of Dachau at the precise moment some of the priests finished their prayers.

Tony Zagier and I had been going around with long machete knives inside our jackets; we could have been caught and executed at any time. At the moment of the Allied troop arrival, I was in service to a sick prisoner. The hour was 5:27 pm, and the man I was carrying in my arms was covered with severe wounds. A loud whistle cut through the air at the top of my head. The whistle sounds kept coming, one after another, with disorienting frequency, and it was unclear whether the final execution was upon us. I wanted to fall to my knees for cover, but I was carrying a human body and did not want to crush him. I rushed to the closest bed and actually tossed him there (such was my fear), then pulled my machete from its hiding place.

Tony Zagier and I had agreed to fight to the end, and he ran over to me. We had no time to think, not a second for reflection. As the Americans moved closer to us with each step, we were losing all our nerve and reason. An invincible force seemed to be dragging all the prisoners toward the front gate of the concentration camp, and we moved with them. We became a disorderly but compact mass of individuals with no reason, pushing blindly toward a will to live, toward salvation, revenge, toward something, like fire takes power over dry material blown only by a gust of wind. Those who were healthy rushed forward, even though they had not yet seen a single American soldier. Others, who were wounded or broken, dragged themselves like serpents on their abdomens. Everyone rushed toward the sounds of machine gun shots, and with every shot, our hope grew.

The Germans flew the white flag of surrender, but it was a trick; in reality, they had other intentions. They had seen the Allies getting close and had put up the white flag only to open fire on the Americans. The camp walls and watchtowers protected the Germans, and they looked down on the Americans' approach. The Yankees, realizing they were victims of German treachery, withdrew to regroup before coming forward again with round after round of bullets, every step bringing them a little closer to us. German machine gun fire could not stop the American movement toward the camp. Both sides fired heavily, bullets ripping back and forth through the air with tremendous intensity. Two Native American Allied soldiers threw themselves with fury against their enemy.

The air was full of prisoners' cries: "Long live the Yankees!"

"Death to the Germans!"

These cries became the answers to the sound of the machine guns. They were bringing our salvation, and also the death of many Germans, those guilty of years of inflicting extraordinary suffering on untold numbers of innocent human beings. One of the Allied soldiers, a man of Polish origin, succeeded in climbing over the wall and attacking the towers, an extremely dangerous but effective maneuver, and the Germans began giving the signal for unconditional surrender. Throwing weapons out the windows and humbly descending the stairs with their arms raised in the air, the Germans begged for mercy from the sky, perhaps believing the Allies would treat them kindly. However, their defeaters forgot mercy and applied the law of justice to a vicious, brutal enemy.

Quickly, German soldiers were caught and lined up along the ditch surrounding the concentration camp. Their swift but just sentence was announced. It could have been, "He who lives by the sword dies by the sword."

They had committed unspeakable acts against humanity as well as acts of treason against their native land. A slight movement and they fell to the ground like wheat before the scythe. It was the execution of the guards. Bits of lead ended the lives of those soldiers who were traitors to the principles of humanity and any form of international agreement. What a stupid tragedy of man; just days before, these men had boasted that they were the masters of the world. Now, today, they did not have enough strength to control their own lives.

Those German soldiers had shown no respect for anyone, not even for God or His commandments, and they had prohibited us from praying under any circumstances. To them, there was no God. They had gloated over an expected victory and had believed themselves to be immortal, equal to or better than any God. When their fortune changed, they transformed from voracious beasts into docile lambs, miserable and vulnerable and now looking for God. They begged for prayer, asking for prayers on their behalf, for their lives and the lives of their families. Some of our worst persecutors, with tears in their eyes, asked for prayers on their behalf, that God might spare their lives. What a marvel is God, bringing wolves back to his flock as domesticated lambs.

For the Polish prisoners, the Americans' entrance had been not only a day of liberation but one of extraordinary pride as well. We were all rescued, and it was the descendant of a Polish family who raised the Allied flag over the tower of the principal building presiding over the entire concentration camp. We Poles, the most oppressed and humiliated, the most despised and martyred by the German military, felt our hearts leap with emotion at the sight of the Polish flag undulating over Dachau. Yells of victory and immortality issued forth. Poland and its people, who had been crushed, divided, stepped on, reduced to ashes and pools of blood, despoiled of our families, our rights, our homeland, our material goods, who had borne the brutal yoke as prisoners, were not mute and silent, but active, fighting, and never defeated. The Americans' presence among us not only opened Dachau's gate but ripped off our chains of slavery. Everything seemed a perfect triumph.

The yell "Death to the oppressors" had been more powerful to us than the voice of the machine guns. However, little by little, those guns forced the German soldiers to surrender. It was the most important act in the dark history of Dachau. The total mass of prisoners, blind with happiness and emotion, lost their fear and threw themselves into one another's arms. We became a bunch of international people who forgot national differences, endlessly kissing and showing love for one other without tiring. In freedom, there were no Poles, Germans, Czechs, Belgians, or Russians, only men, one bonded mass of prisoners, loving every different race and color. And there was only one celestial Father, who was watching over everyone.

As in the days of the gospel, a single voice was heard and understood by all present, a scream of happiness that overwhelmed the murmurs coming from the lips of every person. Men with newfound physical strength picked up those lying on the ground and raised them high enough so that they could see the men who had saved us in the last moments of our lives. Many of them did not have enough strength to yell, "Long live the Allies," or they were too emotional to do so, laughing and crying at the same time, tears spilling over their faces. The ambulant cadavers, who a few days earlier had wished for nothing but death to stop their suffering, began feeling new impulses, a new energy to go on living. At that moment, when the Germans' power was reduced to nothing, the burdens we carried on our chests that had long weighted us with pain began to be released; our pulses revived with new physical and moral strength. The voice of freedom rose above all these events, and our arms were opened wide to every son of the human race.

Nevertheless, only a few hours passed before a dark cloud covered the horizon. From part of the city of Munich, a unit of the Gestapo called Wickig was approaching. By reputation, it was the worst and most frightful division. These sons of the infernal fog were coming with the same idea as the Americans: to liberate us, but in their own way, liberating us from our human bodies and sending our spirits to the Eternal God. Armed from their feet to their teeth, this division was perfectly conditioned and committed to executing the remaining number of us, equaling 30,000 prisoners. According to some statistics, the number of prisoners in Dachau reached 52,000 at its apex; according to other calculations, this number was 62,000. I don't know the reason for this discrepancy in the numbers, other than that perhaps during the few days before the American liberation, 10,000 may have perished.

Quickly, a battle began between the two sides, with the Americans defending the camp. They were grossly outnumbered, and little by little, the Germans were overwhelming them. The longer the battle went on, the more likely it became that Wickig would achieve victory. Making the situation more difficult, the prisoners were mixing in with the defending soldiers, hampering them and making it harder for them to retreat to better positions of defense. Our luck looked bad. However, God saved his own people and protected us. Reinforcements arrived at just the moment when the Americans saw themselves obligated to fall back, and the Gestapo's advance became nothing more than a prelude to their surrender. There was to be a final American victory and liberation.

THE BOMBINGS

WHAT COURAGE, WHAT HAPPINESS THE Allied bombings instilled in the souls of the unfortunate prisoners who had desperately lived between life and death for so long. We saw that our salvation was perfectly dependent upon the destruction those planes imposed. Every bomb dropped caused the material destruction of our enemies and gave us one more ounce of physical strength.

The Germans believed frantically in the superiority of their own race. According to Hitler's doctrine, *Mein Kampf*, the Germans had the privilege and power to conquer, exploit, use, and exterminate other races for their own benefit. This diabolical system, used against their enemies and all the prisoners who were treated as slaves, seemed to confirm Darwin's idea about the survival of the fittest now fully implemented as a forced selection of the race with the weak being overcome by the better, victorious race of Germans.

Then the bombings destroyed it all. Yes, superiority can be discussed. Allied bombing showed brilliant military superiority against Germany in the final conflict, with superior weapons and strategies, though the number of soldiers was fewer. However, even in triumph, no one race was truly superior to all others. There is a well-known saying: "God chokes but He does not drown." He was with us. Germany surrendered, and we were to be liberated.

It is unclear what so many prisoners, kept in slavery all this time, were to do with their liberty. The Germans had systematically worked at turning all the imprisoned men and women into beasts, incapable of thinking or feeling, but the inmates had not lost every human feeling, and they wanted first to express their thanks to their liberators. We wanted to publicly thank the leader of the rescue operations, whose cleverness and perseverance, after God, was responsible for our salvation. Whenever American 1st Lt. William Cowling appeared, the enthusiastic multitude gave him warm and sincere thanks. He was a valiant soldier and a man conscious of his mission, one who knew how to see the totality of events and relate them to the providence of our God.

Climbing to the office balcony, he asked for our attention, telling us he wanted to say a few words. Asking for silence, he said, "The thousands of dead comrades shot down in the camps, and found along the road on my march toward Munich, gave me the idea of changing tactics and direction and arriving as soon as possible at Dachau. With a small group of soldiers and without having an express order from my superior, I came here to the full march, determined to arrive in time."

Happily, he and his soldiers arrived before our execution, and a few minutes before the Germans would have further bathed themselves in the blood of the innocent.

"You now thank me for your salvation," continued the Colonel, "and I do not deny it, but I did with my hands that which was already preordained. You must know that the true Savior is not me, but God. It is He who sent me here on time and saved your lives."

He took off his hat and, in his language, invited us all to pray with him words of gratitude to our true Savior: "Our Father, who art in heaven…"

In a similar manner, Winston Churchill spoke: "God bless you; this victory is yours. In all our long history, we have never seen a more glorious day than this. On this day, we are humble and reverent and give thanks to God Almighty for having liberated us from German domination."

Each prisoner continued this prayer, all of us praying in diverse languages, saying the words of Jesus: "Hallowed be Thy name…" This was our public prayer, filled with fervor and love, directed at our Father, our common Father of all human beings. For the first time, we all prayed, regardless of country, nationality, or creed, in a loud voice and without fear of being beaten, expressing our natural commitment to our Savior and Creator.

Three days after the public prayer, it was decided that a Mass would be held in the middle of the plaza, in the area where so many prisoners had been openly tortured, and an altar was constructed. The Mass would be offered in gratitude to God for those of us who had survived in Dachau. It would also be a fervent plea on behalf of those who had suffered tremendously and gone on to the eternal life. An enormous cross covered in crepe stood over the plaza, and all the prisoners, as well as the Allied troops, congregated to take part in this religious act.

We were to stand in perfect silence, as usually happens during the Sacred Mass, but something quite different occurred. At first, only the voice of the celebrant could be heard, and he made a great effort to ensure that the words of the prayer carried to the far edges of the circle of men and women surrounding the altar. However, as the Mass continued, every second was broken by a whisper, then a sob, and finally a moving and common cry from thousands of men and women realizing that they were not dead, not empty, no longer part of a life with no meaning. The Germans had induced those feelings with their brutal system, and now they were gone. We were sons of God, who was still in His heaven, and we were brothers to one another.

In that colossal gathering of human beings, a block of ice began melting under the influence of the warmth of that prayer, which went to our core. We bathed in our own tears, which flowed abundantly and flooded the faces of those people whom pain and extreme suffering had so harshly tried. This spectacle held pure emotion, in the manner of a lake disrupted by a child throwing a little rock, ripples and circles extending farther outward until not a single soul was left untouched, until the circles surrounded and encompassed every one of us.

THE AMERICAN CAMPAIGN

FROM THE MOMENT THE AMERICANS took charge of the concentration camp, we enjoyed the natural human privilege of liberty. Liberty gives a man dignity, opening locked doors and creating a grand benefit to the spirit – one that does not include pain and abuse. Man is a lover of liberty, but being unaccustomed to showing respect for others, some of the prisoners committed acts that, in the outside world, would have had serious repercussions: robberies, drunkenness, etc. The Americans had guards throughout the camp, but they were familiar with the behavior of rescued prisoners, and they often ignored and permitted acts that would have ordinarily been unlawful. Being a nurse, I wore the white and red armband and could open any door and enter wherever and whenever I pleased. I wanted to see the properties adjacent to the camp. There, I found giant storage rooms containing millions of pieces of clothing, as well as other goods that had been brought to the Germans by those who had been executed.

The Americans did not understand the extent of the prisoners' hunger and set out immediately to feed all the inmates. Most of the prisoners who were still alive were in no condition to eat a full meal, and a bad situation developed that no one could have foreseen. Each prisoner received a can of greasy food and, instead of splitting the cans into a few meals, the starving individuals ate the contents all at once. The result was death for some of those men whose systems were unable to digest so much food; others experienced intense stomach pain and diarrhea. Luckily, I understood this and was careful to eat small amounts; food that I received to feed my sick men was broken into smaller portions. The men did not understand, and were like wolves in their fury toward me; they wanted all the meat from the very start. Denying it to them was difficult, but I remained firm. They did not become ill, and I had the joy of knowing that none of them died under my care. A silent American soldier was guarding my area, and he did not try to interfere with me. He seemed to trust my competency with the other prisoners. We had no way of communicating personally, as he knew no German and I knew no English. Then we realized a Russian medic in the room knew perfect English and could serve as a bridge between us.

From the first days of liberty, I received a type of radio for the sick room. It was in good condition and gave us a distraction and some happiness through listening to music. However, an American soldier in charge of a neighboring barrack wanted this radio. He was in love with a German woman and had promised her the radio even though it did not belong to her. He came into our sick area and, without a word, hiked the object up onto his shoulders and started walking out of the room.

I went to him and in a loud voice asked, "Where are you going? Is that radio yours? Leave that here immediately!" I spoke in German, and he spoke to me in English. He did not understand me, and I did not understand him, but something was quite clear: He was a thief. We owned the radio, and he was not taking it from us.

The soldier yelled and gave me a few punches, and I gave him a few back. The Russian doctor came to translate; he told me the soldier was determined to take the radio to the German woman. If not today, he would certainly come back another day. The American said that he was a soldier and I was a prisoner and the radio belonged to him. I told him the radio was mine and would never be his, that I was a free man and he was a thief. The soldier left without the radio, promising to come back and take it another day.

I knew what his plan would be. I made the radio disappear for a few days, and he was unable to find it. He also did not marry the young German woman, perhaps as a consequence of "no radio." Thank God it was over. The Americans were great on the battlefield, knowing how to fish out the Germans, but they were ignorant of living conditions in a concentration camp.

Along with the mess involved in giving full cans of food to the prisoners, the Americans committed several other foolish acts. We were all barely clothed, and millions of pieces of clothing were in the storage areas, left behind by the victims of German bestiality. Instead of allowing us to dress in these clothes, to begin looking even a bit more civilized and to have what we needed, the Americans thought the clothes were too sad a reminder of the mass executions and burnt all of them in a fire.

We were still starving, and the patients in my hall were in ruined health, victims of bombings, men covered in wounds, with bad odors emanating from their flesh; they needed good food if they were to begin healing. The Americans did not seem to understand that their miserable meal plan of no substance was worsening our health every day. I was truly desperate to help the sick. Giving them water boiled as soup, I put the spoon into the bottom of the pot and stirred and stirred; however, I found nothing but water – no vegetables or meat or anything at all. I spoke in German, and I was in a fury. The devil himself would not have been ashamed of my language or my rage on behalf of the sick men. I abused the Russian-Jewish doctor and the American soldier to such an extent that they left while I continued shouting and spitting into the air.

The next day, the soldier returned with no noticeable difference in his attitude. As I started ladling out the water-soup, the door opened and in came soldiers, civilians, and one young lady. The first soldier was an American colonel who surveyed the situation, and then asked me why I was so insulting to America. I said that I did not insult the country of America and that if he wanted to know why I was so angry, why didn't he come over and stir the water, which contained nothing else to feed the hungry and sick men.

The results were highly favorable. The colonel stirred the water and found nothing. He and the doctor had a conversation I did not understand. Then, I was asked to write down on a notepad the items of food these prisoners needed. The American soldiers who had been giving us boiled water were humiliated, but they did behave like gentlemen, and I did not feel the need to apologize for my cursing. The results were magnificent.

Immediately, the menu became that of a first-class restaurant. Each day, I filled out my menu request card, asking for dishes that would help heal the sick. The cook, although unhappy, gave us food that tasted good and could be eaten, and the men began regaining their color and some of their energy. From that happy day forward, because of my fury, life in our hall took on an aspect of a free, rich hotel, and the sick congratulated me with seldom-seen sincerity. They were content and satisfied, still covered in wounds but healing in the climate of fraternity and mutual love.

Up to that moment, they had ignored the fact that I was a priest. At this point, I proposed to them a Mass of Thanksgiving. Despite the different nationalities and religions – Greeks, Asians,

Communists, Jews, German Protestants, and Catholics – not a single voice rose against it, and I began my preparations. The sick men asked for the priest who would be coming, and none of them realized it would be me, their fellow prisoner and caretaker. When the day for the Mass arrived, I went to my room and dressed in a liturgical way. Then I returned to the room, astonishing the men. There were exclamations and applause in acknowledgment of my vestments and my calling.

Once Mass began, there was a respectful silence and prayerful behavior worthy of admiration. There was no Communion, but there was a long and fervent giving of thanks from all the men present, not only for their renewed lives but for the abundant and delicious menu which their caretaker had arranged through his cursing.

After the Mass, various curious comments continued, not only about the Mass itself, but about their caretaker/priest. Some of the men were quite unhappy that I had "hidden" my priesthood, while others thought it was all right because I had justly been able to kick thieves and other shameful men. More than a few had suspected that I was a strange man who did not seem to fit in with the others nursing them. One of the Jews felt that I was as savage as any of the other soldiers, and a Greek thought I might be normal, but maybe too nice, denying all the gifts offered from outside the prison.

The communists were the most content, forgetting their creed and past affiliation, and speaking with noble hearts and great affection. For them, the caretaker had ceased to exist, and before their eyes an entirely new man emerged. They thought I had been kind before, and now a strong and deep feeling of love was awakened toward their "babushka." They all felt the need to shake and kiss my hands with care and love. From that moment on, a friendship surged between us, the communists and me, one of limitless trust. I was no longer a nurse but a "babushka," a beloved Catholic priest. This was a grand day in my life as a prisoner, one that would never be forgotten, engraved in the hearts of the sick men and in my own for our entire lives.

Our liberators were only slightly enlightened about the terrible situation among the ill and the system of medical attention. As the beds filled, the sickest men were transferred to the hospitals. The medics' attention was exquisite in the barrack for the sick, and there, the men were on the fast track to recovery. However, when they were transferred out, hospital conditions were not good and the ill quickly lost their ability to improve. The Americans simply did not understand the needs of the sick, especially the extra nutrition required to heal. In the hospitals, the care was quantity and not quality.

The lack of good, nutritious food continued to be a real problem at the hospitals. Of course, during the German occupation the food had been worse, but the sick men were so exhausted by their continuing hunger that they became mistrustful of their liberators. Some of them ran away from the new hospitals, while others refused to be transferred into the Americans' care. The Americans decided to close the camp hospital and transfer every sick person to their own new hospitals; no other alternatives would remain. I had no choice but to say goodbye to my dear ill ones and prepare to leave the concentration camp, with the following days to be spent at the grand college of Pullach.

PULLACH

Of the eighty-five Polish Jesuits at Dachau, thirty were still alive. After the war ended, we received an invitation from the Vicar General to travel to Rome, the Eternal City. Before going to Rome, the Jesuits from Pullach College offered their hospitality, though bombs had partially destroyed the campus. It was being rebuilt and offered enough room for us to stay. After our years in the concentration camp, we were happy to receive such a kind offer.

I stayed behind for a period of time to continue helping the sick. My desire to leave the camp was strong, but my desire to serve the sick men was even stronger. Because of his age, Father Boleslaw Szopinski, Sr. was placed in charge of the Jesuits and tried to convince me to go with them. We had many conversations, and he was worried about my well-being. They left, and I did not go with them. I stayed among the sick ones and became the only Polish Jesuit who remained in Dachau.

Father Szopinski wrote from time to time, sending announcements and communicating his desire to see me at Pullach. He became frustrated and finally sent me an order in the name of obedience, which I refused. He had no authority over me, and I felt that serving the sick was more important than my presence at the school. The other Jesuits at Pullach were not having a well-deserved rest as they had hoped but were receiving Jesuit discipline, and they were submitting to many forced jobs now overseen by civil authorities instead of by those who gave us our religious orders.

The Americans expressed their gratitude for my help during this last period of time, especially because all the nurses had taken advantage of their liberty and left the camp. Given a chance at freedom, they had forgotten the needy. When July 18, 1945 arrived, the care of the ill was turned over to the Americans, and I was freed of all responsibility. The next day, I left Dachau to join my comrades, who had been suffering another type of enslavement. The College of Pullach, consecrated to the study of philosophy and theology for young Jesuits, was eleven kilometers from the city of Munich.

Surrounded by beautiful parks and gardens, this college was splendid because of the gorgeous forest that was part of its surroundings. Before the war, it had been full of young students, but by the end of the war, it was almost completely uninhabited, housing only the Fathers Superior and some brothers. Bombs had damaged its walls, and all the windows had been blown out. Once the school's main portion had been restored, the Americans had occupied it as a sort of military garrison. The principal of the college wanted to guard its religious future and had called for novices to be brought immediately. Their numbers were quite meager, and arrangements were made for all the Jesuits in Dachau to quickly be delivered to Pullach.

The head of the college was a man of high ancestry, called Tatenbach, who was quite young and very likable. He had not yet finished his theological studies and, against ordinary custom, was named principal of the religious institution as soon as he was ordained a priest. He was the one who quietly brought all the

Polish Jesuits to the college and, in this way, secured the building for use as a religious institution once again. When the Americans saw that religious men inhabited most of the college, they no longer used it as a military garrison.

The life of the Polish Jesuits greatly improved once they left Dachau, but the lack of working hands to plant and harvest crops at the college produced another difficult situation. What better way to keep the agriculture going than to equip the Jesuits and send them out into the fields? The college officials, without communicating with its director, had already organized work groups assigned to hard labor on the school's terrain. The stupid and obedient Poles went out there every day, just as they had done before the Germans were defeated. As soon as I arrived, one of the men from the ministry, Prefect Korn, took me to find my tools. His plan was clear from the beginning: to gain another worker, one who would work for free. I flatly refused to pick up the tools or work in the field.

I said to him, "I have already worked for Germans enough for free, for five years and eight months under the German Reich, and will never do it again."

This time, instead of gaining another worker, he lost us all. Prefect Korn tried following the German system of brute force, yelling and threatening me with his superiority, but this had no effect. He finally left me in peace, reaching out to Prefect Rectos for help. As soon as Prefect Rectos learned what had happened, he called me in to have a talk, and I made myself available at once.

He was young with dark skin and eyes, and he had a soft and pleasant voice, giving the overall impression of a man worthy of trust. He questioned me delicately, and it was clear that he did not know how the Polish Jesuits had been forced to work in the concentration camp. He ordered Minister Korn to call all the Jesuits in from the fields, and we were told that we would never have to work at such labor again.

The Polish Jesuits began receiving some German marks and weekly portions of goods from the United Nations Relief Administration; it was not enough to make a daily life, but it was a start. The local German authorities were obliged to provide meals for everyone at the college. In this manner, our presence benefitted the Germans at Pullach, who were sustained by our food. We lived in one part of the college; the remainder of the building, which was still in bad condition from the bombings, would cost one million marks to repair. Materials were not readily available, but once again, our presence was like a ring on the hand of the college authorities. We knew where many tons of carpentry materials in good condition were being stored at Dachau. The German authorities were able to procure all these materials with non-existent money, using bottles of liquor and wine as their currency, and so conditions at the school improved.

Beyond the wall surrounding the college was a gorgeous pine forest. I enjoyed going there every day to breathe the healthy, fresh air. I strolled around and took in the beauty of nature in peaceful contemplation. One day, while in the forest, I was surprised to see a large pile of bicycles, some trucks, and some luxury cars parked together. I couldn't imagine where they had come from or what they were doing there. I looked at the bicycles and touched them. The desire to take one filled me, and I separated one from the bunch.

Immediately, I heard a German voice: *"Halt es ist verboten."* From behind a tree trunk, a man appeared, dressed as a civilian but armed with a rifle. He slowly approached me, saying in the same high voice, "You cannot. It is prohibited."

To my question, "Who has prohibited it?" he answered dryly, "the American Army."

The man showed no further interest in talking to me, but I kept asking questions. Finally, he told me that all the bikes and vehicles were gathered so that a loaded truck could run over and flatten them. Then the truck would be set on fire and the entire pile liquidated. He had seen this happen many times, and his job was to stand guard over them.

I asked him, "Why don't you take a bicycle for yourself?"

He said, "It is prohibited."

"Yes, I know, but do you have one at your house?"

He answered, "I do not."

I asked, "Are you a married or a single man?"

"I am married."

"And do you have children?"

"I do, two sons and two daughters."

"And do they have bicycles?"

"No, they do not have anything."

"And does your wife know how to ride a bike?"

"Yes, but she does not own one."

"And wouldn't you want one for your own use?"

"Well, yes, but the Americans prefer to destroy them, and I am afraid to take one."

"Do you know that I have never seen a German as frightened as you? We know these bicycles are stupidly destined for destruction. I will help you take some, the best for you and your family." I did not wait for his answer but put aside some for him and fifteen for me – that is to say, for all the Polish Jesuits at Pullach. I mounted mine and sped as fast as I could to my friends. Within a few minutes, all the bicycles had disappeared, destined for our use.

The salvation of the bicycles was a minute reconciliation between the hated Pole and the more hated German by means of mutual understanding. I had found a bicycle in good condition that carried the name Kaminski, evidence of its origins – taken from the hands of a Pole and now back in the hands of a Pole. Yes, I organized the bicycle heist, taking back all the bicycles that the Germans had previously stolen. These bicycles made an enormous change in our daily lives, allowing us to move about more easily with a larger sense of freedom.

Good trucks and cars were also awaiting the flames, and this seemed unforgivable to me. Among these was a truly luxurious car, and I did everything I could to acquire it so that it would not be demolished. I did not know how to drive a car, so I called one of our group who had slightly better skill. At the sight of the extraordinarily elegant vehicle, he became enthusiastic and applied himself to the job. After he figured out the diverse gadgets, the car began to move and was brought onto the grounds of the college. Others followed with two vans and a truck, also in good condition.

These vehicles brought great service to their new owners. The director of the college, Father Tatenbach, needed a car and had not been able to find one in working order. Naturally, at the sight of this elegant vehicle, his heart filled with happiness, and he never let it out of his sight, for even one day. He loved it so much, it seemed impossible to him to live without it, just like a good husband cannot live without a good wife. However, his days of honey were not to last; over the horizon came the car's authentic owner.

The director had driven into Munich to make some purchases, and had left his car on the road in front of the business where he had stopped. A woman saw the car parked in front of where she was standing and seemed paralyzed with fear, not trusting her first impression, touching the car, looking at it with such admiration and pleasure, never imagining that her stolen vehicle would be returned.

"This car is mine," she said, and her senses did not fool her. This was indeed her car. The Gestapo had violently taken it from her, and now the suspected thief was inside one of the businesses.

As the driver came toward the car, she was afraid, but it was none other than the director of the famous Jesuit College of Pullach, a man well-known for his high ancestry.

She said, "Excuse me, Father, are you driving this car?"

And he said, "Yes ma'am, what can I help you with?"

She said, "Excuse me, but this car is mine." She started talking about its history and how it had been taken from her.

And the priest, who was an authentic gentleman, interrupted her by saying, "Sorry miss, can you prove you are the rightful owner?"

She opened her wallet and took out her papers, which made it clear that she spoke the truth.

The priest did not permit further explanation. Instead, he took the key from his pocket and handed it to her, saying, "Pardon me, miss, I am happy to give back the car to its owner. Please take your key." He feared she would think him a thief, but she asked no more questions and got into her car.

Now the situation had changed completely. The lady who had come from her house at a slow pace was returning in an elegant vehicle, and the grand sir who had driven into Munich began his slow steps walking back to Pullach. She was very grateful to him and offered to drive him back to the college, thanking him for taking such good care of her car. Father Tatenbach had a truck and two vans at his disposal, although he never drove the truck because the Polish Jesuits were constantly using it.

As I mentioned before, there was a great, continuing need for construction materials to rebuild Pullach College. We knew that tons of doorframes, window frames, and other wood was still available at Dachau. We also knew that the Americans, not wanting to leave a trace of the foul German presence, would burn everything. An American soldier guarded the storage area day and night, marching back and forth, a seemingly invincible difficulty to overcome.

Nevertheless, a small detail of us went to the camp. The American soldier on guard was kind to us, and we could see that he had no great love for the carpentry materials. In fact, they were of no importance to him at all. What was important to him was gin or any kind of liquor he could get his hands on. This alcohol turned him into a deaf and blind man, not hearing or seeing anything that passed in front of him. We went to tempt him many times, bringing him those bottles that made his heart melt, their attraction to him more powerful than the military rulebook itself. Thanks to this lucky coincidence, we were able to take everything we needed for the restoration of the college, as well as extra materials for distribution to needy families in the area.

Our truck provided extraordinary service to the college, carrying necessary materials of every kind. It also gave us a chance to enjoy a noble pleasure, hiking through the beautiful Alpine regions. The most interesting excursion we took was to Lake Starnberg. This adventure could not be called anything other than "sheer insanity." It was along a road that snaked its way forward, between high walls of blocks of rock and unfathomable cliffs, toward a place of earthly delight. We all had dreamed of seeing Lake Starnberg, no matter the cost, because God had given this corner of German land the most incredible beauty. However, none of us had the necessary driving skills. Most of us had acted as chauffeurs, but no one had enough skill to drive that big colossus on that type of mountain road.

Despite our ineptitude, we were determined to go, and each of us tried our luck, driving the vehicle slowly, very slowly, balancing on the rock edges for some miles toward our destiny: Lake Starnberg. Blessings accompanied us from the beginning, and we had the joy and relief of arriving there without mishap. It has been said that Providence attends the audacious, and we had been audacious beyond reason, driving on that road under those circumstances.

Once we arrived at the lake, we contemplated its green waters and its clarity; its smooth surface gave us profound satisfaction and an atmosphere for serious reflection. The previous day, not a single leaf had been moving, but on this day, something invisible seemed to animate all the plants and trees. The beauty of the lake and the colors of the forest reflected in it, and was seen through softly rippling water that charmed us and filled us with delight and sweet love. We had time to think back over our journey and the grave danger of the trip, and we gave thanks to the kind hand of God who had guided the inept drivers.

We began reviewing the experience and the extremely dangerous places that could have been the death of us. When it came time to leave, we chose a man to drive the truck, one with the eye of a hunter. He had fast reflexes and would be able to see and maneuver around any difficulty on the mountainous road. This in itself was not a bit calming. He inspired our trust because of his steady personality and his total self-confidence, as well as his complete faith in the mechanics of the car. He believed the motor would tell him anything he needed to know, any sort of imperfection that existed. However, the motor could not speak and remained mute during the next dangerous adventure in our lives.

Fortified by our trust in the chauffeur, we got into our seats for the grand return journey. Before starting to move, however, we thought it was a good idea to commend our lives and souls to God and His angels. From the beginning, we noticed that the motor was working awfully hard, though we tried to attribute this to the hill we were climbing. However. even under God's protection and with the chauffeur, we began having a bad feeling. In truth, the motor was not choking from the climb, but from a lack of oil; the axis was totally dry and taking on the color of fire.

We called this to our chauffeur's attention, and he made everyone quiet with his famous saying, "If you do not understand motors, stop bothering me on the cliff's edge because everything is fine."

We opted to be quiet and not bother the man. We continued on a few more miles until the truck came to a complete and final stop. We got out and, in our ignorance, began examining the truck. One thing was evident: we were also out of gas. Our brains came to a complete stop because none of us could turn water into gas. To make matters worse, the radiator was not functioning because it was out of water. We were stuck in the middle of a narrow, mountainous, extremely dangerous road with no ability to move forward or backward, with no gas, no oil, and no water.

The sun was already preparing for its well-deserved rest, its horizontal rays shining upon our faces. We were sadly considering spending the night under the stars on the cliff's edge, covered only by a blanket of sky. Suddenly, while we prepared for an unpleasant night, a car came quickly around the mountain curve, driven by a man who had a young woman as his passenger. The car did not even attempt to squeeze between the truck and the mountainside; instead, the two individuals got out of their car and expressed a lively interest in our predicament. As the man saw our precarious situation, a smile crossed his lips. Without a word, he turned his Volkswagen around and left us. He drove to the nearest gas station and came back quickly, bringing a container of gasoline and a box of oil, then taking charge of filling the tanks.

He said, "The water you can get yourselves from any stream."

We saw that our truck was like new and that we would be able to continue our trip back to Pullach. Almost all of us talked and yelled at once like a choir: "*Danke schoen, danke schoen*" ("Thank you, thank you.").

So many *danke schoens* embarassed the man, who replied, "*Gluckliche reise*" ("Good luck with your travels"), then climbed back into his car and drove right through the tight pass and on toward the horizon. We were enthusiastic to keep going, except that we needed water for the engine, or the truck would not run. Some kilometers from where we were stalled was a small stream with crystal water, but we had no container. We tried to use our socks to carry the water, but they hardly produced a few drops. We could not move the truck, and so we stayed there for hours until the lights from another truck's reflectors broke the night.

It was a powerful truck transporting various merchandise from Munich to Starnberg. Behind the wheel sat a Bavarian driver, fat as a toad, and with two big curls of a mustache under his nose. We could not understand a single word of what must have been German. "Blah, blah, blah," he continued, but he was clever as a fox, and he did not need our commentary to tell him what was wrong. The first thing he wanted to know was if we had enough money to continue our journey. When we said we did, he gave one of us a container and told us to fill it with water, which we did. He filled the tank without difficulty and, after a few tries, the engine started humming. We thanked him for his help and, trusting the ability of our chauffeur in the darkness, headed in the direction he indicated, toward Pullach.

Instead of arriving back at the college at 6:00 or 7:00 p.m., as we said we would, our trip ended at 11:00 p.m. We were truly safe at last, and considering all our foolishness along the road, we should have been presenting ourselves at the doors of St. Peter rather than to our own gatekeeper. Discussing this trip some years later with German friends, we decided we must have had the luck of fools being protected by Divine Providence. None of us could say why thirty Polish Jesuits, exposed to the worst by our own doing, defeated the obstacles and came back safe and sound, while twenty-eight young students had died and were lost on the same cliffs along the road. Those students had an expert driver who followed the same path, saw the same cliffs and drop-offs, and rode in an excellent bus, one destined to tip over the edge, killing them all. No one knows God's plan. Is it possible that he did not want any more of our blood or our Jesuit bodies killed on German soil?

In Pullach, we could rest and enjoy our freedom, and we enjoyed the bicycles. We had the opportunity to ride out and measure the distances between cities, taking advantage of the good roads. Not a day went by when we didn't test the bicycles' resilience, as well as our own. The landscape was irresistibly inviting, and it would be a lack of courtesy to the Creator and to nature to not record this important fact.

Among the Jesuit Poles were three young men who had not yet been ordained priests, although they had fulfilled all the requirements. Among the German students was one who awaited his vows while others, functioning as priests and on happy days, could offer God's immaculate Host. Valery Kawski came up with the idea of approaching the Polish bishop in Munich and asking him to ordain the four students who were waiting. We took this idea to the director of the college, Father Tatenbach, who, considering the circumstances, accepted the plan gratefully.

The Polish bishop, Jozef Gawlina, had special jurisdiction over the Poles in Germany, and needed only a few small religious items to fulfill our request. He needed the Episcopalian symbols, which we could obtain from the German Bishops in Munich. I was sent to bring back these items and, within two days, I presented myself to the gatekeeper at the Episcopal Church of Munich. There, I asked to see the Bishop. I waited an hour, and he did not appear. In the end, he became available, and I greeted him courteously, with all the reverence his high rank in the Church of God deserved. I let him know the reason for my visit.

From the beginning, there were difficulties. He was concerned about the Polish bishop who would administer the ordinations to the three Jesuit Poles and the German.

He kept saying, "You say he is a Polish bishop? How Polish? How can a Polish bishop ordain Jesuit Poles in Germany?"

I answered, but he proceeded to openly make fun, using humiliating words directed at the bishop.

To him, this was a complete comedy, and he laughed and exclaimed, "Ah, a Pollack, a Pollack, a Pollack bishop comes to administer priestly ordinations in our dioceses. Who gives him the authority?"

I explained to him that the authority came from His Holiness, yet he continued in a sarcastic way.

Tired of his stupidity, I told him I had not come to listen to his objections but to fulfill a promise to the director of Pullach by bringing the religious symbols back with me. He said that, unfortunately, he did not have these items in his "palace" because everything was at home with his family. He gave me the name of his street and house number, and I believed every word; I went and easily found his address.

A woman opened the door and said there were no such religious items in her house. She went to ask everyone in the house just to be sure and, in a short time, returned to say that there was nothing. I could not imagine the monsignor being wrong, but I returned to the gatekeeper. I asked to exchange a few words with the bishop who, once again, made me wait for a long time. However, I was determined to bring back the necessary insignia. I had to arm myself with patience and wait until he felt like seeing me.

He finally appeared, followed by a large black dog. The dog went ahead of him, as though before the queen; he was black like coal and large as a calf, producing fear as he came forward. However, he was docile as a lamb; he approached me for all sorts of petting and gave me a copious licking. The monsignor deigned to sit on the edge of the couch and play with the dog, paying no attention to me whatsoever. Of course, his attitude made my blood boil, and still, I could not get his attention. After he was certain I had reached the peak of humiliation, he explained that I had to go along another road. He indicated the street and house number where the Episcopalian insignia could be found.

Without delaying another minute, I went to the place and encountered the same response from a different lady, who answered the door and had no idea what I was talking about.

I returned to the Monsignor. When he heard what I had to say, he replied, "You may come back at 3:00 in the afternoon because I cannot give it to you now."

I made him understand that I was not willing to come back at 3:00 in the afternoon, and that he was to give me the insignia now. He said he could not. I was so upset, I said to him, "Monsignor, what you have done today, only a German pig like you could have done." I turned around, found my bicycle, and returned to Pullach.

I arrived back at the college empty-handed, filled with anger and rage about the German priest's joke. I immediately went to Father Tatenbach and told him what had occurred. He listened calmly, worthy of his high rank, in control of himself without manifesting hostility, and told me not to worry any further. He would go to the bishop. The following day, he made his presence known at the church in Munich and, with no difficulty at all, returned with the necessary items.

The ordinations took place in the chapel of the college presided over by his Excellence Jozef Gawlina, Bishop of the Polish Army, conqueror of Monte Casino. I was master of ceremonies. One of the ministers of the college who always made things unpleasant, Prefect Korn, complained and suggested that I was not equipped for this duty.

Finally, I was forced to say, "Father, I am in charge here, and you have no role, so please leave me alone."

He complained to the director, but the director openly took my side and said to him, "Leave him alone. He knows what he is doing." After this, the ceremonies continued to the end without mishap. The celebrants thanked us profusely that everything had gone well.

New Problems

One day, we unexpectedly received the news that the MRP Vicar General awaited us in Rome, and he had given us a choice. We could go to the religious order in Belgium, where they would receive all of us, or we could divide, and some of us would be received in Rome. We split with no problems into two groups, fifteen of us going to Belgium and fifteen to Rome. Father Cieciwa was chosen to lead the group to Belgium, and I was chosen to oversee the preparations for Rome. Father Cieciwa's group had no difficulty; everything proceeded quickly and well for them.

We, however, encountered many obstacles. The only way to cross the Alps was to join an American transport whenever it was going in that direction. I went from one of their offices to the next and received a cold reception, with none of them interested in helping us make the trip. Day after day I went to them, and even though from time to time transports of Italian prisoners were being organized, no one was willing to include us.

Tired of going from office to office, I started insulting one of the officials in front of a lady who walked in with another soldier in military uniform. Perhaps they heard my high-pitched voice. The man approached me and asked for the cause of my indignation. I changed my tone and told him about the matter. The lady paid close attention, and her anger grew stronger than my own.

She gave them a royal lecture for the trouble they'd caused us. The American official, having been so rude to me, suddenly became as docile and obedient as a sheep, immediately willing to prepare transport for all we needed.

I remember quite well what she emphasized in her speech: "To all sorts of Jews, Greeks, and Italians you arrange transport, but not for the Polish?" And she demanded immediate action. The officer now acted like a sweet man who would have everything ready the following day. I expressed my thanks to the lady, and she answered in perfect Polish, "*Niema za co ja go naucze rozuma!*" ("No problem, you don't have to thank me, he learned his lesson!")

I was insane with joy for two reasons: we had achieved transport and were going to Italy and, even better, the young lady of Polish descent had given a sermon to those officials who opposed our trip. I returned to Pullach, yelling at the top of my lungs and announcing to my comrades that we would have transport the following day. We were to be ready at 6:00 in the morning.

They, in turn, yelled, "Finally, finally, we can get out of here!"

The following day, with everyone armed as soldiers for war, we were to pass before the ministry of the college, including the famous Prefect Prusacok and Prefect Korn. We readied ourselves for the appointed hour, but almost everyone became aware of something missing. One of them could not find good-enough pants because he had only shredded pieces of material to cover himself. One was missing his shoes. We were fine enough while we were at Pullach, but we had not been able to acquire anything new, and we did not want to arrive in the Eternal City like bums.

The Germans at the school had a thousand reasons to fall on their knees and bless the hands of the Polish. We were leaving them in great condition, having done much work for them, providing materials, fixing windows and doors, doing everything they needed for the reconstruction. However, thanks were not in order for us. The clever minister, smelling the air and not trusting the Polish, arrived an hour before schedule. Like one of the Gestapo, he did not express gratitude but wanted to thoroughly search every man who was leaving. Naturally, our men who had survived life in a concentration camp did not say a word or resist. They deposited everything at the feet of the less-than-noble Germans.

In this manner, the priests lost many things, including their bicycles. I suppose I should have shown the same humility, but I could not, and I knew how to use my mouth and get physical if that was required. When the German minister came in front of me and ordered me to leave everything I was taking, he expected humility and religious obedience. Instead, what he heard was a firm "no. "

I knew from experience how brutish the Germans could be, but I defended myself and my belongings. There were yelling and enough of a skirmish for a fight, but in fact, it did not go that way. My things, including my bicycle, went with me to the Eternal City.

The German who drove us said, "I will leave you at the station, and I do not care if you find transport or not; you cannot come back to the college."

He may have won, but as it happened, we lost nothing and were only slightly delayed in leaving for our destiny through the beautiful Austrian Alps.

Once we were underway, we allowed ourselves the pleasure of strolling around at leisure. Our train cabin had no sign of beds, but we were comfortable enough lying on the dirty floor to get some sleep. The noise and bumping of the train cars did not keep us from passing the night quite comfortably.

From the moment we left Munich Station, the bright celestial stars shone over us, spilling their rays onto giant blocks of snow at the top of the Alps, which paraded majestically in front of our eyes. Some centuries before, a young Pole, guided by the merciful hand of God, had crossed these same Alps, following God's destination for him to travel with Jesus. With no other angel, Custodio Stanislaw Kostka began his most daring adventure: crossing Anibla. This boy, at the age of fifteen and with no weapon other than his unlimited trust in Providence, and with no meal other than the bread of a wandering beggar, made a conquest like that of Francisco Pizarro, who had arrived at the doors of the golden Mexican Empire. Kostka had traveled on foot, been exposed to every danger and discomfort, and had walked in extreme terrain as a beggar. We were following the same road by train, riding comfortably in a luxurious carrier, one that had been ready to transport us like animals to our death but was instead taking us toward repatriation in the city of Rome, to which our Vicar General had called us.

We arrived at the first Italian station where the convoy stopped. We stepped out and into a small group of people, some with American uniforms, and we walked in different directions to learn the name of the station. It was called "Uscita." The name was unfamiliar, so we asked a gentleman and were embarrassed to learn that it was not the name of a city but instead signified "exit." While we were gone, two American soldiers entered our train car for an inspection. They took my bicycle as though it was their own, never asking about its ownership. They took it not for its cash value but for the utility it would provide them.

One of my comrades came yelling toward me. "They have stolen your bicycle! The Americans have taken your bicycle!"

This news awakened all my senses and I began running with all my strength to the place where this had happened. It was a theft without precedence, as I had never imagined the Americans to be thieves just like the Germans. To think that the Americans dared put their hands on the biggest conquest I had ever made outside the concentration camp – this was unbelievable to me!

In three gigantic leaps, I was standing next to the thief, who was about to climb onto my bicycle. I screamed that the bicycle was mine and the poor soldier, dazed but ready to fight, quickly began screaming back at me. We screamed and, to the violent gestures I used, he answered with more violent ones. When he tired of this and had easily acquired the bicycle, he turned and was ready to take it, leaving the battle.

However, something happened. Like a child having a tantrum, I struck him, not a mortal blow, but strong enough to distract him. I pounced on the bicycle and disappeared. The soldier dusted himself off without much fuss. I had my bicycle, and I felt tranquil and triumphant.

My triumph, though, was quite ephemeral because, within a short time, four other soldiers appeared. In their barbarian language, they told me to hand over the bicycle to their comrade. Another argument began. They spoke in their language, and I spoke in my own; none of us understood anything, and the whole situation was becoming comedy/drama. However, it was understood that they wanted the bicycle and I refused.

Finally, among the soldiers was one who spoke German. "It is good you speak German," I said. "I will not voluntarily give the bicycle back to the soldier who stole it from me even if you kill me."

The soldier who was interested in owning it demanded a document that proved my ownership.

I said, "I will not show my document to a bunch of thieves."

"We are not thieves," replied one of them.

I said, "I do not know if you were thieves in your private lives, but you are defending a thief, and so you belong to a group of thieves."

They went to speak to the authorities and came back with an American official. This captain was a sensible man and better educated. After greeting me in German, he asked for the document proving my ownership. Before leaving Munich, I had acquired from the Americans a certificate stating that I was the legitimate owner of the bicycle. With the paper in hand, the captain settled the argument in my favor.

The soldiers were angry, but they left the bike and document in my hands. My bicycle went back to occupy its place of honor in the train that was taking us to Rome, and it created no additional problems along the way.

THE FORTUNE-TELLING NUN

I HAD MANY THOUGHTS WHILE we traveled. I found myself remembering a religious sister whom I had met during my journey in a town called Konin. The Gestapo was holding her even though she was known in that area for her charitable acts. It was clear they did not know what to do with her. We had never met before, and I saw her sitting in front of a little table, very absorbed in playing cards. She seemed to be reading them.

I said to her, "Oh wonderful, a religious sister telling fortunes like the Gypsies."

She started to laugh and said, "If you like, sir, I will tell you what you wish."

I could not refuse and sat down with her while she read the cards.

What she said seemed to be a revelation offered as something of a joke. "I see that you are a priest, am I right? Be careful because the police seek you and will find you if they have not already done so. A young, blonde woman with blue eyes will cause you great damage, and the police will capture you because of her. A long life of suffering in jail awaits you, many sufferings, I repeat, many sufferings. The death penalty threatens you, but you will not die. I see you in the company of two women and two men, traveling in a small space on a train, and after this, you will go to a large place with many people who are more dead than alive. That will be a place of terrible suffering, where many will die of pain and hunger, and you will reach a point of death, but you will not die. After this, another long trip, not by land or sea; I don't know how you will travel, but you will be happy and surrounded by many young people."

I said to her, "Sister, what you are saying is really frightening. How do you know these things?"

She answered, "The cards say it clearly."

I said, "I do not believe in cards."

She said, "I do not care whether or not you believe. I only tell you what I see."

And she shuffled the cards and dealt them again with the same results.

I asked where she had learned to read the cards. She said it had happened through observations around her for a long time. Was the sister to be proven right? I did not believe in her Divinity or in her methods, but her premonitions all came true.

I was arrested because of a young blonde girl, and I traveled by train with two men and two women. My life became one of constant suffering. In Dachau, I was at the point of death more than once, but I did not die. I traveled to Rome, and then to a new continent by air. Against all hope, I lived in South America for twenty years, working with young people, and I have always considered these years to be the happiest of my life.

Toward Rome

We stopped in the town of Botzen and, after some hours, the locomotive blew its long whistle, and we continued on our journey. We took some deep breaths and, accelerating with a "puff, puff, puff," the train started moving. Content with my victory over the soldiers, I began the journey in a good mood. At every station, we found Papal Commission kiosks attending to prisoners and the poor. Every station had a large signboard with the words of Christ on it: "Man does not live by bread alone, but on every word that comes from the mouth of God."

We knew this lesson very well, but we were physically hungry and needed something more practical. We did not think Christ would have posted those signs if He had taken into account all the circumstances of war.

The train traveled along its route for quite some time, following the Adriatic Sea. On the horizon, two seagulls wheeled across the gray sky. Not a single ship appeared on the horizon of the sea, and a heavy peace hung over the atmosphere, interrupted from time to time by the locomotive's whistle. When we stopped again in an open field, we were told it would be an hour before the train resumed its journey.

I said to my friends, "I'm going to bathe. Who wants to come with me?"

Instead of an enthusiastic response, they laughed and made jokes about my sanity, saying that I had no bathing suit. They continued to make fun of me in general.

Without losing any more time, I exclaimed, "I am going to bathe, and whoever comes with me is as crazy as I am!"

I threw myself into the water alone and lonely, accompanied by much yelling and mockery. While some enjoyed the pleasure of seeing a crazy man in the water, I enjoyed the lovely freshness of the waters of the Adriatic Sea. We had been packed in the train like sardines in a can, and no one thought of toning down their physical aromas or toning up their moral strength with a bath.

Some Greeks were on the train, and they were worthy representatives of their athletic country. They did not make fun of me, but applauded and celebrated the swim warmly, though none of them dared join me. I was completely naked in the water amid howls and congratulations. The Greeks left the train in a mob and ran toward me to pat me on the back in recognition of my sporting nature. They allowed me to cover my wet member and brought me back to the train in triumph, shaking my hand warmly, leaving me content and slightly embarrassed. Only the sons of an athletic nation knew how to recognize the true value of a cold, audacious sport, though their attention was a bit inopportune for me.

IN ROME

Toward the end of September 1945, we arrived in the Eternal City. All of us were lodged close to the Vatican. Being in Rome for the first time, we had a profound thirst to explore and know the city. We beheld Rome, a city where the past fought against modernism, and everything had value and was worth seeing. I left the house where I was staying and threw myself into this new adventure, neglecting to note the name of the street or the house number. I had the desire to walk and wander, to arrive at places completely unknown. It was exciting and curious and interesting.

Finally, I became tired and realized I had no idea where I was going or how to return home. I kept going forward and stopped in front of a trolley, where a group of people was gathering around me to board. They pushed me into the car. I decided to sit and see where it would take me.

Then I noticed the ticket clerk. I put my hand in my pocket but found nothing, not even lint. How was I to explain myself? I could not speak Italian, and I was dressed like a bum looking for a free ride.

The ticket clerk surveyed the situation and did not waste any time. According to his Roman character, using all his authority and strength, he gave my back a big push. In the blink of an eye, I was on the sidewalk. I was treated very roughly and had no chance to explain my situation; the trolley pulled away. I was angry and followed the tracks to the next trolley stop, prepared to use some big words on the ticket clerk, but another man appeared. I decided to try to find out how to return to where I was staying.

I remembered that when I was in Poland, someone had told me it was possible to converse with Italians in Latin, which they could readily understand. I thought I would give it a try. When I opened my mouth and began conversing in Latin, the man could not understand one word. There are similarities in the origins of the two languages, but telling one from the other is difficult. I resorted to using gestures as though mute, and during this time, another trolley arrived. A man who had been watching my gestures came over and offered to pay for my ride, using gestures of his own, telling me he was a teacher of deaf/mutes.

A curious circle was forming around us. Some of the ladies were filled with compassion, saying, "Oh what a shame. These young men are in the flower of their lives and are so very unfortunate."

I was gesturing and trying to find out how to get home when the man said to me, "*Avanti senore*," indicating that I should board the trolley.

One of the ladies looked as if St. Anthony had just performed a miracle. She said to the man, "I thought you were mute, but you speak quite well. How is this possible?"

He said, "Madam, pardon me, but I am not mute, and neither is this gentleman. We both speak quite well."

She asked, "Then why did you act as though you were mutes?"

The man explained that I did not know Italian and that we had no other way to try to understand each other, so we made gestures.

The woman laughed so loudly that others asked, "What is happening?"

What a spectacle. The trolley started moving forward, and I was on board. The whole scene came to an end. The Italian man took a stack of papers from under his arm and paid for both of us, and we had our trolley ride.

We went to Rome like astronauts in their spacecraft circling the globe, and we had entered our second orbit when the ticket clerk came to ask us to pay for a second time. The man paid, and we traveled around the city a third time, with him paying again, not knowing the reason for the ride or exactly where to land. I interrupted our silence on the fourth trip to ask if, by any chance, he spoke French. He jumped up, and in French we ended our mute experience; the silence between us was terminated. He must have thought we had finally reached our last stop and could launch ourselves directly to the moon.

We did not understand each other very well in French either, and naturally, he could not believe my stupidity, that I did not know the street or house number where I was living. I'm not sure what his feelings would have been if he had known I was a Polish priest, but seeing me in a bum's jacket and a wrinkled shirt with no money made him sympathetic. Happily, it occurred to me to say the word "Vatican" because I could be able to find my way from there. This resolved the matter. He quickly found another carriage to take us there, and once we arrived, I recognized my surroundings and my house. I thanked him for all his kindness and everything he had done for me. He gave me his card; I was to call him if I was ever lost. Having acquired enough knowledge of the city, I would never again get lost in such a stupid manner.

I took advantage of my bicycle for taking trips around the

city. I did not wear a priestly cassock, and so riding the bike was easier. I knew I would have no opportunity to use it while riding, anyway. However, as they say, "Everything good is cut short, and much that is bad has no end." This saying seems to have been perfectly true in my life.

One day, as I returned joyously from riding around the city, I stumbled upon Father Assistant Antonio Preseren. He was certainly kind, and obviously far along the slope of old age. He was known for his religious humor and his resistance to any advances during the post-war period.

When he saw me entering with my bicycle, he could not refrain from suspicious exclamation: "Oh my, Father, you are modernized."

He looked at me with such distrust, perhaps even disdain, as though I was so modernized as to be beyond saving. I didn't really pay attention to his attitude, and I placed my bicycle in its place, giving it a well-deserved rest (until the next day). Then I went to my room.

Being alone, I began reading a book. Then, suddenly, an interior anxiety overtook me. This could only be attributed to the comment and attitude about my modernization, and I began thinking about this matter more seriously. Now, I could see that the priest's exclamation was not about the innocence of a child, but about a mature man whose mind may have held dark philosophies, theories, thoughts of mercy, and possibly scandal. But what scandal? The bike? Surely, not for a priest who had returned from a concentration camp and for whom the bike allowed the luxury of riding rather than using his feet like all the pious ones. I reviewed the incident, my clothing, and the bike, but did not find sufficient cause for scandal. I tried to think about this through the eyes of the Father Assistant, who, like a good priest, knowing that I had not received any virtuous or religious training while in the camp, was worried for my religious life. He had used the word "modernized" rather than *"corrupted."* With all my soul, I tried to understand his point of view.

When I was invited to the Father Vicar General's office, I knew it was because of the bicycle. I kept thinking that if Pope John XXIII had seen me riding around on a bicycle, instead of saying, "You are corrupt," he would have said, "I am happy this priest is beginning to live again by keeping up with the times." He was a man of advanced age, but he thought as a younger person.

The Vicar General preferred to speak in French, and because there was no crime scene, he asked his careful questions gently and with paternal love.

We talked a little, and then he asked, "Do you have a bicycle?"

I answered, "I do."

He asked, "Whom does it belong to?"

I said, "It is mine."

"Where have you brought it from?"

"Germany."

"Then, is it German?"

"No, it is Polish. It was stolen by German thieves, but it is Polish."

"How can you say it was stolen from the Polish by the Germans?"

"Because I have clear testimonies that attest to this."

"May I see them?"

"I do not have them with me."

"Where are these testimonies from?"

"One of them is from the bicycle itself, where a Polish name is written quite clearly."

With this, he was satisfied, and the first part of the interrogation was over. The second part began with this question from him: "Do you usually use the bicycle?"

"Yes."

"What do you use it for?"

"To travel."

"All right, but where do you go?"

"I just ride around and get to know the city."

"Do you use it to go places where Mass is being held?"

"At the moment, no, but soon I plan to use it specifically for that purpose."

The vicar was perfectly silent. He was taking deep breaths, and I knew this was not the end of the dialogue. He did not want to decide too quickly. After a short rest, which must have been psychologically stimulating for him, he said, "Perhaps you have become aware that certain priests are not pleased with your riding a bicycle around Rome."

I answered that I did not know about other priests, but that I had surprised one older priest and did not attribute much importance to what he had said. I told him, "Your reverence knows well that people of that age cannot really be trusted because their beliefs are ancient and do not go along with the times."

He said to me, "But, that is the problem. The fact that they become scandalized is worse."

I answered, "The fact that they become scandalized does not tell me anything because they are elderly, and the gospel does not mention scandals by the elderly. Instead, Jesus promised special punishment for those who scandalize the innocent: the children. He did not seek to punish anyone for scandals created by the elderly because they punish themselves with their dumb opinions."

My explanation did not please the vicar, but despite it all, he had a smile on his face when he said, "Let us leave the gospel aside and consider this from a more human and practical point of view. It is true that the use of a bicycle is not motive enough to require punishment for scandalizing the elderly. On the other hand, the elderly find it difficult to change older opinions which they have been taught. To avoid anything like this from continuing, don't you think it would be better to keep the bicycle locked in the basement?"

I answered, "Oh, that cannot be because I have serious reasons to utilize it every day."

"And may I know these reasons?" he asked.

"Yes, of course. I was in a concentration camp, and no one came out better from there; they came out worse. I came out much worse. While there, I had lost my faith, although I did continue to have some moral feeling, but not much. On the positive side, I had never had any kind of temptations, due to my physical fatigue. Now, things have changed. The temptations of life have returned to me, and they are abundant. I want to avoid them, and the only means I have to do so is the bicycle."

Then we both went very quiet, and I was allowed to keep my bicycle.

I am making light of the events that took place in Rome. However, the next chapters in the book are not to be taken lightly. They are most serious.

LUCKY SATURDAYS

MY LIFE IN EIGHT PRISONS and two forced labor camps, and finally in Dachau, was for me not only a foundation of atrocious suffering but an opportunity to see the world from a completely different perspective. Many people, when they fell into the Gestapo's hands, thought that life was over and that nothing but death awaited them. I, on the other hand, felt an awakening of some ideas that would never have entered my life had it not been for the war. It had always been said that Germans were clever, yet during my imprisonment I became aware that this was not true. They were brutal people with shallow intelligence, poorly equipped to command others. I don't know whether I was smarter, but I could see that someone clever could easily outsmart them. On one occasion, I might have escaped from prison. Another time, everything was ready for my escape, but I changed my mind on behalf of others. Those opportunities could have been referred to as Lucky Saturdays.

My greatest luck seemed to arrive on Saturdays. One Saturday, I thought up a crazy idea, and Providence blinded the guards so that I was able to accomplish a dangerous mission. Saturday luck accompanied me throughout my time in the Lodz prison. It was no less so at Ostrow, where there was not a single herb to eat except on Saturday, when I could always find a piece of bread.

In Kotzine, it was on a Saturday when I was chosen out of one hundred to help the chief of the work camp with simple chores.

On Saturdays, a package sometimes arrived from my beloved sister-in-law Helena Kozmin, the only family member lucky enough to escape the Germans. She was struggling on behalf of her two daughters, Zosia and Irene, whom the war had orphaned, but she never let more than two weeks go by without trying to send me something. I know her character well and can imagine her saying to her children, "This would taste good to us, but we are not going to eat it. We are going to send it to our Czesiek." The daughters would ignore their hunger so that their uncle might have something better to eat.

Providence seemed absent at times, especially when I was thrown into insanely dangerous places. However, as I think back on my survival, I find that God was always with me, keeping me under guard. The best example of this was at Ronau, where I had been accused unjustly, brought before the authorities, and questioned harshly for many hours. They began to search my body, for something was right in front of them; they were blind and could not see it, and they could not prove anything against me.

Dachau was the last place on my journey during my life as a prisoner. It was a terrible place of inhumane suffering and extermination. It was said that God's entrance would be prohibited there. God did not seem to be with us, but perhaps the Blessed Virgin was there on His behalf, entering and extending her veil of protection over some of us. By the end of the war, many had confessed that she was always with them, hidden but not gone, involved in the course of our lives and in the hearts of those who trusted in her.

Her first favor was sending a German priest to me, not a wealthy man but one who would bring some pieces of bread. He seemed to forget about me during the week, but on Saturdays he gave me a large piece of bread. During my work outside the camp walls, I never encountered any chances to find food. Nevertheless, on a Saturday, the unpredictable happened. We had finished our jobs and were starving and exhausted as always. We were about to start the march back to the prison.

I was filled with bitterness, reproaching the Virgin Mary in my mind, saying, "How is it possible that you have forgotten me?"

Suddenly, I felt a strong pain in my stomach. I broke from the line and ran to the guard, begging to be allowed to go to the bathroom. He could see the pain on my face, but he screamed at me to get back in line. My cramps were so strong that I threw myself at him. He finally allowed me to run, and I got there just in time. Next to me was something wrapped in dirty paper. I took it in my hands and unwrapped it. My eyes almost left their sockets. There were some pieces of bread, half in good condition and half rotten. I knew it would take too much time to eat them, though my stomach had been relieved and I was no longer in pain. Therefore, I tore them into bits and stuffed them everywhere in my clothes. I was able to eat them later.

This is not a fairy tale, nor do I want to exaggerate the protection of our Virgin Mary. I never asked her to give me stomach pain to obtain bread. However, if that was more convenient and natural for her, I cannot object to her malice. She did not call upon a miracle when one was not absolutely needed, but she knew how to provide a starving man with food.

Something Small Has Become Large-Scale

For those of us who witnessed Hitler's Nazi formations, men in perfect uniforms, boots, and gloves without a stain, brilliantly parading before the eyes of so many spectators, it is almost impossible to comprehend that each day, they were murderers. You have read the stories from inside Dachau and beyond of the millions of lives lost. I am now talking about the Germans as master thieves, master criminals without shame. It seems that a single person cannot use rational reasoning to understand the degradation they caused, but the facts and evidence cannot be denied. The events of the war have indicted and humiliated the German nation, reducing it from the heights of an eagle to the level of a scavenging bird of prey.

From the first contacts with the Gestapo, in my presence and in the presence of countless others who have narrated their stories, they exhibited their cold-blooded nature while displaying a triumphant smile, stealing not only the lives of men and women but their homes and their goods, which were indispensable to the lives of families. Thousands of citizens from all the countries the German troops occupied could give proof of these acts. Systematic and daily theft from kitchens, halls, rooms, museums, churches, and other religious places showed the Germans to be people who stole and gained wealth on the backs of others. During their exultant military adventure, which was to terminate in a crushing defeat, they took every possible opportunity to fill their pockets.

When Mussolini conquered the Ethiopian Empire, the Italians themselves told a sad truth in the form of a joke: "When a man steals a country, he declares himself emperor, but when a poor man steals something insignificant for survival, he is sent to prison." This truth can be applied to the German nation, which invaded every neighbor. They stole on the utmost scale, and when the war began, they were entitled to the glorious name of conquerors. When poor people, who lost everything to the Germans, turned to the black market as their only means of receiving food and continuing to live, they were locked in prison cells and treated as the worst of thieves.

Goebbels, himself, in the magazine "*Das Reich*," published his news, and anyone who knew the facts and the truth would have been filled with rage. To justify Hitler and his military, Goebbels made the argument that the attacks on Poland were a German obligation, that the invasion was done to save the poor Poles from dying of hunger. From this alone, and there are hundreds of other facts to support my opinion, it is clear that Goebbels and Hitler had the same father: Satan, the father of all lies. The entire world knew that war was waged against Poland because it was a nation opposed to the realization of Hitler's dream of taking over the world. As far as the Goebbels article is concerned, in only six months the Germans stole so much wheat and other grain and fruit from the Eastern territory of Poland that the wagons could have reached from Kiev all the way to Paris. They went on to steal every art treasure, every machine, and all the food from Poland's people. The goal of helping Poland was not the reason for the start of the Second World War. The Germans took the forests, the land, the homes and lives of anyone and everyone in their paths.

I can't possibly present the total damage that Poland suffered at the Germans' hands. If one believed what was written in *Krystall*, a somewhat shady publication that was generally accepted, and that was written on behalf of Germany and edited in Hamburg by Cajus Bekker, the German losses were extremely high. It said that Hitler had launched 1,875 planes of different caliber against Poland; among those, 285 were completely destroyed and 279 were seriously damaged and incapable of further use. This did not include aircraft launched from German marine vessels. This was the response from a starving country that needed German rescue.

On October 3, 1939, Governor Frank published an order from the Führer, directed at the German army, from his head-quarters in Krakow: *"The only way to handle Poland will consist of exploiting this country without any consideration, taking all the edible products, their prime materials, the machinery, their institutions, etc., necessary for the German war economy, and to ensure all categories of workers are to be sent to Germany, to reduce conjunctively the Polish economy at the absolute minimum for simple survival of the population, closing all the cultural institutions, in particular schools and technical colleges with the purpose of stopping the formation of a new Polish elite. Poland will be treated like a colony. The Poles will be slaves of the German Grand Reich."*

In 1942, Frank wrote (in response to this maniacal order), *"Strength has been used to rip everything from this province that could possibly be taken."*

From many sources, it is clear that Poland was not the only country offering such a magnificent opportunity to the Germans.

France lost riches of every sort. Let the tons of grain taken serve as an example, the value beyond 184,500,000,000,000,000 francs.

In 1943, Russia, a friend of Germany's in the past, experienced a loss in stolen livestock alone of more than nine million cows, twelve million pigs, thirteen million sheep, and what else? Who will ever know?

Italy lost millions as well. And there were many others. This was the reason Germany's army was so well-supplied on all fronts and could maintain itself for all those years. In addition, the lack of resources in most other countries made it impossible to mount a revolution against the Germans. The entire world looked upon Germany with astonished eyes and admired its "iron discipline." Despite the bombing of their countries, daily life continued for many people. Admiration of Hitler's plan and of Goebbels' published words was forgotten when more than twelve million people from different countries were offered on the German altar like a commodity. Those twelve million workers, brought from all over Europe, working for Germany and its hated army, were sent with ease to places where society had no responsibility. These people did not represent any value other than slaves to a master. They received payment in the form of the loss of their own blood and lives.

The Organization

Following the testimony of one of its first prisoners (his name is John, but I do not recall his last name), the inauguration of Dachau occurred in March 1933. The first prisoners were employed in the drainage of an enormous swamp, which is now the region where Dachau exists. The construction and opening of Dachau were received favorably by the inhabitants of the neighboring town of Dachau, which gave its name to the famous camp. They saw a brilliant future ahead, and there was not a single protest. On the contrary, people living in the area expressed sincere gratitude to Himmler for this addition to their community.

Those same people have now adopted an attitude completely contrary to their support of the concentration camp, Dachau, trying to defend their honor and innocence: "*Wir sind uberal belogen worden*" ("We were completely duped", they now say.

But can we believe their perfect ignorance when all those cruelties were carried out right under their noses?

When it came to the organization of Dachau, there were two spheres of control: external, in the hands of the Gestapo; and internal, in the hands of the prisoners themselves. The camp administration was more or less in this form:

Higher than all the rest: Lager Commandant

Following his orders were: Politic Department, divided as follows.

Camp Section: This section was formed by
    Lagerfurhers
    Raportfurhers
    Blockfurhers
Personnel Section: This section was formed by
    Stabscharfurhers
    Personnel Department
    Transportation Department
    Crematorium Department
    Radio Department
    Labor Department
    Espionage Department
Administration:
    Food
    Clothing
    Room
    Finances
    Internal section
    Kitchen section
In the *Political Department*, two groups existed:
    S.S. Hospital (Internal Hospital)
    S.S. Security Group (Station for Malaria)
The strict internal structure was composed of elements, including officials and prisoners:
    Lager Commandant
    Lagerfurher
    Raportfurher
    Blockfurher

VernehmungsFührer: Office of the political division, responsible for security matters, discipline, justice, and punishments

CommandoFührer: In charge of the worker groups and transportation

> *ArbeitseinsatzFührer*: Chief of the works
>
> *Lageraltester*: A prisoner, like a head of the camp
>
> *Lagerschreiber*: Secretary general of the camp
>
> *Schreibstube*: Office for work
>
> *Blockaltester*: Chief of the barracks
>
> *Revier Capo*: Chief of the hospital
>
> *Stubenaltester*: Chief of the apartments

All those directly above were at the disposition of the Political Department.

No doubt, among the commanders of the Political Department, the most noticeable ones were Pietrowski and Weiss. Among the Lagerfurhers, the weightier figures were Zill, Radwitz, Jarolin, Trenkle, Hoffman, Jung, Kuhn, and Rupert. Trenkle and Kuhn also had duties as *Raportfurhers*. Along with Bachler, these names were engraved deeply in the minds of the Polish priests while they were in control of us. The complete vigilance of the concentration camp was in the hands of the S.S., led by a man named Totenkopf. However, the S.S. did not have much personal contact with the prisoners.

Helping the Germans in their dirty work were the *Schwerverbrecher*; these were prisoners who were criminals, pleased to serve the Germans. They were employed in all positions of importance, such as *Lageraltester* and other titles. These men carried out the orders of the *Verwaltunstab*, the true owners of the lives and deaths of the prisoners.

A typical situation follows, when the *Unterscharfurher* (underFührer) were served by subordinates, prisoners who readily took part in the elimination of other prisoners.

The *Unterscharfurher* would ask the subordinates, "*Wievel personen haven sic hier heute?*" ("How many people are here today?")

Let us suppose the answer was, "*80 herr, underscharfurher schon, gut morgen aber ich mochte hier nur 60 schen.*"Eighty, sir, underFührer this morning already, but, tomorrow, however, I might see only sixty here." The number of people had to be less each time the question was asked; in this way, thousands of prisoners were eliminated by the subordinate prisoners themselves.

Without exaggeration, it can be said that the lives and deaths of the prisoners rested in the hands of the *Lageraltesters* and the other officers. These people were ordinarily of poor education and had been drafted from among the prisoners themselves to carry out these jobs. Almost all were of the communist party and learned to specialize in the art of flattery, boastful to their grand masters, adapting to the vigilant conditions of the moment. They protected and defended their positions at the cost of their comrades' lives. Their bloody hands performed most of the cruelties inside the camp. In addition, most of them were perfect instruments for their bloodthirsty chiefs, from whom they received their daily orders. They followed orders, but also had every opportunity to use cruelty at their own initiative.

The system of work was divided into three camps:

Internally, within the camp;

Semi-externally, working with the S.S. in the camp;

Externally, on plantations, farms, and fabrics, working entirely outside the camp on land owned by the cities and the town of Dachau.

In front of the work commands, there was always an officer, almost always a communist. The most famous among them were Kuno Reike and Jules Schatetzle. Schatetzle was sent to another camp in 1944 because of his plan to organize a conspiracy of some kind while in Dachau.

The internal camp was divided into blocks and *Stuben*. Each block had a *Blockaltester* (block-oldest), *Studenaltester*, *Blockschreiber* (block writers), and *Stubenschreiber* (room writers). All their duties depended on the structure of the S.S. Work in the offices gave a prisoner the best chance for survival, as those positions offered the easiest conditions. For that reason, there was constant fighting among the groups for those positions. Of course, the S.S. were insanely happy about these fights and rivalries, and were pleased when the men lacked solidarity.

For easy recognition, the prisoners carried symbols on their chests; each had a different color and a different meaning:

The Polish wore the letter "P."

Jehovah's Witnesses wore the color black.

Jews were marked with the Star of David.

Homosexuals wore a pink triangle.

Politicians wore the color red.

Gypsies wore the color blue.

Criminals wore the color green.

JUST THEM?

MY FIRST ENCOUNTER WITH JEWISH people during the Second World War occurred in Golina. Those were critical circumstances, with the Gestapo persecuting so many. I had the opportunity to help save the life of a young man (while endangering my own life), and the young man's father gave me a gift of thanks, a small, exquisite mirror so that I might see the different aspects of my own face. On the back of that mirror was a completely naked woman, but I did not appreciate the gift because of its decadence.

Then, in the city of Kalisz, I had an opportunity to help a Jewish woman, the daughter of a wealthy family that swore to end her life because she had converted to Catholicism. She said to me, "My parents have sworn to kill me for accepting the teachings of Christ, but no power can keep me from Him from the moment I have known Him." She spoke with such firmness and faith that I helped her go her own way, although she would continue to be exposed to a thousand difficulties.

When I was condemned to the workforce at Kotzine, I worked alongside seven Jews who had been sent there for the same purpose. Unaccustomed to physical labor, I was falsely accused by one of the men of being lazy, a denouncement that almost cost me my life.

At Dachau, I offered my blood for transfusion into a young

Jew. We shared our blood, and he recovered from that day forward. Apart from that experience, I had very good relations with the Jewish medic from Moscow and another group of Jews at the camp. By far, the largest group of Jews came from the Balkan countries – men, women, and children whose numbers were between 1,000 and 1,500. They thought they were coming to Dachau to begin a new life; all of them were sent into the gas chamber.

There is no doubt that the Jewish community is correct in letting the world know about the atrocities committed against them: six million dead at the brutal hands of the Nazis. However, many people were taken from Polish territory, and the number of Poles who were killed is largely unknown. When people refer to the Holocaust, they think of the killing of Jews; I would caution them to remember the hellish sufferings of all the people, including a terribly high number of Poles in the concentration camps and the infamous ghetto of Warsaw.

Many years after the war, I attended an exhibit in Springfield, Illinois, which told of the events of the Holocaust. I was deeply disappointed in the lack of attention paid to people who lost their lives and who were not Jewish. There was a martyrdom to the Jews and a sincere public response of compassion on behalf of their suffering, which is entirely accurate and good. However, there were so many millions of others. According to *Der Weg* from Bern, Switzerland, the number of deaths from executions in the camps was eleven million. Other numbers are as follows: outside the camps, 5,500,000; from bombardments, 2,860,000; from military operations alone, 14,450,000. In total, 33,810,000 human beings.

Why did the exhibit not mention the number of Poles? How many people were killed trying to help others of every nationality being taken by the Nazis? How many were killed by collaborators within our own cities?

Throughout my life, there have been discussions of why the Poles and the Jews had hatred toward one another. There is no single answer. I know that the relationships between the cultures had not improved after the war, when the Jewish families were the only people who were a tribute at the time of the Holocaust and beyond.

There are many stories of this hatred. "Why do you hate the Jews?"

"Because they are Jews."

"Why do you hate the Poles?"

"Because they are Poles."

And there are good stories of Catholic children who had lost their parents in the Warsaw Ghetto and were adopted by Jewish families – Jews who had migrated to the United States and inherited the farms of Polish families. I would emphasize the Lord's commandment that says, "Love one another because if not, the two of you will go to hell; you for hating me and I for not loving you."

NEITHER ONE NOR THE OTHER...
THEN, WHO?

WHO DOES NOT KNOW ABOUT the events that occurred in the multiple concentration camps during the Second World War? Thinking about them from a moral or philosophical view, we have the impression that it would be better to descend into our graves than to leave these memories to the next generations. However, the war itself is, by far, the best teacher of the evil man who is capable of committing a crime when life is lived without moral guidance or Christian principles.

Nevertheless, Hitler's own attitude is invited into countries that seek to cover everything as though the war did not exist. Many who lived through the war have said, "Future generations will not believe this."

Two generations have already passed, and not only have people forgotten about the atrocities of the war, but there are new efforts to ignore the truth and, in so doing, to sanctify evil. Who of today's German youth knows their real history? Just as the German government has cleaned up the blood of the cadavers in the concentration camp of Dachau and many others, so does that same government make substantial efforts to not tell the new generations about the true horrors of the war. If their purpose is to erase an embarrassing defeat of their country and create new roads for the glorious triumph of the German empire, another Hitler will gladly walk down these new roads.

The German, fed throughout many years by the revolutionary idea of his absolute superiority among all nations, began believing that he *was* a superman and that Germany's destiny was to dominate the world – a world willing to submit like slaves to a superior culture. Hitler did not invent this philosophy, as slaves have existed throughout history. However, he was able to crystallize it very well, enforcing his will with brutal force, violence, and complete indifference to suffering.

According to Christ's teachings, we are compelled to feel compassion for the weak and to be moved by human tears and misery; we recognize man's defects and ask pardon for his faults. These are noble characteristics that reflect the greatness within Christian virtue. In Hitler's theory, however, these qualities are humiliating defects to be loathed and rejected, qualities that weaken and degrade the "superman," whose destiny is to be master of the world. To the young Hitlerian, the brutal mistreatment of others and the discovery of new ways to exact suffering are like cold rocks, piled toward a peak of aspiration, in the formation of his strength and greatness. To anyone outside this system, it is impossible to comprehend these men who were converted into true beasts, feeding on any human weakness and coldly spilling human blood.

When Hitler rose to supreme power in Germany, the land was already well-prepared for the cultivation of his aspirations. The German people had been raised by their own philosophers, in centuries past, to feel exalted above other men. In such circumstances, Hitler had nothing more to do than ignite the wick, leaving all Europe in flames, and to press a button so that figures would show up and dance to the music of their musician.

At the beginning of his career, Rosenberg was already invoking the greatness of Hitler in *Volkischer Beobachter zum 34 Geburstag XX* ("Volkischer observers to the 34 Geburstag XX") on April 20, 1933: "He is hated and loved, just like everyone of greatness."

Henrich Hoffman, the photographer of the greatest men in the political world, mentions in his book, *I Was Hitler's Friend*, the high compliments from Lloyd George referring to the Führer's persona: "Thank God we have such a wonderful Führer."

Winston Churchill seems to have surpassed all fawning when, in the *Times* of 1938, he published an open letter to Hitler: "If a comparable disaster to what happened in Germany in 1918 happened to Great Britain, I would beg God to send us a man of such strength and temper."

The capitulation of France was another motive to praise the greatness of Hitler; Keitel exclaimed triumphantly, "You are the greatest military leader of all time."

It is clear that in such an atmosphere, Hitler's wings grew along with his tiger's appetite, helping him believe that God called upon him not only to lead the world but to *be* a god to new generations. When an insane man is in the company of other insane men, he benefits greatly from the climate of support and the compliments of other high-ranking men.

I can imagine Hitler's interpretation of the words of Jean-Paul Sartre as if they were said directly to him: "*Il faul tuer pour gagner le ciel*" ("We have to kill to win heaven"). Those words were his plan of action. Kill to ensure other countries would follow him. Kill to ensure that the fruits of those countries, bathed in blood with millions annihilated, would be his. Kill any type of individual or nation that resisted his plan.

However, Hitler alone cannot be blamed for the incomparable injustices that occurred, as he was not on an isolated island. He was only a man who lived, thought, and acted upon his own impulses and who was supported and influenced by many around him. He was the principal engine of his movement, but he had many collaborators, including Himmler, Bormann, and Goering. Himmler was chief of his operations and was deeply responsible for the perpetration of war crimes. Henrich Hoffman's book quoted him as saying, "I was Hitler's friend."

Himmler was a provincial man, selfish and sly, who compensated for his lack of intelligence by devoting himself to Hitler. Like a diplomat in agriculture, a formerly peaceful owner of a poultry farm, he had a face for all situations. With the motion of his small hands, he signaled the elimination of millions of human lives and changed the template of the European continent for years to come.

I actually fared better as a prisoner living under the supervision of the Gestapo in the concentration camp than did many civilians eliminated by the S.S. Gestapo and the S.A. (*Sturm Abteilung* Stormtroopers), who massacred them quickly without a single exception. The S.A. was an assault unit and the party's strong arm; they organized and participated in spreading all types of terror. Their crimes were particularly effective among civilians. Everywhere they went, their crimes empowered them.

Within the concentration camps, the worst men were the "block testers" (those who had been in the block the longest) and the officers who interpreted the orders of their bosses. The lives of thousands of human beings were in their hands. They were the real killers of their brothers. Their indoctrination was tragic. Imagine them receiving orders from their bosses and somehow justifying and carrying out those orders. A vicious circle was formed, with the Gestapo officers giving orders and responsibilities to their subordinates, and the subordinates blinded by obedience to those who ranked above them.

Adolf Hitler was not a dry, rational man. He was a passionate demagogue from whose mouth flowed words of promise, capable of dragging men with cold hearts toward a golden future. Germany's youth lined up to follow him, and German families gave tacit permission for their children to take up a nationalist movement. In this way, Hitler had a malignant effect on the spiritual lives of his followers, dominating adults and children with his propaganda. Young people in particular displayed a frenetic enthusiasm for him, parading and screaming, "*Heil Hitler*," which echoed on the plazas, in the streets, and in the valleys and mountains, quickly becoming a symbol of fidelity to a supreme master.

This enthusiasm penetrated the walls of religious convents as well, creating a common line of thought and collaboration. I once spoke with a Catholic priest, a man of advanced age, who confessed with sadness what had happened in his convent. Hitler's political program blinded the religious youth who lived there, enough so that out of eighty-four students, only three remained in the community. The remainder hung their cassocks on pegs and threw themselves into the fight for the Führer and his high patriarchal dreams. This fanaticism – claiming for itself the supreme sacrifice, the youth of a nation – was not limited to small circles. Its rings widened and extended until they reached the top of the hierarchy, the heads of the Catholic Church. Some of them were faithful sons of their country, but they were not obligated to follow Hitler's course. They quickly followed Hitler, adhering to his manifesto and providing support for his military aims.

Evidence of church support is clear in the pages written by Professor Gordon A. Zahn in *German Catholics and Hitler's War*, Sheed and Ward, New York, 1962, referring to the time of Hitler's aggression into Czechoslovakia. Mr. Zahn writes, "The arraignment in the fight of Sudetenland in 1936 has been accepted for the goals with an effusion of enthusiasm. It can be largely attributed to the telegram of congratulations sent to Hitler from the German Cardinals, in which they express their feelings of sincere happiness caused by the stop of an imminent armed conflict."

Preceding this telegram, Cardinal Bertram, a national leader, sent a letter to 300,000 Germans in Sudetenland who were members of the Diocese of Wroclaw. In the letter, he asked for unconditional submission to the powers of Hitler as their moral duty as citizens.

Dr. Zahn, a Catholic man, could not understand the position of the German episcopate, which seemed to openly oppose the words of Pope Pius XI. In his encyclical, *Mit Brennender Sorge*, which spoke against German aggression, Dr. Zahn writes, "That extraordinary help in legally protesting a consciously revolutionary and authoritarian regime, along with blind obedience by the civil authorities and moral approval by German Catholicism, has served as history would prove in the years to follow, to ensure universal help for German aims during the second world war and even before it began the cruel march of true German aggression."

The cruel march began on September 1, 1938, a day dedicated to the cause of the war. Throughout that time, the bishops spoke about their desire to encourage Catholic soldiers to comply with their obligations according to the will of the Führer, in making sacrifices and vowing allegiance to his will. After the occupation of Poland and the capitulation of France, Belgium, and Holland, a pastoral letter from eight bishops in Bavaria was published in 1941 and read on the first Sunday of Lent.

Here is a fragment from that letter: "Dearly Beloved…We come to you today with the words of admonition, with paternal love and solicitude, with the purpose of inspiring you toward complete dedication in the service of the *Vaterland*, and beloved *Heimant* country, compliance consistent with our duty and the profound recognition of our mission. We Germans form a great community of life and luck; we Christians form a community of love and faith in Christ."

A Catholic, upon hearing such advice in favor of compliance with duties, could easily conclude that despite the Hitlerian police's anti-religious aspects (something they certainly realized), the church officials remained united behind the military efforts.

Bishop Kampfmuller from Augsburg directed a call to the soldiers at the war fronts in which he highlighted the value of the special sacrifice of Christian soldiers. Taking their strength in faith, he told them that the Christian is always the best comrade, always faithful to the standards, whether in war or peace.

The Bishop of Wurzburg, Mathias Ehrenfriend, believed in his duty to invite his flock to trust in God with complete dedication and loyalty. "Soldiers" he affirmed, "comply with your duty toward Hitler and the *Vaterland*. According to the teachings of the sacred scriptures, he said, '…and those who remain at home must demonstrate unity and love, in peace and trust, as a fountain of strength and confidence for those who fight at the front.'" Nowhere in his declaration did he ask whether the war Hitler was waging was a just war.

Keeping in mind these declarations from the heads of the Catholic Church, it is not surprising that the soldiers, without a difference in creed, carried on their buckles the words "God Mit Uns," or "God Be With Us."

After seeing the ruins left after the war, we can understand the prophecy of one of the German colonels who, before the end of the war, had foreseen Germany's complete defeat: "If God exists, we have already lost the war for the barbarities our troops have caused the Polish." His words and the outcome of the war demonstrate not only that God exists, but that He was on the side of the innocents, not on the side of the Germans, despite their belts. Those words crowned the absolute ruin of the Hitlerian regime.

So that the reader may form a clear opinion about the Polish and the importance of moral values that Catholicism provides in life, I will now present "The Polish Prayer on the Brutal Anniversary of the German Attack into Poland."

"Oh Lord, who is the memory of the world, make us always remember the route and purpose of our walk around unknown lands until our purpose is complete.

"Thou art the inexhaustible memory and always vigilant. Make us not forget our faith, nor our tongues, and let us not lose sight of the stars, which guide us in the land of our fathers.

"We beg you remember that our loyalty was shut off with bad faith, and for that, our labored morals were fed with the bread of treason, and we have been given bitter betrayal to drink.

"Count, Oh Lord, how many of us have fallen to the bullets of Katyn and Palmira; how many were incinerated in the ovens of Auschwitz, Ravenbrueck, and Belsen; and how many were devoured on foreign soil, the thousands in concentration camps in the north; how many fell on the battlefields of Europe, Asia, and Africa, in the air and in the sea and in open combat, and in the underground battle in which a man encounters the power of all that is bad.

"Count, Oh Lord, the tears lost by our mothers, wives, sisters and daughters, the infinite pain of their tormented hearts through fear and horror.

"Measure in your hands our spilled blood and the immensity of our sacrifices in vain.

"Allow us the benefits of a permanent peace, and forgive our enemies as you have forgiven the repented thief.

"Make us forget our hate and allow us to love each other like good neighbors and sons of the same Father."

To finish these reflections, it seems appropriate and reasonable to quote the paper written to the German people by Franz Werfel in his *"Die Letzten Hundert Tagen"* ("The Last Hundred Days"), as follows:

"Men of Germany, if we mean to resurrect our souls, we must first recognize our faults. You were men and women of Germany, responsible for the terrible years 1930 through 1945. You were German accomplices of the assassination of millions and millions of Europeans, peaceful and innocent, who did not threaten anyone. You were, men of Germany, committing acts of cruelty that would have made even Satan angry."

IF YOU THINK A LITTLE, YOU CAN

A CURIOUS READER MAY HAVE remaining questions about things this book did not mention. For example, one might ask, "To what do I attribute my long stay in the concentration camp, despite the inhumane conditions in which I had to live?" I would answer that I was at the edge of death all that time due to extreme exhaustion. My lowest weight was sixty-five pounds, all bones and feet.

I think the first reason I stayed alive was that I always divided my bread into three parts and spread the eating of it throughout the day, along with the smallest sip of water. It was very little solid food but something to sustain my body. No one else proceeded in this way that I can remember; others immediately ate everything that was put into their hands.

Another factor was the psychological terrain. I am inclined to believe completely in the influence of the spirit in helping me stay alive. I tried to practice this adage every day: "*Live only for today, and be peaceful on this day.*"

I tried to put into practice the gospel's advice and to not look ahead and think about tomorrow or the days to come. I tried to let the experience of each day guide me and I closed my mind to the possible suffering that might occur the next day. I comforted myself by saying that today was not so terrible, that it was bearable, which let a little light into the deadly situation. Many friends in prison questioned how they could continue enduring such suffering, deconstructing the present with incredible fear for the future. In this way, they could not find any reason to go forward, each day bringing them closer to death. I tried to grab every bit of energy to win the day's battle to live on.

Another psychological factor was the practice of the lessons of St. Ignacio, which, if summarized, could be said as "One of Indifference." On the gate of the concentration camp was the sign "*Arbeit Mach Frei*." The prisoners interpreted this as indicating "There Is No Way Out of Here," which created a profound sense of desperation. Many inmates felt empty, with little or no instinct or desire to continue living in "this hell." However, I found great spiritual strength in trying to practice indifference or equal respect for life and death. Of course, I did not want to die, but I also did not fear death. This gave me a steadier equilibrium so that I was not tormented every moment of every day and night; it fed me optimism.

GOD AND THE SUFFERING OF MAN

A READER ORIENTED TOWARD A spiritual life could ask about the formative value of suffering. It has often been said that suffering is the builder of man's greater character. This is a delicate point and difficult to accept as the truth. Many prisoners taken to the camps had never truly suffered and were completely unprepared for what awaited them. I had experienced very difficult tests from illness, both internal and external, so that when I was arrested, my initial imprisonment did not shock me as much. It is hard to deny that some suffering may strengthen a person's reserve. However, the type of suffering that occurred in those camps, as well as the duration of the suffering, was marked more by dark desperation and the destruction of human will and character. When human beings see only pain and death, and when everything around them is destroyed, when their bodies are reduced to bones with only a miserable, thin coating of skin, no reserve is left in them, no energy or initiative or optimism necessary to continue living. On the contrary, one begins to decompose, and death is very close. Just as moths or silverfish eat every bit of the most precious clothing, this type of suffering eats away at the human soul until no hope exists of repairing the damage.

Having submitted to all types of suffering, I cannot, morally and psychologically, see it as God's Divine Will or submit to it at all without rebellion. Such suffering reduces a man to a vegetative state. If we are to see it all as a kindness from God, He would be a father no one would ever love. For me, the experiences were like a surreal dream that man created. The constant pain and beatings birthed hatred in me, the worst a man could feel in his life. So many years have passed since I left the camp, but this has not lessened. The example of Christ on the cross as a model man in pain does not help me. He suffered for a number of hours, and then it was over. The prisoners in the camps bore pain every day, some of them every day for many years, and God was no longer attractive to them; He became repulsive. This most profound and base result informs my conviction that extended and terrible suffering kills the great character of man rather than enlightens him.

GERMAN MORALITY

WHAT ARE WE TO THINK of the effects of Hitler's movement on the morals of the German people? To know this, one must know their moral state before times of war. My knowledge of this subject is poor, and I do not feel I can answer effectively. It was as though Germans had a double reality. I saw them in civilian life, in the military, and during the formation of the Hitlerian party their character depended upon the circumstances. Before the war, speaking with them on the street or recognizing their emphasis on education, I took pleasure in seeing and speaking with them. They were people of good humor, a bit ponderous perhaps, but natural and amiable, with a slight tendency toward feeling superior as a culture. However, once the war movement began, they were malicious and perverse, often demonic, dealing in human blood, proceeding without compassion, people completely dangerous to humanity. In this light, they were not formed as God had made them in the world. They showed themselves to be the complete opposite of supermen; instead, they were the worst vile creatures born into this world.

No doubt, the Hitlerian movement left a stain on them. They moved at the command of "Kill, kill if you are an authentic German. Kill all those who oppose Hitler's ideas." It was their law: "Kill the weak, the sick, those incapable of working for themselves, kill anyone who is suspicious. Kill as though you are beasts." They were reduced to savages who followed a dark command. If I wanted to judge those who followed Hitler, I would say that, with few exceptions, they deserved the same concentration camps they had established for the innocents they slaughtered.

In my opinion, the great Germans, noble and truly loving of their country, must concentrate all their efforts on positively influencing future generations. They must tell their history fully, everything about the Hitler movement, with the purpose of protecting their youth from those perverse ideas and aberrations that can so easily infiltrate the mind and spirit, ideas without any sense of morality or divine spirit.

Lastly, I do not want to leave without touching on a question that would interest anyone who witnessed German brutality during the war. How can it be that they enjoyed the suffering of others so much, especially when their own hands caused it? It can be said that good people, normal ones, do things that are not always loving. They sometimes avoid doing evil deeds because they fear being caught and punished for their actions. However, during the war, millions of spectators saw Germans enjoy brutality toward others and making others suffer, readily adhering to the philosophy that those acts made them more "super" than any demonstration of compassion could. They did not fear capture and punishment because the movement fully sanctioned their actions. Cruelty was often not required (after all, no one was watching at the beginning of the war). However, by committing violent acts, they could be recognized and rewarded as authentic sons of Germany.

Also, Germans were blinded by the march of their armies and the constant propaganda and repeated promises of a superior race, repeated a thousand times by their chief. They were blinded by victory, believing that the only people remaining after the war would be the German supermen and their slaves. In this way, they lost their conscience, their sense of responsibility, and all their human feelings. They achieved two things: the loss of guilt, which was a heavy burden, and a cold liberty over those who did not have a right to live.

Another explanation for unmitigated violence and cruelty might be that man does not commit evil because he never has a chance to do so without consequences. The Germans did not lack opportunity. On the contrary, they lived and breathed an atmosphere of perversity. And, like normal men, who live and breathe the air without taking notice of it, they pushed themselves toward new brutalities, using their education and natural aggression for evil purposes like a river rushing into a valley.

We could say that the German people saw themselves as dragged toward committing atrocities. The same people might have followed the principles and morals of Christianity, but they were born into the school of Adolf Hitler; they lost their individualism and their laws and adopted an abnormal path while choosing the new "morals" of the Nazi movement. They threw away true morality. The new *Ubermensch* was covered by the protective wings of an ideal, one that would make them supermen. Truly, they never succeeded in being more than what they really were: common and quite miserable human beings.

EPILOGUE

WHEN THE WAR AGAINST THE Germans erupted, a small man by the name of Peter appeared at the Allied military headquarters as a volunteer and registered as a soldier in the twenty-first infantry regiment with shouts of "For the country, for the Faith, and for Mary!" He launched into the war with enthusiasm worthy of a great hero. After fighting courageously for a few days, he fell wounded. However, despite the blood he left in his shoeprints, he continued forward toward the invaders. Finally mortally wounded, he – his body – fell on the battlefield, the rifle still in his hand.

Now began his route toward a new life. In the starry palace of St. Peter, the blessed Saint was ready to go out for a brief stroll in the gardens adjacent to the heavens. By mistake, he left the keys to the Celestial Gate with his helper, a little angel. The angel, proud of all the trust his patron had shown him, began playing with the keys in his hand. Then, he came up with the idea of opening the gate, just to take a look at the road that came from earth toward the heavens.

At a short distance, he noticed a Polish soldier marching toward him with braveness, proper to men who have been in the fires of war. The angel looked on with attention, interested at the same time by the uniform and what the man carried.

The small man Peter approached the doors of heaven and,

seeing a little angel, reverently saluted him with the profound religious words: "Praise be to Jesus Christ."

The angel responded, "Always and Forever."

The little angel, seeing the Polish soldier in the correct posture and praising Jesus with such reverence, opened the door widely for him. Peter, taking advantage of the situation, slid in delicately and, in a second, found himself in heaven with a gun in his hand.

Once there, he was fascinated by such beauty as he had never seen in his previous life. Strolling along quietly, he suddenly found himself in front of a bearded gentleman who looked at him with an evil eye. Peter saluted the unknown man, who looked at him from head to toe and who, without responding to his greeting, yelled at him with indignation: "And you, who are you? Where do you come from? What are you doing here?"

The small man, Peter, although feeling as if he were sinking into the ground beneath his feet, straightened his chest and raised his head. He did not lose the proper character of a brave soldier and answered, "I have come by order of obedience to you. I am a volunteer of the twenty-first infantry regiment, fallen while defending my Polish country, my Catholic faith, and my Mother Mary. My name is Peter Cichowiak, and I have died on the Wisla River, a place you can see from the sky."

St. Peter, unhappy with this explanation, looked at him with an untrusting eye and replied, "That you are, Peter, I know. Being your patron, I have witnessed your baptism, and I know that you are a Polish soldier. I also know that because of the uniform you are wearing, you are a volunteer, and I can see that in your conduct. But what I want to know is, how did you get in here without my permission?"

The small man did not like these questions because he did

not wish to compromise the little angel who had allowed his entrance there.

Then St. Peter continued his investigation. "It is not only that you have trespassed the privileged terrain, which is forbidden to any living human being, but you have entered with a gun in your hand. May God forgive you because I will not. This is a crime never before committed in my domain. Who has ever seen such audacity and arrogance as this, to enter the heavens with a rifle in hand?"

To come out victorious in this argument, the small man Peter attempted to make St. Peter see the plight of a soldier during the war. He responded, "What kind of soldier would I be if I left my weapon behind? It is true that I was born without my rifle. But, being a soldier and in the war, it would be shameful and a sin to die without my rifle."

St. Peter did not listen to this defense. On the contrary, filled with anger, he exclaimed, "Get out of here with your gun and do not come back until I call you." Then, a bit more tranquil, he continued, "Naturally, you cannot return to earth, as you are dead. For now, you can wait in the Milky Way. Move immediately when I say move. I know what I am saying. Now, get out of here." But St. Peter was wrong in thinking that he had a frightened child before him, one who listened to his yelling without thinking.

The small man Peter, without turning around, remained firm in his place and reflected upon the idea of leaving in such a disgraceful way. Suddenly, he saw the Virgin Mary passing by, in the company of some angels and saints. Without wasting any time, he ran toward her and knelt at her feet, begging for help.

As soon as the Virgin Mary heard the case, she turned to St. Peter, saying, "Leave him here, St. Peter. It is true that he has committed a fault, but he has already repented."

And St. Peter, as harsh as he was, courageously answered her, "That cannot be, my Grand Lady. He must get out of here immediately."

She said, "But St. Peter, I see you do not know that I am the Queen of Poland. And you also have not realized that this soldier is Polish, one who has died in defense of his country, his faith, and me. You see his uniform? It is soaked in blood."

St. Peter said, "Yes, I have seen it, Ma'am, but I reign here, and I am the one who has the keys. Without my permission, no one can enter heaven, nor can they stay here."

She replied, "Well then, be it as you wish. If you want to throw out the soldier, I will no longer remain here."

He said, "Be it as you wish, Queen of the Sky." Turning to the soldier, St. Peter asked for the devotion book that his mother had given him. The soldier took out an old, worn book and gave it to Mary. St. Peter said to her, "Of course, you may take everything that belongs to you, Gracious Lady."

Mary, turning the pages of the book, stopped at the page where the litany in her honor began and read aloud, "Queen of the Angels, of the Apostles, of the Martyrs, of all the Saints…" As her voice resounded, the skies began a terrible movement. From all corners of the heavens, the voices of the angelic choirs were invoked.

St. Peter, seeing this frightening movement, quickly realized that his palace would become empty and that all were abandoning him. Then he realized his mistake and that he would be left alone as a dry tree. He knelt at Mary's feet, begging her, "Oh Lady, let the Polish soldier stay here with his rifle in his hand, but do not leave the heavens."

In this way, the Polish soldier, volunteer of the twenty-first infantry regiment, who had fought in defense of his country, his

Catholic faith, and his Mother Mary, Peter Cichowiak, remained in heaven with his gun in his hand and an old, worn prayer book, which he used as a diary.

The small man Peter lost the battle with the Germans, but he won another one, the most important one: the battle for heaven. And while he enjoyed the company of his Queen in the sky, Warsaw, the place of his death, continued fighting against the invaders. The Polish people laughed, despite the blood that ran on their streets. They mocked their oppressors, who were killing thousands, millions of people, destroying their homes but never achieving the destruction of the Polish spirit.

THE LAUGHTER OF WARSAW

Great is the City of Warsaw;
A thousand days of horror pass.
As long as the horror lasts
Warsaw fights, and it laughs.
Although it is today bloodied,
With blood, memories, it engraves;
As lightning amongst the clouds,
Fine, mocking, always shining.
With blood, it pays these tears.
But a single day does not pass
Without new words that appear
On the posters and walls:
"Warsaw Fights and It Laughs"
Every day the walls
Insult the oppressors:
To Hitler and the "Eje Rota."
The high post of kinterna
Announces "hospitably"
That it remains reserved
Only "For the Germans."
Massacres, hangings, and scaffolds,
The Infernal Night covers us.

419

And nevertheless, Oh Warsaw,
Laughter adorns your ruins.
Who laughs, wins.
To be desperate, it is a sin,
For who has hope
Enjoys victorious laughter.
Today is for the Germans.
Tomorrow for the Polish.
The liberty – we will have.
We shall sing, "Carmagnolia."
Laugh, Warsaw, laugh, laugh…

Front gate of Dachau

Fabisiak, a 28-year-old newly
ordained Jesuit priest, weeks before
his imprisonment.

Chester Fabisiak, Prisoner No. 29697
(identity card and document from Dachau).

Dachau today.

Dachau Concentration Camp Memorial Site.

International Memorial at Dachau.

Church of the Mortal Agony of Christ at
Dachau Concentration Camp Memorial Site.

Boy Scouts

Age 28, Ordained

Age 63, became a U.S. citizen.

Age 81, in the nation's capital for
the dedication of the United States
Holocaust Memorial Museum.

Father Chester Fabisiak, age 81, in the nation's capital for the dedication of the United States Holocaust Memorial Museum.

Three little brushes recovered posthumously. One of them was the brush that Father Chester kept in Dachau. This was "dangerous and strictly prohibited."

A Brief Biography Of Father Chester Fabisiak, SJ

Father Chester Fabisiak, SJ was born on **June 11, 1911**, in Poznan, Poland.

On June 18, 1911, he was baptized into Christ.

In **1927**, he entered the Society of Jesus, and in **1939** he was ordained a priest.

In **1939**, he was taken prisoner by Nazi SS commandos.

On **April 29, 1945**, he was liberated by Allied forces from the Dachau Nazi concentration camp near Munich.

After liberation, he served over twenty years as a missionary in South America, primarily in Bolivia, Venezuela, and Ecuador.

He completed his final 30 years of the missionary devotion in the United States.

Father Fabisiak proudly became a U.S. citizen. Daily, he expressed the everlasting gratitude he held in his heart by helping men, women, and the future generation. He taught the children and teenagers, whom he loved.

From **1966 to 1969**, he served in New York City.

From **1969 to 1974**, he served in Michigan.

In **1974**, he came to the Springfield Diocese, serving the parishes of Saints Peter and Paul,

St. Mary, Taylorville IL, St. Mary, New Berlin Il, and St. Boniface, Quincy Il.

From **1981** until his death, he lovingly served at Blessed Sacrament Parish, Springfield, Illinois.

With God's grace, Father Fabisiak was able to provide his services to the last day of his life.

Some of the highlights of his ministries at Blessed Sacrament included celebrating the early morning Mass at 6:20 AM, ministering to the elderly in local high-rises, and making his services available to all in need, which was his joy. Preparing children for the Godly, spiritual life was his passion.

December 9, 1996, Father Chester Fabisiak, SJ.

At rest with God on the Feast of the Immaculate Conception.

CPSIA information can be obtained
at www.ICGtesting.com
Printed in the USA
BVHW071032100319
542252BV00001B/157/P